LIVING IN THE ROCK N ROLL MYSTERY

Reading Context, Self, and Others as Clues

H. L. GOODALL, JR.

Southern Illinois University Press

Carbondale and Edwardsville

Library of Congress Cataloging-in-Publication Data

Goodall, H. Lloyd.
    Living in the rock n roll mystery: reading context, self, and
others as clues / H.L. Goodall, Jr.
        p.   cm.
    Includes bibliographical references.
        1. Communication and culture—United States. 2. Rock music—
Social aspects—United States. 3. Ethnology—Methodology.
4. Goodall, H. Lloyd. 5. United States—Popular culture.
I. Title. II. Title: Living in the rock and roll mystery.
P91.G65   1991
306.4'84—dc20   90-36646
    ISBN 0-8093-1610-2   CIP

The paper used in this publication meets the minimum requirements
of American National Standard for Information Sciences—Permanence
of Paper for Printed Library Materials, ANSI Z39.48-1984. ∞

For Sandra

If human beings are, indeed, organisms with selves, and if their action is, indeed, an outcome of a process of self-interaction, schemes that purport to study and explain social action should respect and accommodate these features. To do so, current schemes in sociology and social psychology would have to undergo radical revision. They would have to shift from a preoccupation with initiating factor and terminal result to a preoccupation with a process of formation. They would have to view action as something constructed by the actor instead of something evoked from him. They would have to depict the milieu of action in terms of how the milieu appears to the actor in place of how it appears to the outside student. They would have to incorporate the interpretive process which at present they scarcely deign to touch.

—Herbert Blumer

Any truly creative text is always to some extent a free revelation of the personality, not predetermined by empirical necessity.

—Mikhail Bakhtin

The artist is always an evangelist. . . . He wants others to feel as he does.

—Kenneth Burke

Contents

Part One—The Detective's Metaphor: A Personal Introduction to the Mysteries of Context, Self, and Other

Part Two—Listening for the Weave of Clues: The Three Voices of Context

Acknowledgments

This has been a difficult and astonishing project in part because my life has been difficult and astonishing while completing it. I want to acknowledge here my debt to those who stood by me when standing by me was all that could be done and was exactly what I needed: my wife Sandra, to whom this book is dedicated and for whom it was written; Drew Thompson, musician, pal, brother I never had; the WHITEDOG band, including Drew Thompson, Mike Fairbanks, I. B. Alexander, Mitch Rigel, Rob Malone, Mark Sanford, Michael French, the Hankster, Mark Puckett, and Roadie Dave; Michael J. Foley, Ben Poole, Sandy and her mom, Rita and David Whillock, Tom Addington and his happy family, the Stewdog of Ithaca, the folks at A. B. Stephens Music in Huntsville, Alabama, and Butch McGhee, Executive Director of Muscle Shoals Sound; to the participants in the 1989 Alta Conference on Interpretive Approaches to the Study of Organizations, especially Eric Eisenberg, Larry Browning, and Len and Michelle Hawes; to my new colleagues at the University of Utah, for spurring me on and reading drafts of various essays, particularly Mark Neumann, Bryan Taylor, Mary Strine, Steve May, Bob Tiemens, Dave Eason, Doug Birkhead, Dante Orazzi, and Jim Anderson; to Gerald M. Phillips, for sponsoring and at times mentoring this volume; to the "anonymous" reviewers who provided questions, insight, and poems for me to read and think about; to the good people at Southern Illinois University Press for their hard work and belief in this project, particularly Dan Gunter, who added much to the mix of this word music, Susan Wilson, who saw it through and gave me some room with the title and tunes, and Kenney Withers, who has consistently encouraged a new vision for scholarly writing and who has helped me to achieve it; and, as always, to Barry Hannah for coming out with a new autobiographical novel just when I needed to read one.

Parts of this book have appeared or been presented elsewhere. The author wishes to thank:

Ablex Publishing Company, for permission to reprint material drawn from Gerald M. Phillips, ed., *Teaching How to Work in Groups,* (1990), which appears here as chapter 4;

Sage Press, for permission to reprint material drawn from James A. Anderson, ed., *Communication Yearbook 13,* (1990), which appears here as chapter 5;

Southern Illinois University Press, for permission to reprint material drawn from Gerald M. Phillips and Julia T. Wood, eds., *Studies Honoring the Seventy-fifth Anniversary of the Speech Communication Association* (1989), which appears here as chapter 2;

The Southern Communication Journal, for permission to reprint material drawn from my essay "On Becoming an Organizational Detective" (55 [1989]: 42–54), which appears here as chapter 3.

In addition, material included in chapter 1 was originally presented at a Department of Communication Colloquium at the University of Utah; material included in chapter 8 was originally presented at the Alta Summer Conference on Interpretive Approaches to Organizational Study; and material from chapter 10 was originally presented at the International Communication Association convention in Dublin, Ireland, and at a Department of Communication colloquium at the University of South Florida.

Introduction

MYSTERY AND THE METAPHOR OF THE ORGANIZATIONAL DETECTIVE

Mystery begins in a feeling, something deep, poetic, and sweet.

You get caught up in it. You get caught up in it *fast*. Little raptures of being alive ripple down the back of your neck, trickle like ice crystals doing an unknown, familiar dance across the constant heat of your spine. This is what it is like, this is where it begins. Mystery is like a seductive voice deep into the way cool and hot of the music that you suddenly discover is singing to you, directly to you, only to you, breaking you away from what you thought you were, which until that very moment you thought was the whole and substance of your life. Mystery changes all of that because mystery changes you. Mystery defines you in the casting of its spell, in something as simple as the enchantment of a voice, a voice inviting you to dance, a dance that promises something you will always remember or, maybe, that you will never forget.

These are the senses of the power and pull of mystery, the whisper of its voice and the sensuous lull of its prose rhythms, the surround for the private investigations that constitute the public music of this book. Mystery is used here in both straight and delinquent senses, to denote both a way of expressing and a way of experiencing what I will call the rock n roll of social life. Why I call the form of social life I examine *rock n roll* (and even spell it this way) is part of the reading, part of the rhetorics of motive, part of the assemblage of semiotic clues, that join you and me, reader, in working out the terms of this mystery.

Working out the terms of a mystery properly begins with various appreciations of what the term means because mystery, as a term, deserves some recognition beyond the experience of its poetry. Within the prose world of the meanings of words, this means acknowledging the presence of other voices that are heard in this discursive definitional space. I am tempted to say—following Bernard McGrane's (1989) defi-

xi

nition of anthropology—that our definitional boundaries should begin this way:

Mystery *is* . . . and mystery is *relative.*

And just leave it at that. Let the space it takes to move through the points of the ellipsis invite your participation in the text. What you think it means, and whatever you think it means, it means, reader. Burden of proof in this crime of definition is strictly on the reading you provide. Read this way, even without the cool assist of the background music, and you experience the truth of the second part of the sentence, *mystery is relative*—relative to the reading of the clues you provide, which itself is relative to who *you* are, as a person, as a reader, as a scholar of mysteries, and as a participant in the rock n roll of this text of social life. The sentence also spells relative in both directions: relative to the clues I provide, relative to who I am as a person, a writer, a scholar of mysteries, a participant in the rock n roll, and so on. Such is the real and true nature of our dialogue, and we could just leave it at that.

But my editor probably wouldn't like it. Neither would some of the readers, one of whom, a reviewer for this book back when it was still a manuscript (remaining here anonymous because that's how she wanted it), once put it like this in an otherwise very flattering letter to me: "Geographers have four categories of lostness: (1) you think you know exactly where you are, (2) you know you're heading in the right direction, in the right corridor, (3) you know you're lost (known lost), and (4) you think you're not lost, but you are (unknown lost)." It occurred to me when I read this passage that she was—in addition to asking for some definitional boundaries—also describing four ways of experiencing mystery, or rock n roll, or other altered states of consciousness. And she is right. Part of my job is to make a map that will help a reader move through and into the territory and that will invite participation and exploration of its mysteries, its voices, and the experience of its borders.

In that spirit let me describe two ways of constructing a map, two ways of doing the cartographical task. Each one of these ways should be considered as its own path, and each one will at first seem to offer a different way into the realm and being of mystery. But, as I will show, each one, when considered in light of the other, provides a resonant source of help. Read together as mutual sources of meaning in the construction of the meaning of mystery, these divergent paths suggest deeper interpenetrations.

Gabriel Marcel's Reading of Mystery

Gabriel Marcel (1949a, 1949b, 1950, 1987) was an award-winning French dramatist and a reluctant, if prolific, philosopher. For him, mystery is a way of approaching participation in the existential drama and phenomenology of everyday life. Mystery, for Marcel, is contrasted with "problem" as an essential difference of Being, a difference that informs how and why humans view their own lives as well as the lives of others, and provides a locus of motives and reasons for behavior, choice, and speech. Mystery encourages us to see ourselves as integrally connected to others, as co-constructors of a developing narrative of life in which the narratives themselves become intertwined, entangling with them our sense of Being.

"Problem," by contrast, encourages us to divorce our experiences and sense of self from others. To view experience as a "problem" is to divide the narratives of "us" from the narratives of "them" and to see in that division of narratives a natural superiority of the observer (I) over the objects of the observations (them). Our task is not to engage or mingle with "them" on the level of narrative, but instead to create narratives that "solve the problem" suggested by that original division.

To see the interpenetrations of the texts of life as mysteries is to see in them tensions of self *and* other, a drama of narrative structures upon which are constructed larger narratives of Being and within which lie, always, "a question in which what is given cannot be regarded as detached from the self" (Marcel, quoted in Gallagher 1975, 32). For Marcel, the purpose of narrative participation and the spell of dramatic tension are inextricably linked to the processes of knowing and of making known, of seeing and living the connectedness, of artistic creation and self-realization. To be able to confront the mysteries of living as mysteries, to enter and to participate in them, is to be involved in that creative process, and to be involved in that process is to realize the interdependence of self and other(s).

I believe Marcel's philosophical worldview holds particular promise for the practice of interpretive ethnography informed by the dual, sometimes conflicting, emphases of radical empiricism (Jackson 1989) and existential phenomenology. It provides a way of understanding why ethnographic narratives constructed out of the mysteries of self and other(s) are distinguishable from ethnographic narratives that view the other (and the other's culture) as a "problem." It is indeed how the author lives through the experience and writes about it that shapes the knowing and showing evident in the text. Thus, it makes a difference, and a very important one, whether that experience is viewed as an existential, phenomenological mystery in which truth "is in the interstices as much as it is in the structure, in fiction as much as in fact" (Jackson 1989, 187) or as a "problem" to be addressed or corrected through various but specific applications of scientific reasoning in which truth is revealed, constant, and binding.

Marcel's stance toward mystery as the philosophical premise one carries into the research experience parallels my own. In my previous interpretive study, *Casing a Promised Land* (1989), I explored the writing of mystery and the mystery of writing as inextricably intertwined and established as my ethnographic task the telling of stories that featured self, Others, and context as coproducers of the stories. I didn't know Marcel's work then, but I was nevertheless informed by its ethereal spirit, a sort of asynchronous rock n roll collusion of secret words and music, if you will. Discovering him, through the generous influence of my colleague Mark Neumann, was like discovering I had a spiritual kinsman, a person in a distant land speaking in a foreign tongue who had, with a very different purpose in mind, arrived at strikingly similar conclusions.

But his is not the only path through, or map of, the territory of mystery.

Kenneth Burke's Reading of Mystery

For many years I have been an avid Kenneth Burke fan. His wisdom and insight serve as a formidable intellectual challenge as well as a constant professional reminder that eclectic rhetorical criticism is far more than a tool for fine-tuning the stereo systems of thought; it is also a dramatic way of experiencing life.

Burke, too, locates in the pervasive sense of mystery the essential motive for social constructions of realities:

> Mystery arises at that point where different kinds of beings are in communication. In mystery there must be *strangeness;* but the estranged must also be thought of as in some way capable of communion. . . . The conditions of mystery are set by any pronounced social distinctions, as between nobility and commoners, courtiers and king, leader and people, rich and poor, judge and prisoner at the bar, "superior race" and underpriviledged "races" or minorities. Thus even the story of relations between the petty clerk and the office manager, *however realistically told,* draws upon the wells of mystery for its appeal . . . All such "mystery" calls for a corresponding rhetoric" (1969, 115; emphasis mine).

Burke's argument is not about the doing or writing of interpretive ethnography. It instead addresses a context in which particular doctrines drawn from Marx and Carlyle allow us to give a reading to rhetoric as a naturally occurring persuasive discourse, always about the revealing and concealing of sources of consciousness. It is in respect to how consciousness is arrived at and displayed that I think his argument can be appropriated to our discussion of mystery.

Burke begins with the observation that mystery is derived from the recognition that there are different classes of beings and, as a corollary, that there are also different classes of rhetoric inherent to the experiences of those beings. We are indeed separated by our own languages, vocabularies, sensitivities to meanings, and representative cultural codes into different classes of language users/abusers. To appropriate Max Weber's original phrase for our discussion of the borders of self and Other that mark the empirical territories of mystery, we and the persons we are studying are always "suspended in webs of significance that we ourselves have spun." But significance is also a source of difference, and just as a working surface of connectedness reveals a deeper existential mystery, so too does a sense of knowing and naming something reveal the equipotential for what George Steiner calls "alternity," or "the uses of language . . . for misconstruction, for illusion and play" (1973, 224); in turn, this alternity makes us "subjects and agents of our own existence" (Jackson 1989, 187) and experiences. In fieldwork informed by radical empiricism, by immersion and participation in the lived experiences of everyday life, different classes of beings do not share contexts and languages to become like one another, but instead mark the borders to preserve individual and cultural identities, to maintain separate and often unequal readings of reality, and to maintain mystery while constructing narratives that address the mystery but do not always resolve it.

Burke's description of mystery, particularly the last line quoted above, also proposes the need for prose styles capable of attaining some correlation—always contingent because the nature of reality over which rhetoric has domain is always contingent— between lived experience and textual display. Mystery is, read this way, a genre for writing the complexities of lived experience within the framework of immersion and participation rather than "problem" and "solution." It is a way of constructing descriptive rhetorics that reveal the multiple interpenetrations of context, self, and Other as an unfolding drama in which the author—in my case an organizational detective—is an intersubjective participant reading and misreading the clues, not a neutral observer standing behind a one-way mirror or a minor god with a codebook ready to yawn and cipher the one true meaning of the text.

MUSIC AND THE METAPHOR OF THE ORGANIZATIONAL DETECTIVE

The title of this book—*Living in the Rock n Roll Mystery*—is intended to invite participation in the text on several levels. First, a good bit of this volume is dedicated to the proposition that rock n roll is both a form of social life and an analogy for the experience of writing interpretive ethnography. Hence, rock n roll is the detective's music as well as a major source of the mystery of his or her text.

Second, three of the chapters address the fieldwork experiences of playing rhythm guitar in a rock n roll band called WHITEDOG. The purpose of this fieldwork, as of all fieldwork, was both personal and professional. On a personal level I wanted to practice my guitar-playing skills with musicians far more talented than I am, to have the experience of hanging out, playing bars and dances, recording our own tunes, being one of the guys. On a professional level I wanted to experience organizing from the ground up, to get in on the formation of a profit-making organization and participate in its evolution. I was able to accomplish both purposes, but it was in their interpenetrations that the truth of my experience became intertwined with the experience of organizational truth and changed forever the course of my life.

Third, there is a sense in which the organizational detective metaphor inspires a musical surround. My use of the detective metaphor is meant both to include a respect for the direction of intelligence at available texts and to assume the posture of a cultural outsider, a person living at the borders between and among different classes of persons. Either way there is always some music playing, sometimes as background to the ensuing drama, sometimes just a distant radio playing an almost forgotten song. As Zelda Fitzgerald expressed it back in the 1920s, "Most people live their lives by the philosophies of popular songs," and I find this still to be true. So it is that in all of these stories there is a detective and there is music, and there is a mystery text everywhere in-between.

DESIGN OF THE BOOK

Such are the conceptual foundations for the detective metaphor, for mystery, and for music that conspire to make this volume. In addition to these ideas, this book formally addresses three issues central to the unfolding character of interpretive ethnography in communication and cultural studies.

The first issue is one of *presence*. For all of the rhetoric advocating ethnographic tales, the literature that is emerging from the blurring of communication and cultural studies reveals very few field studies. Arguments abound: arguments for fieldwork; arguments for ethnographic techniques; arguments about the importance of interpretive methods; arguments *ad infinitum*. But precious few articles or books have yet been published. The core of this issue is one of presence: how can theoretical and critical work be accomplished without data?

The second issue is one of *voice*. I have taken the position that authorial voice, by which I mean something akin to Kenneth Burke's notion of "the dance of an attitude" that informs our reading of a text, is critical to appreciating the presuppositions a researcher has toward the subject. Through authorial voice, manifested in writing style, readers come to know something important about self, Other, and context. Perhaps more important, recent support for Mikhail Bakhtin's (1984a, 1986) work with the concept of polyphonic voices (including multiple influences evident in the author's voice) and a host of cultural anthropologists' concerns for allowing the Other in research to speak for her or himself (see especially Geertz 1988; Jackson 1989; Rosaldo 1989) provide good reason to believe that the issue of voice is not one of mere style, but one of democracy, content, and knowing.

The third issue is one of *positioning the author within the text*. Here again an abundance of work in literary and anthropological theory suggests that authorial presence is a matter of common concern. If the voice(s) of an interpreter is never neutral, then where the body that produces that voice was standing when the observations were made is critically significant.

These three concerns, then, for presence, voice, and positioning, coalesced to produce an opening, an invitation, for me to participate in the ongoing conversation. What I bring to it is found in this volume, and before proceeding any further I should clarify what I hope to add to the conversation.

In 1988 I was working on an essay (Goodall 1989b) for the volume commemorating the Speech Communication Association's Seventy-fifth anniversary. My editor was Julia Wood. After I submitted my first draft it came back to me with a variety of useful suggestions, including an item that appeared continually in the margins: *Blumer was already here.* She was, of course, referring to the late Herbert Blumer, whose theoretical and critical development of symbolic interaction (a term, by the way, that he always thought awkward) had been appropriated and then virtually abandoned by the communication discipline decades before.

I had read Blumer in graduate school, and then, like most of my contemporaries, had gone on to other, more fashionable thinkers: Burke, McKeon, Habermas, Lacan, Derrida, de Man, Fish, Foucault. However, at Julia's insistence I reacquired an appreciation for Blumer and saw at once that she was correct. His work was not only insightful and pioneering but suddenly, when given a new reading that focused on voice and display of symbolic interaction, seemed to speak directly to issues in the ethnography of communication and cultural studies.

Blumer's work centered on the ways in which symbolic constructions of social reality are created, sustained, and transformed in everyday activities. His critique spanned a wide variety of social and professional sites, from an early concern for the influence of movies on conduct to race relations to a concern with the whole development of the field of sociology. Throughout his life he argued for the primacy of social activities (*not* shared cognitive processes) as the definer of social meanings and for the absolute necessity of dignifying the individual interpretive processes by making them both different from and greater than mere "objective" analysis of behavior. It was also true that he was somewhat of a hell-raiser in his field, a man who stood confidently outside of what was then the objectivist, quantitative, behavioral mainstream and who called into question the whole notion of "variables."

I liked him. And when I returned to read him, this time for clues to the mystery I was then involved in rather than as a routine case assignment in graduate school, I learned to appreciate not only his vision but also the clarity of his writing and his refusal to rely on copious footnotes to make his case. He was clearly a man ahead of his time, a pioneer not only in the methodological position of symbolic interactionism among the social sciences but also in the cause of viewing humans as complex social beings with dramatic inner lives worthy of our deepest interpretive talents.

So it was with great pleasure that I rewrote that commemorative essay, and, at the same time, decided to make it part of a new project. The project is this book, which, as I have already mentioned, attempts to address three central issues in communication and cultural studies—context, self, and Other—as well as to address three issues relevant to interpretive ethnography: presence, voice, and positioning. But it is also a project dedicated to recovering the interpretive and writing processes that inform part of what was lost when symbolic interactionism became, as a professional topic in the discourse, less fashionable than postmodernism, poststructuralism, and feminist theory.

This is not to suggest that all that needs to be done is to place Blumer's words into the ongoing dialogue. Nor does it imply that we should turn away from poststructuralism, postmodernism, or feminist theory. What it means, simply, is that we should be able to look again at the clues in Blumer's work (among others), clues that suggest, given the current poststructural, postmodern, and feminist dialogue, a reexamination and renewed appreciation for the interdependence of self, Other, and context in studies of humans as symbol-dependent co-constructors of social and professional realities.

Context, self, and Other. Three relatively simple words that hold, share, or refer to what I consider to be both the essence and the *difference* of communication and culture. More important, given the status of the ongoing dialogue, these three terms demand the satisfactions of inquiry directed toward appreciating their interdependence and complexities within the advances that have been made in interpretive social science, particularly descriptive rhetorics, since Blumer.

Part 1 of this volume begins with a descriptive rhetoric, a narrative of context, self, and Other that introduces rock n roll as a form of social life and interpretive ethnographic research and writing as rock n roll. In this text, reader, rock n roll is not just a musical style but also a social attitude that informs a wide variety of social and professional constructions of reality, including the doing and writing of ethnography. The point of this essay is to call into question certain tendencies, certain stereotypes, certain words, evident in our talk about ethnographic research and writing, and to juxtapose against them the position and voice of the scholar interested in making the connections make a certain mysterious, musical sense. From this foray into the interpretive dilemmas of context, self, and others emerges the second essay, a more or less traditional scholarly treatment of self, other, and context, the original essay that sparked this project. The goal here is to do justice to the professional literature, and through an interpretation of it, to locate in an essay by Wayne Brockriede, "Arguing about Human Understanding" (1982), the tensions of the recovery project and its dialectical and dialogic processes.

Part 2 is concerned with listening to the clues that form the weave for three voices of context. Let me hasten to add that I am not suggesting that these are either *the* three or the *only* three voices one can find in descriptive rhetorics of context. These are, simply, three studies I have done in voice about context and they are represented here as ways of rocking, ways of making the tune hum, not as the nature of rock or the total hum. Hence, chapter 3 displays mystery as the central vocal mechanism to a context of intrigue and deceit, a voice that I hope comes across much like Margo Timmons of Cowboy Junkies when she sings "Song for Elvis," perhaps with overtones of Raymond Chandler. Chapter 4 uses the voice of a "voyeur" to describe an indelicate case of group decision making whose tune was a tourist's view of the Grand Canyon or Venice Beach; think of David Lee Roth's video remake of the Beach Boys' classic "California Girls." Chapter 5 employs the familiar voice of the participant-observer to unravel the tangle of culture involved in a computer firm's mix of software and softball, but adds the rock n roll dimension of a "lead ride"—the guitar soloist's venture into hyperspace (in this case hyperreality).

Part 3 addresses writing the autobiographical mystery through the detection and manifestations of self. Its three chapters are autobiographical reads of self dedicated to the propositions that individuality is based on history, memory, and relationships with others and that who we are, or think we are, when we do research matters very much. Chapter 6 should be considered a transition chapter that moves us from the mysteries of context into the mysteries of the contextualized self. It attempts to locate the writing of autobiography as part of the interpretive ethnographer's overall project and addresses central issues of style and *ethos* that necessarily become part of any text of self. Chapter 7 is about the mysteries of culture within my "life education"—the truth of my experience intertwined with the experience of truth—in a family dynamic that shaped and formed my self-identity, that provided several of the "voices" I speak through in my own work, and that created the bases for many of the questions I now ask about communication, organizations, and culture. This chapter also reveals why I find patterns so intriguing and why multiple readings of the same contextual data are so much a natural part of my critical apparatus. Chapter 8 is a rock n roll furtherance of Chapter 7, a tale that was difficult for me to write and may be difficult for the squeamish among you to read. So please heed this warning: chapter 8 is dangerous.

Part 4 of the volume is concerned with participating in the mystery while observing others. Specifically, the two chapters that make up this section address issues of interpretive ethnographic technique in uncovering and then recovering the read of self and context in the Other, and then trying to figure out who you are as a researcher/participant/observer from the other's view of persons and things. Chapter 9 is about the cultural detective as a tourist in the culture, examining sites of critical meaning as if they are experiences that induce us to participate in them, like roadside attractions or museums. Chapter 10 brings us back to the experiences of context, self, and Other while participating in rock n roll culture and is a view of the audience from the perspective of a member of the band.

Part 5 consists of a concluding essay that tries to summarize and extend what has come before it. In it I am back to basics such as presence, voice, and positioning, as well as the mysteries of context, self, and Other.

This is a work of interpretive ethnography. Unlike other forms of scholarly writing that police strict borders of fiction and nonfiction and that privilege facts over imagination, this work seeks to blur those distinctions, to call into question the whole notion of privilege and borders and police actions.

That said, let me now say that everything in this book is true—true to *my* experiences. I have changed some of the names of persons and businesses and have been vague about the precise locations of others. I have juxtaposed the world I have perceived against a world I have imagined. While it might be nice to fully separate the two worlds, and to use only real names, it has been my experience that this separation occurs only among those who have lived a truly unexamined life and who do not respect the dignity of Others.

Any resemblance between this work and real persons is purely intentional. Any resemblance between what is contained in these chapters and real life is also purely intentional; furthermore, it is the best I can hope for.

PART ONE The Detective's Metaphor:
A Personal Introduction to the Mysteries
of Context, Self, and Other

1

The Fool, the King, Louie, Louie, and I: Mystery, Ethnography, and Rock n Roll in Cultural Studies

Kudos in our fields today is gained primarily by devising a striking theory, or elaborating a grand theoretical system, or proposing a catchy scheme of analysis, or constructing a logically neat or elegant model, or cultivating and developing advanced statistical and mathematical techniques, or executing studies that are gems of research design, or (to mention something I am not treating in this essay) engaging in brilliant speculative analysis of what is happening in some area of social life. To study through firsthand observation what is actually happening in a given area of social life is given a subsidiary or peripheral position—it is spoken of as "soft" science or journalism.

—Herbert Blumer

The scientific consciousness of contemporary man has learned to orient itself among the complex circumstances of "the probability of the universe"; it is not confused by any "indefinite quantities" but knows how to calculate them and take them into account. This scientific consciousness has long since grown accustomed to the Einsteinian world with its multiplicity of systems of measurement, etc. But in the realm of artistic cognition people sometimes continue to demand a very crude and very primitive definitiveness, one that quite obviously could not be true.

—Mikhail Bakhtin

Their training has become an incapacity.

—Kenneth Burke

THE AMERICAN ORIGINS OF ROCK N ROLL AND INTERPRETIVE ETHNOGRAPHY

In a paper read before the American Sociological Society in 1953, Herbert Blumer described three types of social theories: (1) "that form of social theory which stands or presumes to stand as a part of empirical science"; (2) that "type of theory [that] might be termed 'policy' theory

3

. . . concerned with analyzing a given social situation, or social structure, or social action as a basis for policy or action"; and (3) an "interpretive type [that] seeks to develop a meaningful interpretation of the social world or of some significant part of it." Of this third type he adds:

> In every society, particularly in a changing society, there is a need for meaning-ful clarifications of basic social values, social institutions, modes of living and social relations. This need cannot be met by empirical science, even though some help may be gained from analysis made by empirical science. Its effective fulfillment requires a sensitivity to new dispositions and an appreciation of new lines along which social life may take shape. . . . This type of social theory is important and stands in its own right. (1969, 142)

These words were spoken in America after we had conquered the world and dropped the atom bomb, prior to Elvis Presley, and a decade before the beginning of our debacle in Vietnam. It was a thoroughly modern—as well as modernist—America, a relatively safe place for grand categorical schemas that sought to divide the world into knowable, manageable units, that sought (with William Levitt of Levittown fame) to build squarely divided suburbs as a major hedge against communism ("No man who owns his own home can become a communist—he has too much to do!"), and that intended, with the help of God, Myth, and Science, to construct a rational new order, a new form of civilization, in which all that could be known could be made into a technology, manufactured in mass, and used; in which all that could be used could be purchased; and in which all that could be purchased would soon be obsolete.

But there was another America, one that had known a quite different heritage. It continued, more or less peacefully, alongside the dominant order, it offered songs instead of science, and it did not aspire to suburbs. It was often poor, mostly black, and what it sang—in addition to the dirges, the ditties, gospel, and ballads—was the blues. For more than two hundred years, or roughly from the beginnings of the industrial revolution in America, a time when the ideal machine began to render most human labor variants of human slavery, there were expressive and musical sources of cultural rhetoric whose purpose was both to create and to share human feelings, communal senses of place and displacement.

Together these cultural forces—the rational/technical and the emotive/sensual—would continue to shape two sides of the American experience. However, that experience has been altering rapidly, transformed by the quickening pace of the information society; by the advent of wars in the Third World; by the arms race; by sexual, racial, and material revolutions;

and by the steadily increasing influence of mass media and geopolitics on the events and understandings of everyday life, which has made possible the new global community, horrible, fantastic, and unimaginable as it is. In this new context, what had once been a source of entertainment and relief became transformed into a new form of social and political life.

I have long felt that this "new form of social and political life" is summed up in the term *rock n roll*. For whatever rock n roll is, and it is certainly more than its music, it has occurred as a cultural force at precisely the time in history when the rational, orderly, highly technologized and bureaucratic spirit has been at its zenith, standing in wild, frenzied, revved-up contradistinction to "a world perceived or sensed to be well-organized and predictable" (Marcus 1986, 78). That as music—by which I mean both the lyrics and the copresent, interdependent sounds—rock n roll has consistently taken as its subject precisely these tensions is neither surprising nor particularly revealing; however, as a form of social and political life capable of influencing everything from style in clothing, language, and living to the meaning and feelings we associate with historical periods, movements, and other world events, rock n roll is the expression of important cultural values. However, to limit the study of rock n roll to its status as a producible, consumable commodity, or to discuss its cultural relevance solely in terms of hegemonic and economic concerns, or even to approach rock n roll as the embodiment of "youth" or as some sort of master trope, is to offer useful but decidedly incomplete readings (see Grossberg 1986 and the critical responses to him in the same issue).

The ways one studies cultural phenomena and the ways one writes about those same phenomena are inextricably intertwined. The method of study and its expressive voice jointly determine how the data are displayed, as well as how conclusions, however tentative, are drawn. It is within the world of the word and its forms of expression that understanding is created and embraced, making space for human susceptibility to the various inducements of meaning. Hence, the study of the cultural phenomenon of rock n roll as a new form of social life requires more than a mere retooling of the technologies of the word capable of expressing its life, more than simply altering the avenues of approach to the subject, more than applying a theory of this or that in the there-and-then to what happens in the here-and-now; it requires a more basic, revolutionary action.

Such a revolutionary action must also occur in the scholarship of the period. For it is not merely that rock n roll has entered existing forms of social, political, and professional lives, but indeed that rock n roll is a new form of life itself, altering in its course all existing institutions and forms of understanding. Rock n roll is more than music, or music in relation to culture, or even music in relation to politics; *it is a way in which people are induced to know, to be, to do, and to act.* Similarly, attempts to understand it require subjective immersion rather than objective distance, for rock n roll as a form of social life must be experienced to be understood. By this I mean lived through rather than merely observed and examined, read as a text in which the reader is a presence and the text is drawn into the mix of his or her life, rather than as a text in which the reader is absent and the life is abstracted into arguments that could just as easily be made without reference to the subject at hand. To do this, to accomplish this, requires a form of expression equal to the experiences of its subject, and such a form of expression is interpretive ethnography.

The thesis I offer in this book is that interpretive ethnography is to cultural studies what rock n roll is to social life. Furthermore, both interpretive ethnography and rock n roll must be understood as part of a larger and decidedly more historically relevant tradition that has always reserved for dominant forms of art the role of the fool—the rebellious, truth-telling commentator who speaks in riddles and rhymes while in service to the king, a person whose outrageous costumes amuse and instruct the audience while providing a useful and necessary outlet for major sources of cultural frustration.

That is the project that inspired this book. It is a project that involves issues of research and writing as partners to scholarly understanding rather than as individual components in a scholarly process. It is a project that positions the researcher within the text and reveals voices through which the researcher can speak, and which in speaking reveal different aspects of context, self, and Other. And it is a project that attempts to recover, within the scholarly traditions of rhetorical analysis and symbolic interactionism, those domains of context, self, and Other appropriate to the study of culture and its forms of social life.

In this chapter I will first outline five observations that underscore my approach to understanding social and organizational life and that justify my interpretive and decidedly ethnographic approach to doing research. Then I will examine some impressions about the relationships among lyrics, music, and culture, as well as among context, self, and Other, that help explain why rock n roll and high technology emerge as emblems of a new form of social and organizational life.

THE SET-UP: JAMMING WITH THE LIT

I begin with the observation, not original but nevertheless instructive, that certain tensions govern the practice of everyday life (see de Certeau 1984; Lefebvre 1971). I get up, wonder about where I've been, think about where I'm going. While I grind the beans for my morning coffee, I listen to National Public Radio to catch up on disasters and art. My wife comes in from her morning walk and tells me she ran into a friend who told her that the Dylan concert tickets go on sale today, and there is already a line forming for them. I consider this in light of the fact that I am in the middle of preparing a presentation, and do a quick calculation: tickets on sale now = good chance for good seats versus presentation not completed to satisfaction = bad public performance and resultant sulking. With this logic I postpone my decision about getting in line for the concert tickets, take my coffee to the word processor, and change the channel to *the* rock n roll oldies station in Salt Lake City.

My second observation, also not original, is related to the first: among these tensions in the practice of everyday life we tend to pursue what we perceive as useful or necessary to maintaining our balance, using actions to relieve stress, reduce uncertainties, restore equity, make a difference, create change (see Bersheid and Walster 1978). I make coffee to help me wake up and feel alert; I listen to NPR to participate, at least in a tertiary sense, in the world; my wife tells me about the Dylan tickets to inform and persuade me; I do my silent calculation of cause and effects to handle the data; I turn on rock n roll . . . why?

My third observation is, following Freud, that we respond equally well to the real and to the imagined, and that in addition to the lives we lead we also live lives we don't lead. This is an important assumption because it includes the previous notions of cultural tensions and functional utility but lets them play out at the level of abstraction, fantasy, and dream. While I am grinding my coffee beans I think about a conversation I've never had with Susan Sarandon; my wife reports that while she was exercising she heard a song on her Walkman that reminded her of "me" (which one? I am tempted to ask); when I turn on the rock n roll station I see myself playing guitar and being a star. What makes this level interesting is that its tensions and senses of utility have internal (reasons within its own domain) and external (reasons that give to others about the connections between this domain and the other one) logics, thus adding geometrically to the complexity of our daily lives.

My fourth observation is drawn from the relics of General Systems Theory and is best expressed this way: *Everything counts*. However, contrary to the original orderly and rational engineering intentions of systems work, when applied to the human experience this principle takes a very different semiotic turn. It presumes neither innocence nor neutrality, grants meaning, purpose, and reality to anyone who wants or claims it, and favors no privileged secondary readings beyond the immediate authorship of the experience. I like to think of this as an essential pre-postmodern condition, a theoretical soul, if you will, that moved into the world after that body of literature died, was cremated at conventions, and planted in the forgettable sentences of basic texts.

But back to the principle of *Everything counts*. This means that it matters what kind of coffee beans I choose to grind (at least to me), what brand of walking shoes my wife wears on her walk (at least to her), and why I would play only a 1957 Fender Stratocaster with the new Lace sensors when I played live rock n roll with the band WHITEDOG. This sort of detail is important, and unfortunately usually absent, from social and organizational theories, and that importance is one major reason why, in sentences like this one, I call myself an interpretive ethnographer.

My fifth and final observation, partly derived from Marshall Sahlins's (1976) definition of culture and partly influenced by how I write about organizations and communities, is difficult to articulate, but it sort of goes like this: persons and things are connected, context is always important, and no matter how straight or fair we try to be, what we see and how we locate meaning in life depends upon who and what we are and what we want, believe, and fear ourselves and others to be. Or, in summed up Buckaroo Banzai form: No matter where we go, there we are.

What these five observations add up to is a symbolic interactionism of a third kind (the first being Blumer, the second being his first-generation social science interpreters). Embedded in them are sources of appreciation and critique of social and organizational theories, and a subtle justification for interpretive ethnographic approaches to the study of social and organizational processes. During the remainder of this chapter I'd like you to keep these premises in mind while I do something else. What I plan to do is to follow a suggestion made by Greil Marcus in a critical response to an essay by Lawrence Grossberg called "Is There Rock after Punk?"

> Even if the theorist can never be sure of what messages socially objectified but (within the realm of esthetics) subjective listeners glean from a text as they use it, the theorist can begin to get a sense of how listeners use such a text. . . .

Ultimately, there is only one way to play the game. Beginning with the most specific confrontation with the fragments and interstices of the performance in question, one must remain within the arena of that confrontation for a long time—daydreaming like a worker commuting to a job—and then, betting on the unconscious ability of any listener to absorb the most extravagant suggestions from the most formally . . . impoverished text . . . , one must make the most far-reaching claims for the text: *the text as it cannot be deciphered.* That is, one must make one's claims on the terms of . . . "the grain of the voice," which deciphers nothing, but makes the confrontation between listener and performing artist—the way the singer sings a certain word or nonword, the way the guitarist enters a chorus, the way a drummer leaves it—real. (1986, 80)

In other words, go to the source, immerse yourself in it, and try to figure out what it means. This is what I call doing basic research, and for me as an interpretive ethnographer, it requires getting out of the office and participating in the culture, acquiring new skills and associating with new people.

VERSE FIRST?

In a world socially constructed out of words and actions and their absences and silences, the lyrics of social life hold particular appeal. As far back as the Wisdom Books of the Talmud, verses that were meant to be sung have conveyed cultural beliefs, knowledge, and a sense of permanence in change, but it is in Zelda Fitzgerald's memorable statement (see Milford 1970) about the influence of radio broadcasts of music during the early 1920s that we get a full sense of what at first appears to be a whimsical allusion. She said, and meant: "We live our lives by [in the dual sense of alongside of and within] the philosophies of popular songs."

In my studies of organizations that make up the high-technology environment of Huntsville, Alabama, these philosophies were and are present and meaningful. I do not think it is an accident that the country music message is there but rare in a computer software firm, or that "oldies" rock n roll is the choice a whole new generation of listeners has made, judging from where they tune their office stereos. If we are what we eat, wear, and drive, there is reason to believe that we might also be what we listen to, particularly when what we listen to enters our lives on a regular and rhythmic basis, and the lyrics that come with the music find their way into what we say when we talk to each other about money, love, and the working life.

I should say here that I think Charles Conrad (1988) is right to locate work songs within the broader cultural frames of a Weberian *Weltanschauung* and to argue that their lyrics are clear evidences of hegemonic and occasionally hegemonically demonic forces. I also agree with Lawrence Grossberg (see especially 1984, 1986) that music must be seen as indications of and support for cultural processes and with a variety of researchers (see, for example, Chesebro et. al. 1985, Weisman 1985, Gonzalez and Mackay 1983, Roth 1981, Knupp 1981, Booth 1976, LeCoat 1976, and Kosokoff and Carmichael 1970) who have presented convincing cases for viewing music as a rhetorical process or transaction that connects audiences with their own or an imagined past. Stith Bennett's (1980) highly original field study of the group dynamics of rock n roll band formation and the desire to produce a "sound" further reveals ways in which social, organizational, and cultural forces coalesce around a core concept of music.

In an essay published in *Communication Research,* David Bastien and Todd J. Hostager (1988) use the idea of jazz as an inventive and social art form to describe organizational innovation. They write that "jazz is more than just a style of music that is captured in our collections of records, tapes, and compact discs. It is a celebration of the process of creating music, a form for musical innovation that engages performers as active composers in the collective invention, adoption, and implementation of new musical ideas" (582). Using videotapes of a live jazz performance and interviews with the performers, Bastien and Hostager reveal some principles of innovation potentially useful for understanding social and organizational processes.

I thought that was pretty neat when I read it, and I still do. What we have here is yet another approach to understanding how communication works as an organizer and emblem of cultural forces, as well as a micro-study of how communication works while work is being performed among a team of people who respond to certain symbols and signs and not to others, and how they create new variations on old themes.

Central to this study is the presence of music *and* social processes contributing to the meaning each has for the other, for the performers, and for the audience. Bastien and Hostager conclude that jazz musicians rely on conventions to "constrain their behavior, reduce uncertainty, and diminish turbulence" (1988, 598); these conventions are interdependent with the "level of musical structure," which in turn influences "musical choices available to the players" (598). The result is what is termed a "centering strategy," a way of returning to a commonly understood, stable and enduring theme leading into and following from innovative solo performances that require greater levels of individual and collective risk and uncertainty.

The same could probably be said for a jam session with rock n roll musicians (Eisenberg 1988). The important idea here is not that music is the key to understanding organizational innovation, but that our discipline is willing to recognize that *going to the source of a performance and asking the performers what they were trying to do, and even trying to do it yourself, is an acceptable way of doing research.* Furthermore, this study shows that an interpretive account of an organization can be done in a context other than a bureaucracy, which further suggests a strategic connection between rational and intuitive tensions that play at work and that work in play.

All studies are valuable, no privileged readings are allowed, but, as the summer 1989 hit by the rock band Poison puts it, "Every rose has its thorn." With the exception of Bennett, these studies have been products of scholarship that observe and classify, however artfully or completely, versions of the everyday world according to an academic plan, locating the meaning of the words and music in the language of our culture rather than in the language of the culture(s) producing and consuming them. These studies, in other words, try to make sensible the score without first having played the game. Furthermore, they have done so within the formats of academic scholarly writing, formats that have not changed much since the advent of electricity. This last point is important not just because it privileges ethnography, that rock n roll tale-telling rebel that has been loosed among the classical crowd (see Van Maanen 1988), but because it provides insight about why scholarship leaves out some of what is missing in our appreciations of culture and music.

Consider, for example, what a rhetorician does when she or he studies rock n roll. I choose rhetoric to pick on because I was reared on it and revere it, and I want to point out that my use of rhetorical methods to understand rock n roll has a long history. My first graduate school paper— for Gerry Hauser at Penn State—was an argument for viewing relational correspondences between Plato's *Phaedrus* and Meatloaf's rock n roll song-epic "Paradise by the Dashboard Lights." This interpretive tale aside, the point here is that a rhetoric person, like an archaeologist or an anthropologist, looks for—and at— artifacts. Find the artifact (in this case lyrics), and, using Some Prominent Theorist's work on Some Prominent Notion, interpret it. Then use the interpretation to repair the Prominent Notion, or to glorify it.

Obviously, a rhetorical approach works for all sorts of artifacts. However, when it comes to a performance art that creates an interdependent, ongoing, and changing relationship between performer and audience—such as rock n roll or teaching the strategic uses of nuclear weapons or managing a technical documentation department for a software firm—the processes of communication that work with and against the artifacts are equally important.

"LOUIE, LOUIE" AND CULTURAL PERFORMANCE

For the purposes of illustration, I give you the lyrics from one classic piece of rock n roll, first recorded by the Kingsmen in 1963:

Louie, Louie, whoa baby, I said way ta go,
Louie, Louie, whoa baby, I said me gotta go now.

Now if you read these lyrics sans music, even if you use Bob Greene's (1988) documented original source material, you can make an interesting but decidedly incomplete argument about the metaphor of a sailor going away from, thinking about, and then coming home to his true Jamaican love who has (he assumes) faithfully waited for his return. Maybe use Kenneth Burke to discuss the sort of midnight urge for consubstantiality that these lyrics seem to represent, or, to be really flashy, select some Continental French or German neo-Marxist university-trained existentialist to provide the glow for a reading of what a garage band in Seattle, using a poor, black songwriter's words, really said and meant circa 1963.

No matter what rhetorical reading you give to the words, that may be what the songs says, but not what it *does*. Nor even is it what most Americans think the song is really saying or even is about. I don't know about you, but I grew up singing lyrics nothing like the original ones, and they had to do with sexual positions for what today we would call the aerobically fit among us, and they featured the large "F" word, albeit garbled. Now a rhetorician could find a lot to write about here, this time borrowing premises from a host of sociologists or psychologists, but what would be written and published about the words real and/or imagined would not capture the spirit, the emotions, or power this song has when it comes on the radio or is played, live, at parties and concerts.

It is not that rhetoric as an idea can't cope with it. In fact, I think it can through a renewed appreciation for and exploration of the cultural tensions and aesthetic dimensions of rhetoric's expressive domain. But even with that as a basis for a reading of rock n roll, rhetorical criticism as it is practiced in our literature is conventional while the true subject of rock n roll is breaking with conventions. No matter what reading we give to the "it" of rock n roll, until we approach it on its own terms—words and music, communication processes and relationships among performers and with audiences, aural and visual images located within historical, cultural, political, and economic domains—we are missing important points if not *the* most important point.

This is why I began this chapter with reference to one of my intellectual heroes, the late Professor Herbert Blumer. When he says that the effective fulfillment of an interpretive social theory *"requires* a sensitivity to new dispositions and an appreciation of new lines along which social life may take shape" (1969, 142; emphasis mine), he is, I think, speaking both of the experience acquired by the author *and* of the ways in which those sensitivities and appreciations should be recorded or transmitted. In the case of rhetoric, culture, technology, and "Louie, Louie," you need more than artifacts and method; you need to immerse yourself in as much of the experience as you can seize—if you really want to learn what the songs means, you need to learn how to play them as well as listen to them—and you need a way of reporting the experience that reflects not just the immersion, but also what you've learned.

Without this commitment to understanding a culture on its own terms, we are engaged in little more than academic neocolonialism— the imposition of us, our values, language, and sense of appropriate style, on them. Or, to put an appropriate Burkeian twist on this, derived from his comments on how language shapes us: we aren't doing research, we are letting research do us.

IMPROVISATIONAL RELICS AND BLURRED GENRES

Having meant precisely what I've said, it's now time to explain what I mean. Where do you go, as a rhetorically informed interpretive ethnographer, and what do you do when you get there? These are tough questions because there are no exactly right answers, but fortunately for me some inroads have already been made.

Perhaps the foremost commentator on rock n roll as a cultural force was

Lester Bangs (see Marcus in Bangs 1988), whose critical work appeared
in magazines such as *Rolling Stone* and *Creem* primarily during the 1970s
and until his untimely death, from complications in the heart and lungs
from the flu and Darvon, in 1982. He wrote cultural scholarship in the
form of "music reviews" and used his reviews to meditate, publicly and
with great rhetorical charm, on the relationships between music and life.
He wrote in a stream-of-consciousness street jargon that both assumed
and created cultural commonplaces and was marked by the presence of
insight. Consider his definition of work:

> . . . to go out an' hafta assume what we used to call Manhood, which involved
> going at the same time very day to some weird building and doing some totally
> useless shit for hours on end just so you could get some bread and have
> everybody respect you (1988, 7).

Or consider this one, about what rock n roll is really all about:

> All those early songs about rock 'n' roll were successive movements in a suite
> in progress which was actually nothing more than a gigantic party whose
> collective ambition was simple: to keep the party going and jive and rave and
> kick 'em out cross the decades and only stop for the final Bomb or some
> technological maelstrom of sonic bliss sucking the cities away at last. (1988,
> 64–65)

I wish the quote stopped here, because it puts into one sentence my whole
point about the real relationship between rock n roll and technology, but
to do justice to Mr. Bangs, here is the rest of it:

> Because the Party was the *one* thing we had in our lives to grab onto, the one
> thing we could truly believe in and depend on, a loony tune fountain of youth
> and vitality that was keeping us alive as much as any medicine we'd ever take
> or all the fresh air in Big Sur, it sustained us without engulfing us and gave
> us a nexus of metaphor through which we could refract less infinitely extensible
> concerns and learn a little bit more about ourselves and what was going on
> without even, incredibly enough, getting pretentious about it. (1988, 65)

These words of wisdom appear in a review called "James Taylor Marked
for Death," in which Mr. Bangs recorded the change that was then occurring in rock n roll, a change away from the "Party" to what he feared
would be "I-Rock" music, "the soundtrack for our personal and collective
narcissistic psychodramas" (1988, 66). For those of us who prize this sort
of critical insight as further testimony to the postmodern among us, to
the tendency of a hypercapitalistic society to develop an all-consuming
appetite for images that can, as Stuart Ewen (1988) points out, replace

substance with style, it is instructive to read the following passage in that
same 1971 review:

> The trend toward narcissistic flair has been responsible in large part for smiting
> rock with the superstar virus, which revolves around the substituting of *atti-*
> *tudes* and flamboyant trappings, into which the audience can project their
> fantasies, for the simple desire to make music, get loose, knock the folks out
> or get 'em up dancin'. It's not enough just to do those things anymore; what
> you must do instead if you want success on any large scale is either figure out
> a way of getting yourself associated in the audience's mind with their pieties
> and their sense of "community," i.e., ram it home that you're one of THEM;
> or, alternately, deck and bake yourself into an image configuration so blatant
> or outrageous that you become a cultural myth. (1988, 67)

Ahead of his time, I'd say. But the more critical issue here is the source
of his insight. What is it that he did, as a researcher, that gave him a way
of ciphering the clues to this cultural mystery? Was he born knowing how
to do it, or was it something he acquired, learned? According to Greil
Marcus, Bangs "defined a critical-journalism based on *the sound and lan-*
guage of rock 'n' roll which ended up influencing a whole generation of
younger writers and perhaps musicians as well. . . . [H]e . . . also led
two rock 'n' roll bands active on the Manhattan club scene . . . [that]
Lester said accounted for his approach as a rock critic" (Marcus in Bangs
1988, ix–x; emphasis mine).

Notice here that the act of criticism was informed by immersion in the
culture and active participation in it. Lester Bangs was, aside from the
doctoral pedigree, an accomplished interpretive ethnographer. Perhaps
more important, he sought to be, in his own words, "a contender if not
now then tomorrow for the title Best Writer in America" (1988, x). As
Marcus notes, "perhaps what this . . . demands from a reader is a willing-
ness to accept that the best writer in America could write almost nothing
but record reviews" (x).

I'm not ready to accept that conclusion, but I do think it represents
evidence for the truth of Clifford Geertz's observations (1983) about
"blurred genres." However, to blur the genres means essentially to blur
writing styles and techniques, which, although an interesting development in the history of rhetoric, is no more important than the Beatles'
appropriation of the British national anthem to begin their song "All You
Need Is Love," or a computer terrorist injecting a "virus" into a system.
What is far more important is that by blurring genres what was previously
ineffable becomes expressible. And the result of that articulated presence
is a new appreciation for, and perhaps understanding of, the subject.

BEING THE FOOL, PLAYING THE KING

Now that I've sketched why I think interpretive ethnography and rhetoric can help us understand the relationships between rock n roll and social and organizational life in our culture, I want to share with you how the blurring of those genres opened up new ways of seeing, being, and knowing through research.

For years while I was engaged in the study of high technology organizations and the collective mindset that is Huntsville, Alabama, I neglected to take field notes on music. It was always on, always there, and always alluded to or used to provoke commentary in otherwise ordinary conversations. But I overlooked it because it was so pervasive. If I thought about it at all I thought about music as a part of the environment, rather than something next to it, a source of commentary on it.

About when I completed *Casing a Promised Land* (1989) it occurred to me that there was another story going on here. At first I saw it as "the other side of high technology" and tried out the idea of music as a pressure valve in the machinery of culture, a way of gradually reducing stress or, at parties and concerts, of blowing off steam. I think this works, but it is incomplete. There is more going on here than that. Rock n roll is not fully explained by the metaphor of a pressure valve because contemporary, side-by-side tensions of modern and postmodern culture aren't fully explained by the metaphor of a machine. This is also a service economy that chooses music while people are legally defined as property, and workers as slaves (see Spence 1989, 162–80), and a high-tech context that weaves song lyrics through the real and symbolic traffic of a fast but highly regulated public life. These are different combinations of words, and they invite different interpretations of meaning. By saying those words aloud I also learned to see things differently.

I used to drive down the main streets of Huntsville and see signs for computer companies and missiles and solid-rocket boosters, then I noticed that some of those signs had been replaced with advertisements for oldies radio stations, live rock n roll bars, and expensive stereo equipment. Signs and their semiotics had altered, but I was so busy writing I hardly noticed. Now the denizens of high-tech research parks sported album-cover hairstyles that ran the full range from Euro-punk to New York hip while still wearing the corporate uniform of starched white collars and designer rags. Things, and persons, were loosening up.

This perception, and the words that created it, also accompanied me when I went shopping. Suddenly, everywhere was the 1960s music again; even the top-forty stations were playing remakes of old hits. The oldies compact disc sections in record stores grew, in the space of a few months, from a rack at the end of the alphabet to alphabetized sections that read like they did when I was back in high school: Animals, Beatles, Cream, Dylan, Jimi Hendrix, Janis Joplin, Stones, Who. It was clear that those who own the music rights were tuned in to this renewed source of cultural appreciation. Then I started noticing video soundtracks, which increasingly read like Kasey Kasem's rock oldies show, and saw that the lines at movie theaters and concerts featuring sixties musical groups included teenagers for whom that historical period was roughly equivalent to what World War II and big band music had been for me, and I wouldn't have been caught dead at their age doing that. Company picnics and Christmas parties featured rock n roll.

I was on the edge of something. It had something to do with the character of the community I had been studying, and something to do with rock n roll music, and although they had always been here together, it was as if they had suddenly crossed a threshold. But my inability to be more precise was a major clue in this new investigation. This would not be a matter of finding the words to describe and analyze the text, of giving a reading, spinning webs of significance, and of walking away. That would not solve the problem. But what would?

OUTRO AS INTRO

Thus confused, I began asking a very different sort of question.

Lester Bangs said that "you can say that to love the questions you have to love the answers" (1988, 25). But love is very much a participatory experience, and it was clear to me that if I was to understand what was happening here I needed a fuller form of participation.

Rock n roll, like interpretive ethnography, is not a spectator activity. Even in video or at live concerts, the audience comes dressed and hyped up to be part of the show, participates by tapping a foot, singing aloud, screaming, dancing, or just nodding out. But to watch the audience is to privilege consumption over production and to miss something in the context that links self to Other. It is to give a partial reading, and one that I think favors the rational and reflective over the emotional and spontaneous. It is also to look at the backs and behinds of people instead of their faces, and to observe the heat rather than to feel it.

Rock n roll is not about physics, even though it exudes heat and motion; nor is it about chemistry and biology, although chemicals, pheromones, and sexuality pervade the environment. Rock n roll is not even about music, either, when it comes down to it, at least as music is understood as just another art form. To appropriate Max Weber's phrase for my own purposes, this investigation is ultimately not about the spider, or the web, or even the fly caught in the web, but about the whole of the ecosystem that supports this possibility; it is about the evolutions of culture and nature, of life-forms and forms of organization and technology that coalesce in time and space as interdependent, interpenetrating forces meaningful in the connections among their processes and relationships. It is about desire and satisfaction played out in cultural performances that say something about what it means to live for today on the rim of tomorrow in a modern and postmodern society where the truly blurred genres are fact and fantasy, and the essential questions are not "Why?" and "How?" or even "Where did we come from?" but "Who are you?" and "Is it cool?" and "What's on next?"

It was at this moment in my musings that I first got that odd tingling sensation on the back of my neck and down the well of my spine, felt the pull and call of mystery, heard the detective's music. There was no way out.

Now that I knew this, I needed to do something about it. Find my way *in*.

To make a long story into a few short sentences, I joined a rock n roll band. We called ourselves WHITEDOG and learned to play no-compromise rock n roll. This is what I call doing real-world social research. It required reacquiring skills I hadn't used in twenty years, spending money on an instrument and amplification and the rest of the apparatus of the business, and striving to fit into a group that practiced three or four nights a week and played for money and beer whenever it could.

This is how it was in the beginning, anyway.

I thought I was only following my academic instincts, playing the undercover cultural detective in a rock n roll band. Immerse yourself in the culture, I said, learn to sing its songs, play its chords, jam with it a bit.

Yeah, that's exactly what I said. What I thought, too.

So, as a follow-up to my study of the high-technology companies and government agencies in Huntsville, Alabama, I went undercover again, this time as a rhythm ace in a rock n roll band. The aim was not fame but *verstehen,* an understanding of the social and political life and appeal of a service organization that satisfies a particular desire within this culture.

Again, this is what I thought in the beginning. This is where it begins. How could I know that one year later I would look back at that innocence, that academic instinct, that desire for being alive in the mystery and music of fieldwork, and see not just the beginning of a research project but the end of life as I had known and practiced it?

But I am getting ahead of my story. I apologize.

I want to conclude this chapter by returning to my thesis about the cultural role of rock n roll (and interpretive ethnography) as a new form of social life. You will recall that I mentioned that rock n roll played the fool to technology's genius, and as a fool it could sing the truth while wearing a fool's clothing. This time around, however, the king is not a nation but a dominant ideology of technological capitalism (and formula-driven research reports) that is the currency of the mixed media of the side-by-side modern and postmodern eras. I think it is important to recognize that rock n roll (and interpretive ethnography) grew out of the working classes (how else do you define field research?) in England and America and is the inheritor, both musically and culturally, of the enslavement that influenced the development of the Mississippi blues and before them the slave songs, the dirges, and the ditties. I think it is also important to see the connections between the recent Soviet and Chinese sponsorship of forms of capitalism to make their economies more competitive, particularly their technologies, and the virtual explosion of rock n roll as a force within those cultures. And I haven't even mentioned Japan and its insatiable appetite for American rock n roll (see Iyer 1988) or the mass purchase of rock n roll records by East Berliners that memorable weekend when they began tearing down the Wall.

I do not believe these are merely correspondences in time, but neither do I feel I am quite ready to make any of this into a causal argument. There is clearly a lot going on, and this is the first chapter of these private investigations of a form of public life. What I keep coming back to, though, particularly when I think back to how I played rock n roll before a live audience, is this notion of tension between the fool and the king. I think what I am about to read to you from the work of Lester Bangs invites some very intriguing questions, good stuff to go softly, rhythmically, into that dark night. It goes like this: "Rock 'n' roll . . . is all just a joke and a mistake, just a bunch of foolishness. . . . What's truest [in it] is that you cannot enslave a fool" (1988, 74).

THE VOICE(S) IN THE TALE(S)

There are many descriptive rhetorics available within the public and private lives of rock n roll. From balladeers to rap artists, from skiffle groups to heavy metal, from country crossovers to Philly soul, it is through the presence of the individual voice, however awkward or strange its cut against the mainstream or its neat fit into it, that the creative mix of music, culture, and technology finds expression, comments on life.

The roar and swirl of the everyday is everywhere, and the experience of it is always personal and close. There is no such thing as a tranquil process, no more than there is predictability and uniformity in matters of passion. For even if our outward actions can be described in categorical displays and our experiences reduced to mere behaviors in public places, the meanings we have for those actions and behaviors are generally far richer than the simpler words we use to describe and categorize them. Something essential gets wiped out and the rest is enslaved, and with what got wiped out goes some essential part of understanding the experience of being human, even if that experience is sung in the rage of a low, solo voice, even if that voice is chronically out of tune.

How else can you explain Bob Dylan? Or Lou Reed?

And where would we be without them?

Interpretive ethnography seeks to liberate the human voice in humane scholarship, just as rock n roll liberates a major source of the soul of public life. This may be its call, its inspiration, but there are more practical matters that should concern those of us who labor in the fields of scholarly endeavor. For it is out there in those fields, within that mysterious *sursum corda* mix, that interpretive ethnography seeks to display aspects of culture in its naturally occurring, often confusing, always enabling, dialectical, dialogic maturity. Here is where we resist enslavement, sing songs, and tell tales. Just as Mikhail Bakhtin (1984a) found in Dostoevsky's characters the polyphonic qualities of discourse about social life, so too should those of us who study public life strive to give voice to the polyphonic discourse in which we immerse ourselves.

When we do that, the stories we share must inevitably deal with the same three elements of dramatic penetration—self, Other, and context. Issues of self go beyond the classical questions of authorship to the marrow of who we are and to who we are in relation to those whom we study and strive to understand. When we ask questions of the self in ethnography, we are asking questions not only about where and how we position ourselves as authors within the text, but also who we find ourselves to be when we get there. I am speaking here of our autobiographical selves, the stories we weave as threads into contexts that are themselves but a multiple weave of autobiographical texts. For what else is a rhetorical situation but what happens when two or more persons meet? And can any tale from the field be told accurately without involving those aspects of autobiography that teach us who we are, what we favor, and what we ignore? To give voice to a text is, in part, to give voice to the self who composes it.

Issues of Other are always even more complex. If the self assumes autobiography, then considerations of the motives and actions and meanings of Others assume biographical qualities. If we are proud enough to answer the call for explications of self, then we must be brave enough to answer a similar call for details about the Other. Who is this person, these persons? Who does the Other claim to be, and where did the Other come from? The Other, individually and collectively, comprises a voice(s) in the polyphonic stir of culture, and its representation within ethnographic texts is always problematic. Their songs, all of them, are about the flesh of identity inside the flash of behavior.

The voices of context are those most often missing from communication scholarship, and they must be recovered if interpretive ethnography is to make good on its promises. I am speaking here, of course, of *place* of public discourse and deportment, its poetic and physical dimensions, the meanings it holds for self and Other, its permanence and its change. But I am also speaking of context as the sum of the tale, as the story that gets told after all the dramas have been enacted, of the sense of place that lives on beyond its own immediacy and purpose. I am speaking, then, of context as sentences that comment on the weave as well as the weave that is used to make utterable the sentences.

Such is the fabric of this text. It is rock n roll as public life gotten at by means of private investigations called, grandly, interpretive ethnography. But it is still just rock n roll. And you, reader, can place the appropriate accent anywhere in that sentence you feel it belongs.

Let us begin on familiar ground, in a sort of standard blues riff played out in a moderate tempo in the key of C, in the scholarly voice of an earnest student of communication and culture singing carefully to an audience of his esteemed peers. And let's go into it now as easily as you turn this page . . .

2

Trouble at the Border:
The Mysterious Disappearance of Context,
Self, and Other from Communication Scholarship

Symbolic interactionism provides the premises for a profound
philosophy with a strong humanistic cast. In elevating the 'self' to a
position of paramount importance and in recognizing that its
formation and realization occur though taking the roles of others
with whom one is implicated in the joint activities of group life,
symbolic interactionism provides the essentials for a provocative
philosophical scheme that is peculiarly attuned to social experience.

—Herbert Blumer

The search for one's own (authorial) voice. To be embodied, to
become more clearly defined, to become less, to become more
limited, more stupid. Not to remain tangential, to burst into the
circle of life, to become one among other people.

—Mikhail Bakhtin

Here truth is not scientific but metaphorical.

—Kenneth Burke

THE BORDER METAPHOR

In the concluding section of an essay entitled "'What We Need
Is Communication': 'Communication' as a Cultural Category in Some
American Speech," Tamar Katriel and Gerry Philipsen (1981) offer the
following observation:

Our study of American "communication" has led us to think of ethnography
less as a journey into a foreign land or culture, and more as a journey into a
no-man's land, which is neither the territory of the self nor of the other. As
every Israeli child who was taken on that mandatory field trip to the border
knows, one cannot risk more than a few steps into unsettled territory.

In doing so, however, one becomes aware not only of the existence of the
other's territory, but of one's own, and the concept of territory in general. The
ethnographer, like the careful tourist, pays his or her tribute to the border at

22

designated spots, but the border stretches and winds between these spots as well, and it is in this unmarked territory that the "person" searches for a sense of personal meaning. (316)

My essay begins with this observation for three reasons. First, I want to use the metaphor of the border and its place in relational definitions of self and Other to further an argument about the centrality of context to both processes and products of human understanding. Second, I will examine our professional literature as a cultural artifact that reveals both ontological and epistemic dimensions of the problems of self, Other, and context that are inherently connected to accepted forms of scholarly research and writing. Third, I invoke a Brockriedeian interpretation of *human understanding* as a source of critique for a dialectical (and dialogic) bridge between readings of the cultural category of American communication and the personal experiences and reporting habits of communication researchers.

My purpose in this chapter is to build on rich intellectual traditions to suggest that a new frontier of communication research and writing is available for scholarly exploration. At this frontier, new questions arise about the relationships between and among researcher, subject, and context within the broader scope of historical, cultural, and social processes that create and constitute *meaning* as the core human experience of "communication."[1] Toward this general objective I will derive major assumptions, questions, and methods from the enterprises of cultural ethnography, anthropology, family systems psychology, and the philosophy of communication that are at this historical juncture converging on meaning-centered, postmodern conceptions of the connection between knowledge and its representation. By attending to the promise of this new frontier I will show that all accounts of "communication," "understanding," and "research" are interpretive episodes capable of providing readers with narrative details about how we know about what we see when we situate the study of communication in contexts marked by the presence of self and Other.

1. This essay must acknowledge a heavy intellectual debt to George Herbert Mead and Herbert Blumer. While most readers will recognize that most of these arguments are embedded within the scholarly traditions that have worn the label of "symbolic interactionism," my formal acknowledgment here is intended to extend these ontologic and epistemic traditions to include considerations of literary, relational, and representational concerns that are featured in this chapter.

NO-(WO)MAN'S-LAND: THE ABSENCE OF
CONTEXT AND THE NEGATION OF SELF AND
OTHER IN COMMUNICATION RESEARCH
PRACTICES

Victor Turner observes that "meaning arises when we try to put what culture and language have crystallized from the past together with what we feel, wish, and think about our present point in life" (1986, 33). Viewed this way, meaning can be both a constrained response to a situation (as when a certain language "fits" a ritual) and an inventional opportunity to overcome or replace those constraints (as when a revolution, innovation, or discovery is articulated as such). Meaning, then, suggests an array of possibilities in any situation, that array being limited by cultural standards, personal history and preferences, and whatever occurs within the situation that prompts a meaningful response.

To be meaningful, experience must include three sources of potential information: knowledge of and about self, knowledge of and about Others, and knowledge of and about the context in which meaning can be attributed to the experience. This is not to suggest that each one of these sources of information is real, complete, or accurate. No matter how completely we believe we know ourselves or Others or understand a situation, such knowledge is at some level always necessarily ego-centered and is therefore, by definition, partial.

TWO VIEWS OF SELF

Viewed monistically, a self is contained within an individual, and the nature of self, while never open to purely empirical scrutiny, is nevertheless a category under which falls, depending upon your linguistic assets (theory), a variety of sentences, phrases, and descriptors. For some, knowledge of self is "organic" and may be located in a particular region of the brain. For others, knowledge of self is a linguistic category shaped by cultural and environmental influences, definable only by its outward manifestations of behavior. For still others, knowledge of self is a product of organic and environmental influences, an analytical category that nevertheless maintains that the individual actor is a hero-villain capable of exercising choice to overcome negative predispositions, a poor economy, illness, or family neglect.

Each of these conceptions of self is grounded in a preference for individuality. In them an individual self is the inheritor of certain traits and capacities and has the native ability to develop, change, or maintain them. Knowledge *about* the self, then, is knowledge *about* an individual actor, a person, a choice maker, a user of words, a performer of observable behaviors.

Viewed dialectically, however, knowledge of self is never achieved alone. The self is not presented to the world in isolation but in consort with other selves. For family systems theorists (Haley 1976; Kerr and Bowen 1988; Phillips and Wood 1983), "the individual" is a convenient linguistic construction that often obscures the fact that a structure of interlocking relationships—rather than autonomous psychological entities—is the base for whatever empirical, behavioral, or internal states are used to describe a self.

This view of a self as an actor within webs of relationships reveals that knowledge *about* the self is always interdependent with knowledge *about* Others (Blumer 1969; G. Mead 1934). It also reveals the centrality of communication as a bridge between or among selves and places at the forefront of communication theory the issue of linguistic representation of human experience. Knowledge of and about how a person, a self, interacts within a particular web should proceed dialectically within an evolving context. We therefore confront two issues simultaneously. First, how can we make sense out of the action? And second, how can we make the action sentence-able?

The primary issue of sense making, then, is relational, not individual. What are the structures of family, friends, enemies, and so on, that contribute to the observed performances? If meaning is a broad cognitive construct, and if situated meaning among persons is aimed at least partly at reducing the uncertainty of the setting and partly at reducing the anxiety of the self, then dialectical conceptions of self—who am I in relation to the Other? what are the likely reponses the Other will make to me? etc.—seem far more appropriate than individual ones.

The second issue is as important as the first, at least as far as scholarship is concerned. The issue is not merely how to make sense out of a performance, but how to make such a performance sentence-able.

First, it seems clear that to capture multiple selves within contexts requires fuller participation of the selves being captured whose experience can and should be articulated *by* them rather than *for* them. Several options are currently available, including multiple authorship of the essay or book; an account of the experience written by the researcher's subjects and included within or as an appendix to the text; and experimentation with alternative genres for writing scholarship, including drama, dialogue, fiction, interview, and debate.

Second, knowledge of the researcher/writer's self must be included in scholarly accounts of others' experiences. If we insert ourselves into the context we will learn to see our observational and critical processes as part of the reading we give to whatever happens, and the written (or other form of) account will provide richer testimony to the complexity and connectedness of how meanings are constructed through communication.

Third, alternative media may be cultivated for presentation of scholarly work. Our generation of scholars has available forms of expression previous generations did not, including all forms of electronic media. Consider, for example, a video of a corporate culture—say, the BBC's series "Decisions"—as a way of revealing what the discussed persons and things look like and do, complete with oral endnotes, if you like. The result would be a new use (for communication scholars) of an available means of persuasion that could further our understanding of what an individual took as data for interpretive conclusions; it would also be a permanent account of both the data and conclusions which could easily be made available to others for critical scrunity.

So, in summary, a knowledge of and about self is understood within a web of relationships. To get at those relationships, to bring to their internal dynamic a source of external critique, should be a natural aspect of communication research. To do such research requires expanding the way in which research projects are carried out and reported by actively engaging the participation of those studied, by acknowledging the researcher's knowledge of self in the experience, and by broadening the scope of what constitutes a scholarly contribution.

THE PROBLEM OF THE UNDIFFERENTIATED OTHER

Knowledge of and about the Other in communication research is one of the most troublesome concepts in our literature. Historically, speech scholars have defined the Other as the audience, a collective group of generally passive listeners about whom the speaker had attitudes, strategies, and motives and toward whom the message of the speech was directed. With the advent of group and interpersonal research the concept of audience shifted—mostly along the lines of the individual psychology discussed above—and the interpersonal Other became, in the communication process, a partner whose personal needs, desires, goals, and motives were to be assessed.

There are both ontological and epistemic concerns that guide research about knowledge of and about the Other. Rawlins (1985), for example, discusses three phases of interpersonal communication research that occurred from the 1940s to the 1970s, using the labels of social integration, individual integration, and situational integration eras to chart changes in the what and how of our discipline's research. In his review, he develops an extensive critique of the terms most often used to describe the ontological dimensions of our knowledge—effectiveness, social conventions and idiosyncratic rules, communication skills and attitudes toward communication, persuasion versus individual freedom, and interactional control—yet curiously absent from his list is any coherent concept of the Other. It is as if, despite our claims to a fundamental concern for communication as the substance of human *relationships,* we carry over into the realm of relational research the intellectual baggage of an individualized, nonintegrative view of the self and Other that form relationships.

The question of the ontological dimensions of the Other—what is this person to the relationship, and what can be known about him or her?—is reduced to a categorical mirroring of our similarly narrow view of the self as behavior: what we are is that portion of what we say and do that can be measured. A more comprehensive, holistic, and dialectical perspective would modify that statement to read: what we are includes what we say and do as well as the *meanings* we (self and Other) have for the experience of those actions within contexts and relationships that we maintain. Viewed this way, the Other is a full partner to the relationship and an equal contributor to the ways in which contexts are understood.

The epistemic issue has been handled primarily as a question of methods for conducting the research, rather than as a question that connects those methods with their results—the written research report. If our knowledge exists in sentences, and if our sentences are constrained by traditional scholarly formats and formulas for reporting research, then the issue of how we come to knowledge is isomorphic with how we represent that which we have come to know. Unfortunately, most graduate training—both texts and course structures—creates an unnecessary and inaccurate bifurcation between "doing research" and "writing up the report" that fails to recognize the connection between knowledge and its representation. The result is, in part, that we have developed sophisticated methods that fit into the traditions of scholarly writing without examining how that writing has likewise contributed to (and obscured) our knowledge. Consider, for example, the representative depth of a good dramatic enactment of a relationship, particularly what it suggests about the self and Other in a context, against any published essay in our literature. Which one better depicts relational reality?[2]

The issue is not whether the questions we ask as scholars can be accommodated by alternative genres and media, for surely an answer—regardless of which one you give—is too superficial. Some very sophisticated questions about human relationships have been evident in plays, novels, biographies, and films for quite some time, but not everyone who has mastered the methods of sophisticated inquiry can write that well. The issue, however, is deeper than that: whoever is able to define the Other is ultimately in charge of what is known.

As researchers/writers we have a relationship with those whom we study. In that relationship we also have the power of the pen, and the authority of our role in society as seekers of truth and beauty, knowledge and understanding, to control what is made known. If our knowledge is constrained by the genre of our endeavors, and if our understanding of others is narrowed by our treatment of them as objects to be seen, counted, accounted for, or manipulated, then we are back to a concept of knowledge of and about the Other as audience for our sophisticated rhetorical charms. We still don't know who the Others are or what meanings they bring to our—and their own—relationships.

THE REDUCTIONS OF CONTEXT

If our research literature reveals anything about the concept of context, it is that we have reduced it to one of mere *role,* occasionally coupled with the researcher's descriptions of a physical environment. Studies are done in which x number of roles (roommates, friends, superiors/subordinates, students, and volunteers) define the context in which the study is

2. Some graduate programs within our discipline allow performance theses that attempt to accomplish precisely these objectives. Specifically, I am thinking here about the arena of performance of literature, in which the actor's ability to research and to produce relational understandings within a definable context is paramount.

to have meaning. Similarly, other studies focus on the artifacts within an environment as clues to what a context is, despite the fact, as Sackmann (1987) points out, that the presence of the same or even similar artifacts in two distinct cultures (for example, the pyramids in Egypt and in Mexico) may give a false sense of shared meaning (the former are to honor the dead, the latter for worshiping the sun).

Similarly, to define context as the role enacted within a physical environment is to ignore the functions of communication in creating and constituting, as Marshall Sahlins puts it, "the meaningful orders of persons and things" (1976). If the researcher is the key definer of the role, as well as the physical aspects of the environment, the meanings ascribed to the relationships manifested in the context by the participants are essentially lost. Think about the well-intentioned but nevertheless neocolonial attitude of early cultural anthropology as an analogue to our research experience. We are learned and trained observers; they are our naive subjects. We give to them a context of our devising and seldom ask if they have thoughts concerning it beyond the narrow purposes of our particular research project. We are interested in findings and conclusions, in rounding out the research experience in a way that will further our scholarly goals.

The conceptualization of knowledge of and about a context is often rendered in the static language of photography: we are taking pictures of a scene; this is what you see in it. But the scene was not the same before the photographer entered, and it changes after the picture is taken. A context is not the picture any more than "the word is the thing" (Korzybski 1933). What is even more confounding is that a context is given meaning in sentences uttered by the participants, who, in turn, are influenced by those utterances to "see" the context in their own interpretive ways. What one person "sees" as the context is not necessarily what another person "sees" (or responds to) in it, even though their roles may be clear to the researcher and to them and despite the fact that they share precisely the same physical environment.

Here again we confront the ontological and epistemic problems of ordinary, everyday experience. There are no easy answers unless we reduce the complexity of the experience, in which case, to what questions are we actually providing answers? Furthermore, if our overall agenda is to take apart naturally occurring experience, to break it down into components, perspectives, dimensions, and so forth with the eventual hope of putting it all back together again and reporting it in a linear form appropriate to scholarly conventions, then we mix in the metaphor of the machine with the metaphor of the organism and render the cultural, the social, and the semiotic—those symbolic, complex, and meaningful processes and relationships—into a technology of scholarship governed by a technique of writing. Given these sources of knowledge, it seems reasonable to assert that, if one is accounting for some event in which another was present, considerations of self, Other, and context should be included. This, of course, begs a question that cultural anthropologists have already confronted in accounts of their own cultural history (see Clifford and Marcus 1986; Davis 1986; Geertz 1988; Marcus and Fischer 1986; Van Maanen 1988). To wit: When a researcher goes into a foreign land and imposes his or her own cultural categories and biases upon the "savages," the result is a "homogenization" of cultural understanding toward the dominant (Western, scientific) model which obscures the meanings of the observed reality (or the copresent meanings of multiple realities) and denies to the observed the opportunity to respond. Furthermore, as Edward Said (1978) has argued, the rhetorical devices used within the genre of Western scholarly discourse value the activity (and active voice) of the author over the activities (and passive voice) of the subjects, rendering the discourse little more than further testimony to an exercise in power rooted in neocolonialism.

For discourse that aims at creating knowledge of and about a people and their practices—the essential task of cultural anthropology—meaning is not an aspect of reality to be observed and classified as if it were any other empirical fact (if, indeed, such a statement can be made of any data). Instead, meaning is derived from one's insertion of self into a setting in which knowledge of self, Others, and the setting all figure into the calculus of what is made known.

Consider, for example, the following argument made by Robert Paul in a *New York Times Book Review* essay in which he considers the dilemma posed by an anthropologist (in this case, Wade Davis) producing two accounts of the same experience—one for a scholarly audience and one for a more general reader:

> The purpose of the revision, so it seems, is to present the author's findings in a form more acceptable to science than the lively first-person narrative in "The Serpent and the Rainbow." Consequently, Mr. Davis has omitted from the present volume the story of the human events and encounters that led him to his findings.

The irony is that this revision not only makes "Passage of Darkness" less interesting to the lay reader, but also reduces its value as anthropology. Anthropologists these days do not imagine themselves to be objective observers of empirical cultural facts, but understand themselves as actors whose research is a complex process involving the construction of meaning, power relations and the placement of oneself and the people one studies within a real continuing social and historical setting. (21 August 1988, 14)

These insights are, in my view, equally applicable to communication research. While it seems unnecessary to point out that meaning can occur only within contexts (Carbaugh 1988; Goodall 1990b; Mishler 1979) and that any study of communicative motives, meanings, practices, or actions occurs within specific cultural, social, and historical circumstances, these self-evident truths all too often seem absent from scholarly discussions in our literatures. It is as if we still maintain that empirical reality is not socially constructed; that power relations among those who do the studying and those who are studied are not important as data to that construction of knowledge; or that placement of oneself—and taking account of that placement—is not a condition of the knowledge that ultimately will be constructed. As a result, what we claim to believe does not surface in our writing and, therefore, is absent from the tangible corpus of knowledge we produce.

COMMUNICATION LITERATURE AS A CULTURAL ARTIFACT

Our professional literature is a cultural artifact, the dominant evidence of our scholarly beliefs and values (Calas and Smircich 1987). In it we find, in addition to testimonies concerning our rituals (presidential addresses, attention to professional conventions, the encouragement of debates between advocates of differing points of view) and rites of passage (tenure, promotions, awards for teaching, research, and service), a curious absence of a common definition for communication.

In fact, for some scholars for a number of years this has been a central, and confounding, concern (Dance 1970, 1980; Miller 1966). Like Yahweh, what gives us life and sustains us seems almost ineffable, so complete a mystery that our scholarly lives are spent contributing to and occasionally revising the sacred texts that we pass on to new generations of worshipers. As new generations prosper, new sects—methods of "proper" worship—

develop among spiritual leaders whose noble quests seem destined to lead us to new truths, and for awhile our sacred texts are dominated by displays of prophecy found alternately in various locations. Still, the meaning of what we study eludes us, and communication becomes—again like Yahweh—sometimes a subject for explanation and inspiration, sometimes an object for critical and scientific scrutiny, and more recently, as a political term that legitimizes our scholarly and teaching endeavors (Mader, Rosenfield, and Mader 1985).

Common to communication as both subject and object is the need to express knowledge in a language that is always removed from the contexts that generate it. There is a world within the word, too. One world is lived in and everyday, full of the made-up alongside the constructed, dreamy and real, felt, random, fragmented, and maybe well planned. The other world—the one used to describe and analyze the mundane world—hovers in the literature as a copresent but virtually inaccessible reality around and perhaps above life, everydayless as reverie and noetic as police.

Communication, as a term and as a discipline, has no intrinsic meaning. Because meaning is found in contexts, as a source of tensions among self, Other, and setting, the study of communication—regardless of method or purpose—must always be context-specific. This does not mean that generalizations cannot or should not be made, nor does it mean that knowledge derived from one particular set of tensions is not applicable to another. It is to recognize that the experience of meaning in doing research is bound inextricably (1) to the assumptions, beliefs, and attitudes of the self as researcher, an actor in a scene that has no set script; (2) to the perceived realities that are mutually constructed between self and Others, including the researcher; and (3) to the understanding that whatever occurs within a specific context may not be experienced or explained in the same ways by all participants. Only the discursive product—the essay or book—legitimizes the role of researcher as author of the experience, and that occurs primarily because "the literature" is where, for our discipline, "communication" and our professional identities exist (see Goodall 1989b for extended discussion).

Perhaps this is why, as the opening quotation from two communication ethnographers rightly points out, when one does "communication" research the experience is more akin to entering a "no-man's-land" than a foreign culture. This is because the border between self and Other, between observer and observed, is seldom clearly articulated. And because it is seldom articulated, there is both an absence of context and a negation of self and Other as dominant motifs in our literature. The border disappears, and with it goes a powerful source of human understanding.

READING A RESEARCH REPORT FOR CLUES TO THIS DILEMMA

Consider, for a moment, a typical research report in any of our professional journals. The researcher reveals no self apart from a name, an institutional affiliation, and the references employed to help make the case. The subjects for the research are seldom named or given relational dimensions (for an excellent exception, see Krueger 1982) and are seldom asked to comment on the report after it is written, despite the fact that it is written about them. The context for the research project is described only by implication: it must have been in a classroom if students were asked to fill out a questionnaire. For the moment I will leave out the long-standing argument about using students to generate conclusions applicable to the rest of the world and concentrate on what this practice suggests about our research culture.

First, the meanings we attribute to what we observe are derived from our dominant literature rather than from the subjects we claim to be studying or from our contact with them within particular cultural contexts. Ours is the scholar's license, evident since Plato, to compare what we see and hear to what we believe ought to exist in some perfect elsewhere that is, in our own time, simply referred to as "the literature." Because "the literature" is a sacred text, its legitimacy is seldom questioned, and when questions are raised they are raised in the spirit of revisionary scholarly pluralism that, over the years, dramatizes various political battles that exude at best a hermeneutical zeal for the "proper" interpretation of a literary reference or authority and that seldom have much to do—or interest in—how that interpretation squares with "communication."

Second, researchers are presented in similar personae, as if the granting of advanced degrees in speech communication automatically inscribed a particular view of reality and way of seeing it on individual characters. Clearly, this is not the case, for one has only to attend any of our annual conventions to see that we each endorse particular sacred texts, few of which are fairly common while most are appealed to, and appealing only to, the particular sect to which we belong. Hence, despite the presence of a sacred literature, within the sects we seldom share even a common language for describing our assumptions, methods, or the results of "communication" research. Why then do we persist in the niggling and self-negating practice of writing our research reports in self-less prose that renders, falsely, a sense of commonality and fully shared beliefs?

What I am after here is not merely the insertion of "personality" or even "style" (because occasionally that occurs despite the limitations of the genre) that marks the individual as a person as well as the author of the experience; rather, I am calling for a fuller sense of immersion in the reasons for, and experience of, conducting the study. Aside from the obvious disclaimers of gaining a reputation, working toward tenure, why are we doing this? What are our motives? What are our goals? When we conducted the research, what were the contextual clues that induced our attention, that led us to believe that we had found something interesting? What were our sources of angst, frustration, or pleasure? What didn't we understand about the context, ourselves, and the Others that is also part—albeit unspoken—of this text? Questions such as these move us closer to the terrain of communication as practiced and experienced than do exclusively distanced inquiries.

Third, there is a bureaucratization of our organization evident from the way research reports are solicited, recognized, and reviewed that values narrow in-group legitimacy over broader cultural values. In a way this is reminiscent of Irving Janis's concept of "groupthink" (1982), in which the beliefs of decision makers who use themselves as the only applicable reality often interfere with the quality of their products. This charge can be substantiated in two distinct cultural practices: (1) the way in which we are asked to affiliate within the profession and (2) the way in which research reports are written and reviewed.

When we join our professional associations we are asked to affiliate with no more than two divisions. What if our interests are broader than that? The only real purpose to divisional affiliation is to gain members to justify program slots (after all, there has to be some method to this decision), but the practice encourages us, I think, to see our professional lives as participating in separate and often distinct categories. In an era marked, as Clifford Geertz (1980) has so memorably phrased it, by "blurred genres" of scholarship and by the encouragement of interdisciplinary and multidisciplinary research programs, such labeling is often merely a structurally convenient myth that has as a side effect a perpetuation of bureaucracy for its own sake.

More important, this local bureaucracy carries over into the politics of journal publication and convention space, the very contexts that we use to define our "literature." As in any culture there is a distinct need for new members to acquire the knowledge and skills and to generally "fit in." Research papers reveal how this is accomplished in three interrelated ways.

First, the research paper must "look like" other writing within this genre. Odd, then, that this discipline named "communication," one that admits to the legitimacy of a variety of expressive outlets—speech, poetry, dance, drama, television, movies, video, cartoons, performances of texts, etc.—has adopted the already conservative standards for scholarship among the humanities and social sciences. We study these other forms, but we have yet to use them as productive vehicles for our own scholarly work. For years this has been an active concern of members of our discipline in the dramatic and performance areas, and it seems to me that their experiences foreshadowed the current discipline-wide problem. When ideas must conform to arbitrary and narrow forms of expression, we are limiting expression and committing to scholarly exile ideas that may well express precisely the sorts of alternative wisdom that can help us overcome our native "groupthink."

Second, research reports must be read and reviewed by persons "knowledgeable" in the field. Viewed cynically, this can be interpreted as meaning the three other specialists who are within the minority who care about or support this idea. However, as a person who has served on editorial boards for various publications, I am not ready to be quite this cynical.

My concern is what counts as an "authority." If we, as a discipline, grant ourselves sole responsibility for the legitimacy or truth of an idea, we further separate ourselves from those whom we claim to be studying, not to mention those with whom we might profitably interact, and further narrow the concept of context to our own literature and professional identities. Perhaps we should consider letting outsiders—such as the students in the groups we use to generate our studies or the professionals working in the organizations we make claims about, or historians, political scientists, literary critics, and psychologists, from whom we often derive ideas, methods, and good reasons—to join the ranks of our "reviewers." Not only would this encourage others outside our field to look at what we do and offer criticisms aimed at improving our work, it would also encourage us to improve the quality, readability, diversity, and scope of impact of our scholarly expressions.

These observations are not meant to demean or devalue our scholarship.

They are made out of a sense of debt to a tradition of scholarship that has served us well, but, to borrow two terms Kenneth Burke (1965) has taught us, this tradition of scholarship also offers "terministic screens" that may be leading us toward "occupational psychosis." What we need is a challenge to our perspective. It is not enough to look back fondly over familiar territories; we need to begin to chart our exploration of the future, starting with a commitment not to confine that exploration to more of the same.

THE DIALECTICAL BRIDGE FOR UNDERSTANDING HUMANS COMMUNICATING

The late Professor Wayne Brockriede, in an essay aptly entitled "Arguing about Human Understanding" (1982), creates a critical stance consisting of three dimensions—the empirical, personal, and linguistic—that encourages a holistic approach to constructing knowledge about human communication. It is unique to our discipline in that it can be used to create the grounds for interpretive, pluralistic approaches to doing research about human communication that invites active and evident consideration of context, self, and Other.

Brockriede's model assumes that "*persons* come to understandings about *things* through *language*" (1982, 138) and that "human understanding embraces all of the methods, processes, and products people use when regulating their uncertainties about the empirical, personal, and linguistic aspects of their worlds . . . [while] deemphasizing such terms as analysis, categories, variables, and boundaries" (137). In other words, one does not have to distance oneself from the experience, defining it and categorizing it according to some preexisting system of critique to arrive at understanding. While such analyses may be performed and may be useful for some purposes, this does not and should not preclude the possibility—or the utility—of alternative forms of understanding.

One such possiblity, Brockriede suggests, is to use the figure-ground metaphor to emphasize that when one dimension of human understanding (say, the empirical) is brought to the forefront, others do not disappear; instead, they become the background against which the dominant figure dances (the personal realm of experience and the words that belong to the situation). The critical products of this pluralistic sense of how the world is apprehended and constructed is different from "monistic" perspectives that "reduce human understanding either to empirical things *or* to personal relations *or* to linguistic experience" (138).[3]

A second feature of Professor Brockriede's essay is his conception of how arguments of and about human understanding may proceed. Working from an earlier framework established by Joseph Wenzel (1980) that distinguishes a vocabulary for three perspectives on argument (logical, rhetorical, dialectical), Brockriede places the dialectical as the figure against the ground of logical products of argument and rhetorical processes for arguing. When this is conceptualized two possible outcomes are established: (1) the either/or, or forced choice, useful for making decisions, achieving consensus, or warranting claims; and (2) the both/and, useful for understanding perspectives involved in ongoing, interdependent, symbiotic contexts in which "the continued existence and health of one member of a dialectical pair is needed for the continued existence and health of the other" (144).

The value of building the dialectical bridge to arguments about human understanding is manifested in three ways. First, one can adopt the Burkeian stance toward linguistic transformations that mark "a person [as] *both* a unique substance *and* consubstantial with other persons" (144). Second, this approach has much in common with "the ancient Chinese symbol of yin-yang, which recognizes unity in dualisms and treats such apparent polarities as dark and light, good and evil, not as separate entities dueling to the death with one another, but as indivisible wholes" (144). Third, acceptance of the both/and dialectical schema encourages a broader range of acceptance in matters of arguments about human understanding, following the lead provided by Toulmin, Rieke, and Janik (1979) regarding aesthetic experience: "accepting one interesting and reasonable interpretation of a work of art does not necessitate rejecting others that are also supported by good rationales" (Wenzel 1980, 144).

The advantage of this figure/ground, both/and, dialectical bridging of the empirical, personal, and linguistic dimensions of human understanding lies in the complexity and sensitivity of its imagery. Consider again the problem of understanding what—and who—creates and constitutes "communication" and what is being "communicated" in any context. First consider the role of the researcher in this scene—her or his motives,

---

3. Herbert Blumer (1969, 140–52, 171–82) argued this point prior to Professor Brockriede, although his concern was primarily with social psychology and not within the narrower context of argument theory.

ambitions, purposes, beliefs, values, understanding of the professional literature, understanding of Others, sensitivity to context, knowledge of self. Now, if you will, consider the Other in the context, both those being studied and those to whom the final product (essay, book, video, film, etc.) will be shown or who are simply imagined as audience for this drama, and try to dig into their individual and collective senses of knowledge of and about self, Other (including you, as the researcher), and scene. Finally, consider the elements of the scene itself—its colors, textures, props, lighting, and so on. Consider it as a partner to the meanings that will be both evoked and ignored by those present, that will be judged or read or interpreted according to other scenes, other places, and other understandings of what it all means.

With all of this going on, and I believe all of this does go on every time we study "communication" within any setting, how can we not appreciate the complexity and sensitivity of an interpretive model that values all perspectives, rationales, and judgments as being potentially useful? As Brockriede has it: "The critic whose emphasis is on interpreting or explaining an experience need not offer any definitive account. A critic who takes a perspectival view cannot do so. He or she interprets an experience within the context of particular times, places, and cultures. The experience under criticism can be illuminated from the criticism of persons who choose to emphasize different dimensions, see the event or process from different points of view, or use different constructs" (1982, 145).

Brockriede's dialectical bridge was intended "to be a useful complement to the traditional approach in such activities as theory, practice, criticism, and research" (147). However, I believe his rationale has two other, perhaps subtler, messages for persons engaged in "communication" research. First, and most important, the humans that are to be understood or interpreted, that provide us with data about their communicative performances, and that serve as the constant ground against which our theories about and criticism about them form the figures (at least in our professional literatures)—these humans are *significant* Others. Within a research context we need to pay more attention to how *they* make and manipulate meanings: because they are our dialectical partners, the depth and richness of our literature depends as much on their involvement and continued cooperation as it does on ours. This means more than simply observing more carefully and giving closer attention to details; it means encouraging experimental ways of representing the research experience, particularly the ways of writing the research report.

Anthropologists have given us the lead by endorsing a wide variety of genres for reporting research—dramas, documentaries, dialogues, interviews, and fiction (not in the sense of "untrue," but as perspectival truth rendered within the conventions of this genre of expression). What they have recognized is that there is a genuine and unavoidable connection between how an experience is experienced and how that experience is rendered in prose. As long as the author is content to work within traditional modes of reporting, the knowledge reported remains exclusively traditional.

The second insight provided by this remarkable essay concerns sensitivity to context. Put simply, if meanings occur only within contexts, then contexts must become part of the description of the research experience. This does not mean, I think, that it is enough simply to state that "subjects for this research were 122 undergraduates enrolled in a basic speech course at a large midwestern university" or to state that the researcher "spent three months observing and interviewing persons at the XYZ Corporation." In either case what is left out is any sense of context as it is lived through by human beings, and what is put into the description is merely a conventional line designed to answer conventional reviewer concerns about *where* or *when* the research was conducted, not what meanings were attributed by the researcher (or others) to the scenes in which the drama was enacted. Context is not a static description of place or time; it is an unfolding of clues, a weaving of a pattern, that at some point becomes part of the articulated presence that is further woven or read into the meaning of the experience.

Brockriede's point about arguments concerning human understanding leaves out nothing that is indigenous to human experience. The beauty of his case rests with its appreciation of human complexity and its urging of all critics to admit to and to account for that complexity. Furthermore, his argument lends itself to the interpretive turn in understanding that currently characterizes one of the newest and most promising movements within the discipline. Although no doubt the essay can be read simply as support for the valuing of interpretive critique, I prefer to read it (or perhaps read *into* it) as having a more radical motive. And that motive has to do with how we report on what we experience when we argue about human "communication."

In the culture that is speech communication and that is represented by our professional literature as a dominant artifact, the first seventy-five years have contributed to a great and noble tradition of scholarship, in part derived from other academic cultures and in part created and sustained by the labor of women and men in our discipline who have advanced what we claim to know about humans communicating. It is no coincidence, I think, that these advances and traditions have occurred historically during a period marked by the rise of modernism and by a broadening of the scope of natural science, which has transformed the image of the humanities and fostered the birth and spread of social science; also, during this period of academic history the worth and legitimacy of a discipline has come to be measured by its numbers of scholarly publications, by its accumulation of dollars in grants, and by the reputations of its researchers.

There have been at least two results of this turn for our place in history. One result has been that universities and colleges have devalued the place of education in their mission, focusing instead on research, with implications beyond the scope of this essay. The other result has been the acceptance of conventionalism and complacency in our chosen method for reporting and judging the value of published research. The dominant artifact of a discipline named "communication" represents a division between what we know and what we do.

ALL ACCOUNTS ARE INTERPRETIVE EPISODES

This is the place in the essay to bring together the two themes that have thus far been developed—the border as metaphor for a context capable of dividing self and Other, and the dialectical bridge of both/and that is capable of revealing a necessary relationship between self and Other through empirical, personal, and linguistic dimensions—and to use them to transform our ideas about communication, research, and understanding.

Communication, Research, and Understanding

In 1977 Arthur Bochner reviewed the current state of scholarship and scholarly journals dedicated to the scientific advancement of communication theory and research and asked the poignant question "Whither?" This review occurred at a particularly important time within the history of our discipline because "new" journals such as *Human Communication Research, Journal of Applied Communication Research,* and *Communication Research* were adding outlets for researchers interested in revising monistic theories of science and charting new inroads into empirical (mostly quanti-tative) "middle-range" work. It was also interesting because the concept of "communication" was described as "so pregnant with meaning, that it stymies our best efforts to circumscribe its boundaries" (325). The "boundaries" were then de facto defined as occurring within seven specific professional journals.

Then as now, "communication" was a territory defined by the borders of professional journal space and scholarly volumes, an existence often described as being "at the cutting edge of theory" but nevertheless an existence in sentences spoken at the margins of society. Put simply, our contribution to the commonweal has tended rather heavily toward issues relevant only within the ivory tower. Furthermore, these contributions serve to distance the study of communication from cultures of persons who do the communicating by failing to enter into a dialogue with our subjects about their feelings, experiences, and insights on the topic of communication. Instead, we force college sophomores (who have no real choice), occasional consulting clients (whose names—and often con-texts—are changed to mask their identities), and the numerous faceless Others whom we have seen and observed within the contexts of our own lives and who become the examples we use to document our own work to accept our definitions of what counts as meaningful when they communi-cate. Our focus—our concept of the Other—is ourselves and our profes-sional colleagues who are united by a language code, not the people who "communicate" outside of it.

In 1984 Julia Wood cautioned us to honor the real world connection by "(1) focus[ing] on communication as a substantive, formative activity in its own right, (2) respond[ing] to human issues and problems charac-tering the world beyond the ivory tower, and (3) develop[ing] research designs and methods that are compatible with the recommended concep-tual *foci*" (3). Her recommendations still seem useful and increasingly necessary. Unfortunately, rare is the article that incorporates them.

Earlier in this essay, I argued for a Brockriedeian dialectical bridge for more inclusive treatments of self, Other, and context when accounting for knowledge of and about communication. That may sound like fairly fancy language, and a fairly complex method, to carry into the market-place. But it is not intended to be. To build a dialectical bridge requires talking with those whom you are studying and being receptive to their interpretations of the context you share. You will exchange ideas, engage in arguments, occasionally reach agreement. Through this give-and-take approach to learning about communication, you will encounter words, phrases, sentences, expressions, gestures, and silences that all contribute to the meaning you will, at some point, walk away from the encounter with. That is one way to conduct real-world research.

The more difficult part will be how to represent the knowledge you gain from the experience. It is intriguing to me that the method I have just advocated corresponds to the way some of the more enduring ideas about communication in Western civilization have been generated— witness, among others, the dialogues of Plato, the observations and lectures of Aristotle, the letters of Cicero to Brutus—yet we have no similar genres available to us for reporting current scholarly research. It is also true that people who do not live within the scholarly community have read these classical works, and they will no doubt continue to read them long after the cutting edge of our work has been dulled by the next fashionable idea or method.

The issue here is both the way we conduct research and the available means of reporting it. While our forebears saw fit to display their work in multiple formats and to invent new genres when old ones could not contain the meanings they encountered, we at the end of the twentieth century tend to be far less open-minded. Our research must look like scholarly research, follow the scientific method or its derivative formulas, and provide at least the image of truth to a world that counts on images. The number of publications and the places where they appear in the literature mean more to our culture than what has been discovered about humans communicating.

As one of my colleagues who is also a departmental chair put it, "If you had to make a choice between two faculty members—one of whom publishes regularly in top journals but whose work has little originality and another who had one really good, truly insightful publication—which one would you tenure?" From his point of view I gave the wrong answer.

If history is our lesson in matters of academic traditions, to transform the current problems of "communication" scholarship will require changes more powerful than arguments can sway. To change the meaning of a cultural artifact means either to change the culture or to change the way the culture itself views the artifact, and that means a societal—more than a paradigmatic—shift. In the history of academic theorizing this sort of change has occurred only when current scholarship could no longer satisfy the demands for knowledge made by its constituents and when the enterprise of teaching became widely suspect as preparation for living in the world. It is no surprise, I think, that these are precisely the conditions of our current endeavors within the academy. What we have to say to the world about its communication is generally ignored and/or belittled, and both the functions and effects of higher education are currently under attack from a variety of internal and external sources. We may be smarter than they are, but we may also outsmart ourselves right out of our jobs when those who pay for our services inquire about the meaning or value of what we are doing and our only response is to point to dusty volumes within which specialists hold an in-group dialogue.

Understanding is the final arbiter of scholarly worth. If a piece of work helps us to understand, it can lay the foundation for intellectual satisfaction and pragmatic improvements. In the world beyond the ivory tower, communication has meaning, very often because it is misunderstood. Helping others understand the hows, wheres, and whys of that misunderstanding is important work and should be seen as worthy scholarship.

Objections to What I Have Argued So Far

Probably some readers are at this point in the essay both shocked and amazed by these assertions. Trying them out on colleagues prior to this writing, I have encountered rejoinders such as "That's not how science is done!"; "I don't care what motives people have for their research, I only want to see what they came up with!"; and "Do you realize how this would look to my dean if people starting writing like this?" Assuming these to be representative criticisms, each one characterizing honest and deeply held feelings on the subject, I will now address them in the hope of clarifying some misconceptions and identifying some problems evident in these pleas.

The concern for whether or not we are "doing science" is simply irrelevant. There is no common conception of what "doing science" is, and accounts of how scientists have behaved and what they have read and thought about while they were "doing it" indicate no one dominant pattern. Furthermore, we aren't biologists studying plants in gardens, nor are we animal scientists studying the behavior of horses in herds (Wyatt and Phillips 1988). We are studying people communicating with other people within specific contexts, people who have meanings for their talk, who attribute meanings to the talk of Others, and who mostly know where they are—and have feelings about it—when they behave this way. Our task is "scientific" to the extent that we get outside the office more often and observe how this miracle at the intersections of culture and nature takes place. Science, after all, is a term whose meaning derives from our practices. It is as amenable to change as those of us who use it.

The objection based on not wanting to know what a scholar's motives are, just what they found, suggests that there is no connection between motive and outcome. It is true that people don't always articulate their motives, but that does not mean they do not have them, nor does it mean that a close reading of their performance could not reveal them. The fact is that when we admit this to be true for Others, but deny its relevance to our own behavior, then we are engaging in little more than cultural elitism (see especially Keller 1985). To acknowledge ourselves, complete with our motives and performances in the scenes in which our research and writing is conducted, seems a small, ethical request for scholarship that maintains "communication" to be the substance of human relationships. Finally, concern for how a dean (or department chair or tenure and promotion committee) will view new scholarship is at best a paranoid reaction to an imagined state and at worst a tragic display of cowardice. The scholar's task is to seek truth and explore both the charted and uncharted domains of knowledge—to create as well as to perpetuate. If this task is defined within the politics of publication and as a way to please one's hierarchical superiors, it is profaned as well as prostituted and says at least as much about the character of the person doing the publishing and pleasing as it does about the person judging the results.

There remains one problem. It is relatively easy for those of us who have job security to advocate change; it is quite another for those without job security to act on it. It is not enough to encourage alternative forms of scholarship among those whose professional characters may be judged noble, creative, and brave but whose professional careers may be damaged during the quest. Endorsement of these research and writing practices carries with it an ethical obligation to pursue opportunities for persuasion with teaching and research faculty, department heads, deans, and other organizational members about the merits of these methods of inquiry and discourse. Within any culture, subcultures and countercultures emerge; the degree to which they are successful in gaining acceptance and creating change depends on two interdependent processes. First, there must be results that are worthy of the order's attention and praise, and second, there must be attempts to alter perceptions of what is praiseworthy. Without the former there is no point to the latter, and without the latter the former may be easily discounted or mistaken. Together these two processes—quality work that reveals a redefinition of communication scholarship capable of broadening our audience *and* arguments presented to others within the academic culture about how such work should be evaluated—provide ways and means of productive change.

CONCLUSION

As we look back in reverence at the progress of our association in its first seventy-five years, it is easy to be optimistic about our accomplishments and its future. This is a discipline that enjoys a central place in both the humanities and social sciences and has as its subject, according to the late Richard McKeon, that "architectonic art capable of informing all disciplines and subjects" (quoted in Bitzer and Black 1970). It is also a discipline that holds as one of its central values the freedom of expression and as one of its principles that the way a message is communicated is as important as its content in judgments of effectiveness and in judgments of meaning. It is also important to examine that progress within the historical, cultural, literary, and social contexts that contributed to its theories and style of reporting research. As we celebrate this time and take account of what we have created as knowledge of and about communication, let us also look ahead to the new frontiers of scholarship *and* to new ways of reporting and displaying our work.

This essay has essentially forwarded a very simple case. It has been a case for examining relationships among self, Other, and context in accounts of communication research. I have suggested that we learn from the experience of cultural anthropologists about the power dynamics inherent in studies of persons within cultures both familiar and exotic and learn to see that relationship as part of the data we use to construct meaningful interpretations. I have shown why family systems theorists have embraced a relational perspective on all accounts of human behavior and asked that we consider their ideas within the contexts of our research, again focusing on the meanings we attribute to actions in the name of communication. And I have argued, perhaps too passionately, for opening up reporting methods for our research in ways that can take full advantage of this frontier.

In essence my thoughts are those of a person interested in pursuing—and in encouraging others to pursue—a *meaning-centered* relational approach to communication. For years this sort of approach has gone under the general label of "ethnomethodology" (Garfinkel 1967; Hymes 1962), and it has recognized the need to expand our research techniques and methods of reporting the results to readers who, through the act of reading, become partners in the creation of meanings within our shared text (see Hickson 1983).

There have been numerous calls for doing this sort of work in our discipline (see especially Ellis 1980; Hawes 1977; Pacanowsky 1988; Philipsen 1977) and some published studies accomplished within this general schema (see especially Benson 1981; Carbaugh 1988; Goodall, Wilson, and Waagen 1986; Katriel and Philipsen 1981; Philipsen 1975). But as yet the interpretive dimensions of this sort of immersion and critique have not greatly influenced the mainstream understandings of what communication research is or does. The new frontier of communication studies aims at a more general interpretation of meaning as the core of human experience and ways of accounting for meaning as inherent in *all* communication research. The idea is not to define meaning, but to evoke it; not to claim that it is a source of perfecting discourse, but to admit, outright, that it is imperfect; and not to perpetuate the scientific myth of control, but to advance a postscientific notion of communication as the process in which and through which self, Other, and context make and exchange meanings (see especially Newman 1984; Tyler 1987).

This essay, then, is making a decidedly postmodern case for the cultural, relational, and contextual primacy of meaning as the conceptual and methodological bases for *all* interpretations of human experience and behavior. This is a large call and a major challenge to existing wisdom, and one that recognizes its place in a side-by-side modern and postmodern, scientific and postscientific world that understands textual strategies as embodiments of worldviews and genres of writing and reporting research as rich with rhetorical implications for viewing those worlds.

I began this essay by evoking a passage from the work of two communication ethnographers, Tamar Katriel and Gerry Philipsen (1981), who observed that ethnography is less a journey into a foreign land or culture than it is a journey into a "no-man's land" belonging neither to the self nor to the Other. I want to return to that passage again, and ask you to read its last sentence again, this time aloud and within the context we have evolved in this essay: "The ethnographer, like the careful tourist, pays his or her tribute to the border at designated spots, but the border stretches and winds between these spots as well, and it is in this unmarked territory that the 'person' searches for a sense of personal meaning."

PART TWO Listening for the Weave of Clues: The Three Voices of Context

3

The Consultant as Organizational Detective:
A Tale Told in a Voice of Mystery

This process (of interpretation) has two distinct steps. First, the actor indicates to himself the things toward which he is acting; he has to point out to himself the things that have meaning. . . . This interaction with himself is something other than an interplay of psychological elements; it is an instance of the person engaging in a process of communication with himself. Second, by virtue of this process of communicating with himself, interpretation becomes a matter of handling meanings.

—Herbert Blumer

This stubborn urge to see everything as coexisting, to perceive and show all things side by side and simultaneous, as if they existed in space and not in time, leads Dostoevsky to dramatize, in space, even internal contradictions and internal stages in the development of a single person—forcing a character to converse with his own double, with the devil, with his alter ego, with his own caricature.

—Mikhail Bakhtin

All Living Things Are Critics

—Kenneth Burke

SUSPICIOUS MINDS, EARLY CLUES, AND LUNCH

His name is Edward R. Seeman.

"Call me Ed," he commands as we shake hands. We are doing the usual male thing with the squeeze, each one of us applying a little more pressure until it becomes just uncomfortable enough for one of us to release. Because he's paying the tab, I release, although I don't want to. *Call me Ed,* you muse. Call me Ishmael, and his name is Seeman. Where's the whale?

Equity thus restored I follow him to a table, each of us eyebrow admiring for the benefit of the other the significant nonverbal aspects of the hostess's rearward appearance. In the background is Muzak. It is going to be one of *those* lunches. I knew there were reasons why I got out of this business.

Ed is about my age but makes better money and spends large sums of it on clothing. Today he is decked out in *Esquire's* full-page three-button double-breasted fall insert from two months ago, the heavy Italian designer influence from the cut of the lapels to the point of the shoes, given added weight by the brand-new Rolex Mariner. I appreciate the thematic unity here, but discount some important points due to a decided lack of originality. For my role I am costumed in standard College Professor from the Eastern Liberal Establishment duds, blue blazer against beige Land's End cotton twill trousers, tasseled loafers, light-blue button-down Sero with, literally, the old school tie.

Clearly there is a cultural clash between us. We sit across from each other as two representatives of foreign lands, and the negotiations begin as all negotiations do, with strategic choices of drinks and food.

"I'll have a double vodka martini," Ed orders, "with Absolut."

"I'll have unsweetened iced tea with extra lemon," I add. In the old days I would follow the alcohol lead but I always felt mildly foolish when I did. Before that, on cases like this one, back when I was just out of graduate school and really poor, I drank the booze because it was free.

Ed leans forward, his Rolex catches the light and sparkles. "I saw Phil Davis at the Heritage Club last week," he grins, "and when I told him about my little problem he recommended you."

Thanks, Phil. I try to restrain myself from saying something like "Phil's an ass, which verifies my initial opinion of you," but instead settle for a milder form of insult. "The Heritage Club, huh? Well, my fee just went up."

Ed ignores it. In the world we are currently constituting there is a tacit understanding clearly in place about his social and professional attainments; I prefer not to reveal as much about my own. Sometimes they come in handier if you don't.

About Phil and his recommendation I am less certain. Phil Davis hired me a couple of years ago to look into a "communication" problem in an aerospace manufacturing firm that ended up being a cleverly masked excuse for a consultant's report that would blame a particular department for something that wasn't its fault. Phil didn't know this, but he played along as if he knew something, which in a way is worse. I didn't play along, ended up going undercover in the organization to discover the truth, and wrote a very different sort of report. In the end nobody got hurt, I got paid, and everyone, including Phil, looked good.

But Phil also knew I had done more, and less, than I was asked to do. So this could mean that Phil thinks I will do the same for Ed, or something else entirely. He could be getting even.

By the time the food arrives—his rare beef and my Cobb salad—I have a vague idea about what Ed wants me to do. The problem is "mid-level managerial dissatisfaction" that is causing "high turnover" and "other problems" (unspecified, but I get the hint that they involve the law). Ed believes this is really a "communication" issue and wants me to do "the sort of thing you did for Phil," complete with a report.

"What sort of thing did I do for Phil?" What I am after here is some sense of the level and depth of the lie Phil probably told this guy about what I did. I am, of course, grinning a good bit, to communicate the understanding that I don't have as if I really do.

Ed gives me a good looking over before he replies. In his eyes are questions about my *machismo,* my ability to do what needs to be done, my attitude toward my work, toward Ed, toward Phil. The choice of iced tea and Cobb salad didn't please him, and I don't seem as willing to go along with all of this as Phil apparently told him I would be.

He clears his throat, wipes his mouth, flashes a million dollar smile. "Phil told me everything," he replies.

"Really?" I try my best to seem impressed.

"He told me that you saw through the bullshit to the sensitivity of the problem and that you did some fancy steps that protected his ass."

"Hmmm." Figures that's what he would have said.

"What's that mean?" He means my "hmmm."

"Hmmm means hmmm," I say. "It's a form of talk that I use when I'm considering something."

He relaxes. "Oh, you mean money." He smiles. "I've been authorized to pay you $5,000, plus any other reasonable expenses."

I chuckle. "Phil must have lied about how much I'm worth."

"I don't think so," Ed replies. "Of course, you will need receipts for the expenses."

"Of course," I say. "I'll take $2,500 now, and the remainder when I turn in the report."

"Fine." He reaches for the corporate checkbook. His signature is huge and illegible. He hands me the down payment.

"I'll keep this in a safe place until I decide whether or not to take the job."

He tries hard to avoid looking stunned. "What do you mean?" His face doesn't know whether to smile or frown, so it does both at the same time and awkwardly.

"I mean I never take a consulting job without doing a little background work first. I learned that a long time ago. It keeps me out of trouble and I sleep better too."

"What sort of checking out? And when will I know?"

I stand up and throw down money for the meal and tip. "I never disclose my methods until I solve the case. I'll call you in a few days to tell you whether I'm working or not." I smile and offer my hand.

He shakes it. This time I do the squeezing. I squeeze hard.

He gestures toward the money I have just thrown on the table. "That isn't necessary, this is on me. I invited you, remember?"

"It was a joint venture. We haven't agreed to anything yet except that I'm not going to cash your company's check until I look into a couple of things. If everything looks like you've said it will and I take the job, you can buy my lunch later. Until then, I pay my own way."

"It was a pleasure meeting you, Dr. Goodall." He frowns in earnest now, giving himself away, but adds, "I think."

"Good. Thinking helps. I'll be in touch."

READING THE PARKING LOT

On the way back to the office I stop in at Ed's company. Happens I know someone who works here, and this person is a mid-level manager. The goal of this little gambit is to see if his words match the territory Ed has been describing. If they do, then the problem is obvious, which means the solution will probably be either too complicated for my skills or too nasty. If they don't match, then maybe it's Ed who is the problem, in which case I think I'd like to know why.

I park my car in a visitor's space and spend a few minutes observing the parking lot. I am big on parking lots as evidence of organizational dramas because in this culture of hypercapitalism and commodity values you are what you drive at least as much as you are what you wear, eat, listen to, or talk about. This contextual logic works on two levels, actually. First there is the sort of general observing I am now doing, and second there are the polite inquiries I will eventually make (if I take the job) about what people drive and what they think they would like to be driving. It was Freud, I think, who told us private dicks that people respond equally well to the real as well as to the imagined in life. Getting both sorts of data on a variety of issues is often very helpful in figuring out what needs figuring out and connecting clues to what Meryl Louis calls "the unique sense of place."

This parking lot tells a mundane tale. All the colors are muted, and virtually everything has four plain doors and standard-issue tires and wheels. Nothing exotic, no flashy colors, no obvious displays of sensuality or mystique. I am at this point in my musing when Ed pulls in. His vehicle is the clear exception to the rule, a RED, current-generation Corvette.

Very interesting.

He combs his hair before exiting the car, and I get the feeling by the way he slams the door that this is the sort of guy who probably doesn't change his oil regularly or even check its level. A very bad sign. If the guy in charge doesn't pay attention to details, particularly those of a maintenance standard, he is probably the sort of guy who makes up his mind without gathering enough information and then expects others to carry out the work without any new resources.

Sounds like why I'm here, and fits how I think he made that decision. But we'll see. I've been wrong before—probably why I'm still living in Alabama.

I wait for him to go inside and then take some photographs of the parking lot for later use. I can't go inside now because if my hunch is correct the person I want to talk to won't want to talk to me with Ed around. So I pull out of the lot in my black BMW (which, in my view, reader, stands for Big Money Wasted) and head back to the office and the relative safety of the telephone.

USING THE PHONE AS A DETECTING DEVICE

"Rick! This is Bud, how are you doing?" This is me, back at the office, and Rick is my contact at Ed's firm.

"Fine, just fine. I haven't heard from you in ages. What's up?" Rick is a fellow writer, and the last time we got together was over a story he had written. That was nearly a year ago.

"I was calling for two reasons. First, I need some information about your place of employment." I pause.

"Yeah? Why?" Precisely the sort of response I expected.

"On account of a guy who wants to hire me to do some consulting for you."

Silence on the other end of the line.

"His name is Edward R. Seeman." Now I am listening with all my might for anything, any clue, any hint of a clue.

"Can I call you back?"

"Sure. I'll be at the office for another hour or so, then I'm heading home. Do you still have those numbers?"

"Yeah. By the way, what was the second reason for the call?" He sounds a little suspicious, and far more suspicious than when we started the conversation.

"To see if you ever sent off that story." If I were Catholic this would be the sort of thing that would drive me to confession.

"No, never did. I've been working on some other things, though."

"Good. Maybe you'll let me see them sometime?"

"Right. Listen, I can't talk now, John. I'll have Marla give Debbie a call about that furniture later."

We hang up.

John? Debbie? Furniture?

What would you think?

VOICES IN CONTESTED SPACE

It is later and I have just finished talking with Rick.

He tells me that Ed is the sort of leader who inspires revolutions against himself. He tells me that, then apologizes for having told me.

Then he blames himself, then he doubts that he has been wrong and blames Ed again.

I ask for details about the "problem," which I do not specify.

Rick confirms what Ed told me at lunch. Mid-level dissatisfaction with the way things are being run, how decisions are made, etc. Some good people have been driven off. The word "communication" is used to mean a lack of some quality, some mysterious "it" that exists as an ideal in most people's minds when all the other words that could be used somehow don't quite do justice to the thing that can't be clearly articulated. A lot of "communication" consulting is really vocabulary building, training people to use language capable of describing a situation in a way that can be productively addressed.

Rick ends a long but clearly practiced description of the situation by telling me that he thinks I should take the job and that our friendship should not get in the way of whatever I find out or recommend. Rick is like that, which is fine by me but makes for awkwardness anyway. I ask him what Ed *really* wants me to find out.

"That I need to be fired, along with two other people."

"And what do you think?"

"That Mr. Seeman is wrong."

I decide, at that moment, to take the case. Sometimes you take the case for money, and sometimes you take the case because you think you can do some good in the world, and sometimes you take the case because you don't know any better. This time it was all three, although at the time I didn't know that.

THE WHO, AND PART OF THE WHAT,
THAT I DIDN'T KNOW

Next day I am at the office explaining to two undergraduates some of the finer points concerning Aristotle's development of the enthymeme when our departmental secretary tells me I have a very important call on line one.

"Yes?"

"Am I speaking to Professor Goodall?" The voice is old and feminine, with a decided edge to it.

"You are. What can I do for you?"

"My name is Stella Mims."

Stella Mims is a name I have heard often in the years I've been in this town. Like many persons with substantial power in a community, she is not well known beyond her name outside of her immediate circle. She is supposed to be smart, tough, and to the point. In an oil painting of her that hangs in the central administration building of our campus, she appears to be a keen but serene lady in her mid-sixties who knows exactly who she is and what she can do.

"Mr. Goodall, I understand that you have been retained by one of my firms to do some consulting."

"That's right." Everyone knows she owns this "firm."

"Yes, well." She sniffs. "Please be advised that I expect a full accounting of whatever it is that you discover, and I prefer that you give me your report in writing prior to delivering it to Mr. Seeman."

Tough. To the point. "Mrs. Mims, that was not part of my agreement with Mr. Seeman."

"I know." She pauses as if caught between two ways of telling the same story. "But it is *my* company, and I think I have a right, therefore, to make this request."

"Yes, you certainly do. Should I assume that Mr. Seeman is not to be told about this phone call?"

"You're very quick, Mr. Goodall. Very quick." She pauses again, as if amused. "Here is my private number. Use it when you are ready to make your report, or if anything should arise that requires my assistance."

I write down the number. The line goes dead.

THE INTERVIEW AS A TOOL IN THE INVESTIGATION OF OTHERS

I am in a large, overly comfortable conference room with five clearly uncomfortable men and two highly put-off women. They are the "mid-level managers" and have just been informed that I am here to do a "communication audit" of their organization, which sounds like a threat, and that they are to "cooperate fully, openly, and honestly," as if they wouldn't unless told.

My friend Rick sits to one side of me where we can easily avoid eye contact. I notice, during my introduction by Ed, that these people are *wearing* their faces, putting on particular looks, masks, and guises. I'm not sure what this means, but I've been in this business long enough to know that it means something. I also notice that Ed has not won their hearts. As a leader he is the sort of domineering, clever badgerer who talks *at,* rather than *with,* his colleagues. Only one person maintains eye contact with him, and she does so with hardened eyes.

When it is my turn to speak I try to appear calm and reassure them that a "communication audit" is mostly a diagnostic tool that is used to help organizations locate problems related to information access, distribution, and control. The idea is not to find fault with a particular individual, department, or operation, but to recommend ways in which information used to run the company can be better accessed and used.

This is bullshit and they know it, although everyone seems to relax a little on the words "not find fault with." I go on to say that I will be conducting interviews with each of them and that I plan to spend some time just hanging around, watching how "information" flows through the organization. "And then," I say, "I will write a final report, issue it to everyone who participates in the study, and collect my check." I smile and everyone chuckles.

"Excuse me, doc, but did you say that *everyone* would get the report?" This from the manager of security, an ex-Marine who, in what I guesti-mate is his mid-forties, still looks like he works out everyday.

"Yes, that's right. I don't think it's fair to give the results only to Mr. Seeman. My recommendations are intended to help stimulate some discussions about what might be done to improve communication, so I think everyone needs to read it."

Everyone seems a little happier except Ed. I can tell he doesn't think this was part of our agreement. I'm not sure what Mrs. Mims would say either, but I've learned the hard way that unless something is ruled out up front it's fair game. And these are my rules.

I begin the interviews. My approach to this part of the investigation requires the help of a colleague. I use Cathy Pence, a faculty member in my department who is trained in interpersonal communication. What we do is conduct separate interviews using basically the same questions, and then another interview with both of us present to work out any ambiguities in our previous assessments. I know from past consulting experiences that Cathy picks up on different clues than I do, which makes her a perfect partner for this sort of work. Besides, she does the quantitative assessments from the questionnaires, work I can't do because, even after all these years, I still can't count.

During my sessions I learn that there is a general and outspoken dislike of Mr. Seeman, and that he is perceived as untrustworthy, disloyal, uncooperative, and ineffective in his managerial duties. He is also de-scribed as being an asshole, a fuck-up, and other cultural terms meant to imply a certain level of emotional involvement with the assessments given. This is intriguing to me because I do not use a single question designed to assess Ed's performance. Our questions deal with general items such as who makes decisions and what information is used to make those deci-sions, etc. Uniformly the blame has been placed on Ed, in part, I begin to see, because he is such an unlikable boss and in part because, according to these witnesses, he has pitted department heads against each other, told several well-documented lies, and turned against at least two department heads when they failed to go along with his ideas.

Cathy's findings are more or less the same, but the more or less is what is interesting to us. What she has found has broader historical and cultural implications for the current situation. It seems that Mr. Seeman inherited this job via personal recommendation from the guy who held the job previously. The previous head was an affable, informal sort of person who lives in the memories of these mid-level managers as someone who could do no wrong, who worked with them to solve problems and to get the job done, and who cared about them and their families. Stories are told about this individual that clearly symbolize his sainthood, against which Mr. Seeman's performance is consistently contrasted.

It should be pointed out here that the previous boss went on to a larger company in another state and that his recommendation of Ed for the job was made despite the fact that his assistant was the inside choice. His assistant stayed on as Ed's assistant for a year, then quit in a bitter, public dispute about allocation of resources. Since then things have gotten steadily worse.

It was time to interview Ed. I ask Cathy to accompany me because at this juncture I am certain that eventually I will need a witness. The interview is conducted in his office with the door closed.

I decide to open the interview with a question about how he was chosen for this job.

"I applied for it after Jeb [previous manager] resigned. He called me up and told me what a marvelous city this was, and what a fine opportunity this would be."

"And then?"

"And then I came down for an interview. Everything went smoothly, and I was offered the job."

"Were there any other candidates?" This one from Cathy.

He flinches. "Not really. The woman who was Jeb's assistant let everyone know that she thought she could do the job, but she didn't have the qualifications to even be considered. I kept her on for a year, and then we agreed that she would be better off working somewhere else."

"And you replaced her with . . . ?"

"No one yet. I don't really need an assistant. I like to do everything myself. And I know this has upset a lot of people because they were used to doing things the old way. But I say I'm in charge and they better get used to the new way."

Cathy looks at me, and I look at Cathy. Then we both look at Ed. I say, "So you think people are adjusting to the new way of doing business?"

He squints, bites his lower lip. "Some are, others aren't. You've probably heard what a bad guy I am because I won't bend, or that I've fired people who disagree with me." He gestures to dismiss all of this. "Bull. I'm the easiest guy in the world to get along with. But I'm also the one earning the big bucks around here, which means what I say goes."

"So where do you think the problems are?"

He smiles. "First, I need to do something about Rick. He complains too much, gets everyone pissed off. Then there's Rita, who really wants to be my assistant because it will mean more money, but she doesn't understand that I need her where she is. And Bob . . ."

I break in. "Do you think these are structural or personal problems?"

He considers the question. "For your report I hope you say they are structural," he replies. "If you say they are personal I'll have to fire some people, won't I?"

"So you don't feel the need to get rid of anyone, even though you've articulated some genuine problems?"

"Naw. They just need to relax and get used to the way I do things. If they don't, they'll be encouraged to seek employment elsewhere. But I don't want to fire anybody. That's bad for morale."

The interview continues for another twenty minutes. Toward the end we ask Ed what he think needs to be done to improve communication. "Nothing," he replies.

I ask him why he has retained communication consultants if he doesn't think there is a communication problem. I also add that he had told me there were communication problems during our initial lunch.

"Hey," he grins. "This is all crap anyway. I hired you because some of them kept saying there was a communication problem. This is paid appeasement: you get paid, I get appeasement. I bring you in, they see it as a gesture, for a while everything gets forgiven. You tell us in your report that we need to have a seminar or something, and then we turn back around and hire you, isn't that the way it works?"

"What if I told you that you were wrong?" This from me.

"I'd say I needed to hire a different consultant."

INTROSPECTION, YOUR FAVORITE DOG, AND WHISKEY

There are times in your life when even your best dog and a glass of your favorite whiskey won't bring any comfort. There are times in your life when what you are works against you, and what you want to become seems impossible.

There are times when your partner wants out of a case because the ante has been upped beyond her ability to pay off on the bet and her cards are just not that good. So you let her off.

There are times when the world seems irreparably wrong, and whatever you do will make it worse. This is when you consider your life as if viewed from a purer, more objective perspective, and slip into the voice of the second-person singular.

MEETING A POWERFUL WOMAN ALONE ON A RAINY NIGHT

It is raining and late at night, and you are in a different city because this is what she requested.

You meet in a dive restaurant that plays static. You are wearing plain clothing. You do not use names. You do not make explicit references to the case. You speak in abstractions, telling stories, using the language of what if. You are here to agree on a story, to make one up if you have to.

She is old and looks very tired. Mostly she is tired of this case because she knows what must be done but she wants to do it in a way that will not harm the company. She can afford no negative p.r. The story she wants to hear wouldn't make you come to a place like this to tell it.

But here you are.

You lay out what you have found in broad strokes. There is a problem at the highest levels of your company and it will not disappear and it cannot be corrected. It is a large problem that is complex because in part it is not this person's fault. Although he is not the sort of leader you would prefer to work under, he probably has the talent to do the job but things, persons, and history have conspired against him. He inherited a job but also a situation that he cannot, or will not, respond to. There is a lot of subtlety in the ranks that he does not productively address. He alienates people who could just as easily be his allies. And he does all of this thinking that he is doing the right thing, that he is working for the best interests of the company.

Now he feels trapped. He knows the score. He is not stupid. He thinks you are working for him because he is paying you. He believes you will write a report that recommends minor repairs and that makes him out to be a scapegoat, the person wronged by the others.

She smiles, faintly. "That is precisely the report I want you to write," she says. There is something in her eyes, but I cannot name it.

"Why?"

"Because that is the version of the truth that is acceptable to me, that is acceptable to him, that won't cause problems, and it is, after all, Mr. Goodall, the story you were hired to discover. I believe that is the report I want you to circulate."

"You mean you actually want me to give my report to everyone, but to write the report in a way that is favorable to him?" I am incredulous.

"Yes. You see, Mr. Goodall, this isn't a classroom where grades can be given at the end of the semester. This is real life where the stories people believe are far more important than the stories they have been assigned to learn. You should also know that I have already retained another consultant, this one a lawyer, who will find fault with the report you write and who will construct another version of this story."

"But *why?*"

"Because it requires many actors telling many stories to make a believable play, some of whom are never seen on the stage." She pauses, smiles again faintly. "And sometimes those who are seen on the stage are only placed there so that a particular story can be told, a particular flaw pointed out."

"And I thought I was the guy writing this story."

"Don't we all, Mr. Goodall? Indeed, don't we all?"

THE EFFECTS OF COMMUNICATION CONSULTING ON ORGANIZATIONAL LIFE

So I write the report we had agreed to and submit it according to plan.

I learn from Rick that the report has circulated and that, oddly enough, it has been received well by the mid-level managers. "They thought you were brought in to bust their butts, so when you didn't they were happy."

"What about their complaints about Seeman?"

"You were being paid, everyone knew that. We've had some fun with scapegoat jokes, though."

"And what has changed?"

Rick pauses. "Nothing. But everyone seems to feel a little better. Mr. Seeman even put out a memo last week thanking some employees for working overtime during a crunch. *That* was big news around here."

"Anything else?"

"Yeah. But you won't want to hear it."

"Tell me."

"Okay. We learned yesterday that another consultant is being brought in. This time, a lawyer. He read your report and said you were full of shit."

I smile. "Maybe he's right."

One year later Mr. Edward R. Seeman resigned. In the newspapers it was reported that he assumed a new post with a larger firm in Virginia and that he would be missed. There was a nice photograph of him accepting a plaque from Stella Mims.

There was still something, something ineffable, in her eyes.

4

Learning to Read the Descriptive Rhetorics of Organizational Culture: A Tale Told in a Voyeur's Voice

Group life necessarily presupposes interaction between the group members; or, put otherwise, a society consists of individuals interacting with one another. The activities of the members occur predominantly in response to one another or in relation to one another.

—Herbert Blumer

The essence of polyphony lies precisely in the fact that the voices remain independent and, as such, are combined in a unity of a higher order than in homophony. . . . One could put it this way: the artistic will of polyphony is a will to combine many wills, a will to the event.

—Mikhail Bakhtin

Men build their cultures by huddling together, nervously loquacious, at the edge of an abyss.

—Kenneth Burke

THE PRESENCE OF AN ABSENCE, THE ABSENCE OF A PRESENCE

There is a sense in which a decision—any decision—exists in sentences. To make a decision implies at least some form of articulation, and articulation implies the use of language. It does not matter if the decision is a matter of personal choice (in which case the sentences will be spoken and heard only within the realm of the self) or public debate (in which case the sentences will mingle with other sentences in realms of argument). What matters when a decision is viewed this way is not the sentence but what the sentence necessarily leaves out, which is its *context*.

I begin this chapter this way because what I sense in the decision-making literature is "the presence of an absence." With a bow to Barthes,

Derrida, and Foucault, however, the last sentence should actually read "the absence of a presence" where "presence" is defined as context in its physical, economic, dramatic, and ultimately hierarchical implications.

The problem I want to address is that we cannot understand a decision without taking into account its context, but the moment the decision is phrased into words anyone who hasn't experienced the context does not understand the decision. Furthermore, it is also true that even those individuals who have experienced the context know that the decision is less than optimal, or at least less than what transpired while they were doing the deciding. My purpose in this chapter will be to give an interpretive reading to this dilemma and to locate—or at least bring into view—potential sources of relief.

THE WORLD WITHIN THE WORD

Consider, for a moment, what constitutes a context. The word "context," read strictly as a sequence of seven letters, two syllables, and an abbreviated history found in the *Oxford English Dictionary,* means "to weave together, interweave, join together, compose." Admittedly this definition is a small sleight-of-hand—the active verb cited in place of the reified noun—but allow me a little room here, some discursive space, if you will, in which to construct an argument. My point here is simply that a context, as a verbal construct, is a process aimed at the manufacture of something. It is the seaming together of otherwise disparate elements, perceptions, fabrics, or words, the piecing together of a whole out of the sum of its parts.

This definition is important for two reasons. Overtly and most important is the sense in which a context refers to a process. Given that studies of decision making tend to dwell on arguments and procedures that produce outcomes (read: sentences), this return to the full-bodied nature of the term "context" provides license for expanding our understanding of the scenes and actors (read: vocabularies and dictionaries) that are also interwoven into the sentences they produce.

The second source of importance for this processual view of what a "context" is lies more subtly in its unspoken aims. Consider the words of our definition again: "to weave together, interweave, join together, compose." The for-whatedness is present, but unspoken, and so—at least as a source of articulated gesture—is absent. This "what is left out" aspect of context is particularly enticing because, like a crazy quilt or a marriage, or a composition, it allows its author(s) license to detail the how of what was finally made as well as what it means. A context, then, is *how we make whats out of otherwise somethings,* and it implies that the making may be made out of the somethings after the decision has been made.

Put together, both of these sources of influence create yet another possibility, or context. While there is always one (or more) context(s), there is never one (or more) context(s). A context does not so much exist as it is brought into being, conjured up out of words that cannot represent the whole of the territory (or do not want to), and once it is brought into being the context—whatever it was—ceases to exist as in vivo experience and starts life anew as a world within the words used to describe it. What is left is the record, the consensual document, a carefully (or carelessly) articulated framework that does not so much explain how the decision was made as it justifies the grounds upon which it was finally discovered.

This last distinction is important, particularly within the broader cultural context of organizational decision making. To make a decision implies a sense of autonomy that is generally not part of most organizational job descriptions. Therefore, decisions tend less to be made than to be *discovered,* a term that carries with it the various personal and hierarchical imperatives that surround the work of task groups and committees, a part of the context that has less to do with the weaving than with the ultimate fit of the fabric into the organizational culture that produced it and the uses to which it will be put within that specific cultural milieu.

This seems to be the place for an example. Let's assume for a moment that you are a member of a task group for a university engaged in strategic planning. The purpose of your group is to come up with recommendations for how the university can pursue its "strategic advantages" within the geographical region it serves. You are given this charge, along with an official document specifying the university's stated mission: "to serve the educational, economic, and research needs of the ———— region."

During your first meeting the chair (appointed by the president of the university) explains that the recommendations of the task force will be examined by the Executive Committee of the University, which will have final authority on them. There is a silence, some raised eyebrows, a bit of coughing.

Let's stop the example here. How would you describe the context so far? Now, how would you describe it to the president of the university? The truth, as you can see, often depends on where you are standing when you see it and the purposes to which the description is put. So does the articulation of a context and its associated meanings.

Let's continue the example. We are now in the second meeting, and each task force member has made a report on the assigned "strategic advantages of the region." You notice that most of these advantages tie into the economic and research sections of the university's mission, but none of them addresses its educational function. You say so, out loud. The chair looks over at her colleague, who in turn raises an eyebrow back at her. In a voice that clearly is meant to admonish you for bad behavior, the chair explains that "of course education comes first, everybody knows that." Properly admonished, you try to make light of the comment, but no one laughs.

Stop again. What is going on here? How is this context evolving? What have you learned about it that you didn't know before? Does this new source of information, and its attendant interpretations, cause you to rethink the previous meeting of the group? When you think this way, does the meaning of the context alter?

Back to the example. You are now in your fifth group meeting. All of the research has been completed (although not to everyone's satisfaction), and the task force is considering how the recommendations should be phrased. In the interim meetings clear factions have emerged, mostly along disciplinary lines. Persons from the colleges of science, engineering, and medicine tend to reinforce one another, while persons from the liberal arts, nursing, and the library form the other side. Conflict has at times been heated. The chair, who represents the Graduate School and who is a mathematician by training, is clearly made uncomfortable by emotional displays, and the representative from nursing has been making a none-too-subtle move to assume leadership of the group by intervening and directing traffic during these heated arguments.

The essence of the dispute is a perception, held jointly by the proponents of the economic and research side of the issue, that the only way new resources can be tapped is by encouraging more research contract work to be done at the university. On the other side are the advocates of the "education first" principle. These individuals believe that by defining strategic advantages as economic and research-based rather than by improving the quality of instruction, the university is buying into a bad habit that will, in the long term, encourage the deterioration of teaching as faculty members are increasingly urged to pursue contract work. Both sides do agree, however, that the current administration of the university is engaged in a desperate financial struggle and that little help is likely to come from the state.

Stop. Define the context. Where do you begin? How do your own personal and professional views interfere with the description? How do you expand the boundaries of the decision-making context to include suppositions about state funding opportunities? About the current financial struggle? About the perceptions (and emotions) of faculty members who see this group as a larger battlefield of values?

Back to the example. After three more tense and often heated sessions, the group is ready to forward its recommendations. Two of the members, however, refuse to sign the document. The chair has accepted a job at another university and has assigned the task of writing the final report to the faculty member from nursing, who accepts the assignment with evident bitterness. The last session is quiet as the group reads over the report. You comment that the language seems very abstract, so that almost anything could be justified by it. Someone else suggests that was the intent. The new chair smiles. In the end, even the two faculty members who claimed they wouldn't sign the document do in fact sign it.

This is where the example ends. The issue of context, however, remains with us. How does the context look from this end of the drama? What changes have occurred? How do you account for them? And what about the recommendations themselves, the supposed object of the decision making? Was it a part of the context or its outcome? Or both, but at different times?

SCENES FROM A FRAMEWORK

What is required here is a *deconstruction,* a taking apart of the whole to examine individual parts, an unweaving of the fabric to better understand the weaving itself. As with any such academic exercise the search is ultimately for essences, and in this case for essences of a vocabulary in which to situate the sense and *sursum corda* mix of any context.

The Physical

Contexts enjoy physical properties. To every decision there is at least one room and it is full of clues. In the academic and trade literatures these clues are explained as sources of power and authority (as in the placement of chairs around or along variously shaped tables or work areas), expertise and recognition (as in the displays of academic and professional credentials, civic plaques, awards, trophies, etc.), and culture (as in emblems and symbols of the unique sense of place and/or subtle individualism that populate the environment and serve as signs or conversation pieces).

To read the physical properties and set pieces of any scene is to bring to it your own sense-making apparatus (however fit for the task that apparatus may be), to penetrate the scene with your own interjections of what things mean (as if that *is* what they mean), to pick up on whatever your own perceptual antennae receive (a necessarily selective and highly individualistic process). In other words, it is to leave out of the interpretation all that is inherently within the scene and to replace what is there with your own stuff.

Viewed another way, to read the physical context is to give life to otherwise inanimate objects, to attribute causes to effects, to engage in the symbolic possibilities of mere symbols. Obviously, differences in individual readings of the same scene and set pieces is likely, and differences between and among the individuals doing the reading are likely to lead to different interpretations. That is, however, not the point. Individual perceptual differences can be a given without being necessarily important. For the purpose here is not to decide what the physical properties of a scene *are*, or what they mean, but instead to grapple with how they move in and out of the traffic of decisions, how they form part of the weave of contexts.

Back to our earlier drama. In it, last time, we witnessed a way of reading a context into a decision-making process that focused on issues and alliances and outcomes, sentences that make something out of the politics of discourse. This time let us add a new and physical dimension to its reading and make something out of physical subtleties that play into discussions.

The room, let us say, is located within the central administration building of the campus. With the exception of the Graduate School representative, every committee member must leave his or her own office, located in various elsewheres on the campus, to get there. This means they must plan part of their day around a time established for the meeting, allowing enough extra time to get there. This aspect of the physical properties of the room includes, for each of the players, a perception of its importance ("Why do I always have to go over *there?*"), certain boundaries for discourse ("Sorry I'm late—I couldn't find a parking place near this building"), and rules for the conduct of the meeting ("We can't begin until Ellen gets here"). Subtly the room establishes itself as a player in the drama.

However, there is much more to read here, for this room is a place rich with interpretive possibilities. Located in the rather plush central administration building, it is done in earth and wood tones and rich carpeting that contrast sharply with the plainness of the glass, concrete block, and linoleum offices that the committee members inhabit. Does this suggest that the most important decisions are administrative policy issues (rather than curricular or communal concerns of the faculty)? Perhaps, and perhaps not. Organizational opulence has long been associated with hierarchical advancement, and the proverbial "corner office at the top of the building" is generally associated with prestige and power. On the other hand, in the real world symbolic displays of prestige and power do serve as inducements to identity, and why shouldn't administrative offices be done up, rather than down, when it is often the place other community and business leaders come to when they come to a meeting on campus? It may be part of the silliness of hypercapitalism and a consumer-oriented society, but it is at least as real as the sentences we use to make fun of it.

The heavy wooden door (no veneer here!) is always closed during committee deliberations. To close a door in America is both a common expression of being cut off as well as a practical articulation of supposed secrecy. Why is this door closed? Is it to add the sense of importance the members feel about the task? To remind them of the importance of secrecy? Or just to shut out external noise? Or perhaps, just perhaps, all of these possibilities exist only because there is a door to the room, a heavy wooden door that closes (or that suggests it can, perhaps should, be closed). As B. F. Skinner would have it, the environment's influences over us cannot be so easily set aside.

There is, stage center, the table. It is a table for a seating of twelve, a cherry table above which hovers a fairly decent silver and brass chandelier, and around which are placed twelve exact replicas of a famous early American designer chair. The table is always clean and bright, and although the university has a no-smoking policy for the entire campus there are two strategically placed ashtrays on this particular set piece.

There are no windows to this room. Instead there are oil paintings depicting scenes from English fox hunts during the Enlightenment, scenes, as one of your colleagues puts it, without women in them except as occasional ornaments to the taste of the Master. What does this choice of room decoration mean? What does this feminist articulation of its meaning suggest as an influence on deliberations, particularly when those deliberations deal with issues of authority? Or is it, as another one of your colleagues puts it, merely what you get when a wealthy benefactor bequeaths a portion of his art collection to the university? Meaning, you suppose, that it is all right to hang anything that is given to you by the rich, something that somehow mingles with the issue of what emphasis should be given to the university's mission.

Seating along the sides of the table is, after the first meeting, strictly territorial. Seats are claimed once and the claims stick forever. The chair of the committee reluctantly assumes the command chair at the end of the room and at the head of the table, saying that she would prefer a smaller, round table; privately you doubt this to be true. The colleagues who know each other sit next to each other, forming coalitions of occupied space that ultimately resemble the architecture of the various schools within the university—engineers and scientists here, liberal arts over there, nurses directly across from their medical school counterparts. What does this suggest? What does this natural ordering, chosen by the participants on account (perhaps) of the shape of the table, do to affect the discussions? How difficult is it to disagree with someone who sits next to your shoulder; how easy is it to adopt an adversarial pose toward the person across the table? In a rounder, more perfect world, would these sources of influence disappear?

It should be pointed out here that the temperature and humidity in this room are controlled by a thermostat that years ago, during the first energy crisis, the university decided to place locks on. Therefore, it is always colder in here than in the rest of the world, a fact that committee members learn to take into account when they plan to meet here. It also becomes part of the routine discussion and more than once provides an acceptable excuse for adjourning early. Here again, the physical aspects of the room are part of the weave of a sense of the context—now at the center, but at other times and in other frames of reference at the fringes or, as we saw in the earlier description, absent entirely— that lives alongside of us, influencing our perceptions of meaning, our judgments of persons, places, and things, in ways that are at once highly individualized and that may, or may not, matter. However, to describe a decision-making process without taking into account the scenes and set pieces that are present in it is to give a reading to the drama that leaves out rich, textual clues.

Also, there is no music in this room.

The Economic

Out of the material world of the purely physical emerges—and if Kenneth Burke is right, emerges naturally—a purely material world made known to us through symbols. Symbols are, of course, the makers of meanings and are therefore the final arbiters of any description of context. However, there is a special, primal, sense of the symbol—how it works to induce cooperation or incite riots—that bespeaks its appeal to self-interest, particularly self-interest defined by material well-being.

It does not require a Marxist orientation to realize that every context can be defined within realms of economics. However, such an orientation (selected from the array of available possibilities or contexts) is helpful. Consider, for example, how impoverished our view of public discord and debate would be without an understanding of the terms of a class struggle. Consider also how the ability to define a class struggle is necessarily— given the widespread mis/understanding of Marx and Engels as well as their interpreters—part of any context in which certain key terms (class, struggle) enter into the realm of otherwise ordinary sentences.

Suffice it to say that decision-making groups are resplendent with economic motives, each one capable of defining a particular context for the information used to construct or discover a decision. But how, then, does the economics of context fit into the material of discourse, dialogue, discussion, or debate?

It seems to me that this fit can be parsed in at least two ways. First, and probably most important, is the articulation of economic interests— cost factors, available resources, determinations of benefits, etc.—in the discourse itself. Admittedly this is a pragmatic answer to a semiotic question, but at least at the level of argument the words spoken must be assumed to count as the foreground of the meanings given to the context.

Second, and clearly the more ethereal of the two, is the quiet, perhaps desperate, sense in which human beings recognize their dependence on economic matters despite their feelings to the contrary. It is within this second sense of economic contexts for decision making that we return to our closed-door meeting.

Among faculty members, economic interests are partially expressed by choice of field and the resultant disparities that follow. Here, for example, we have a physician from the medical school (wearer of a Rolex, driver of a Mercedes, investor in a condo project at Gulf Shores) discussing platitudes with a member of the biology faculty (wearer of a Timex, driver of an old Volkswagen, who, without hope of investing in a condo, is lucky to meet his mortgage every month) who in turn asks a question of an administrator (wearer of a Mondavo, driver of an Oldsmobile, owner of a posh townhouse) who in turn directs another question at you (wearer of a Pulsar, driver of a Ford truck, owner of a small farm twenty miles from town) while engaging in Goffmanesque face-work with the physician. What is going on here, viewed within the framework of economics?

It goes without saying that one's lifestyle is a purchase, or series of them, that serves as grist for the gossip mill in any organization. Does it affect decisions? Perhaps. But I would argue that it does so in subtle, nuanced ways. Notice, for example, in the above paragraph how the administrator does not answer the question posed to her by the biologist but instead directs it at another faculty member while engaging in face-work with the physician. Administrators, in my experience, are very good at this small, but potent, rhetorical ploy. It is as if they are suggesting that they do not so much "decide" as "act upon" the decisions of the faculty. And yet there is embedded within this text a fine economic print, a style of lettering that influences, however subtly, the eye. Administrators are, after all, the final arbiters of any decision, the court to which arguments are brought, the well-to-do who invite you into their offices for the purpose of making you feel welcome (which is to suggest, simultaneously, that you ordinarily wouldn't feel welcome). Their natural (or unnatural, depending on how you read it) allies are the similarly well-to-do, in this case the physician. Wealth seeks its own level, it would appear.

But is this important to an understanding of decision making? I think so. In a world where nothing is ever neutral, where opposites define positions that must, at some point, emerge from self-interest, where people joust in arguments that are at best polite versions of open warfare, allegiances are formed among those who have something in common. Or something in common to preserve. That wealth (and its attendant power) is such a readable sign, worn everywhere from the forearms to the key chains to whispers that follow a person into and out of a room, strikes me as cause enough to doubt its neutrality. It is part of the ultimate weave, which, like the intricacies of its fabric, reveals itself only at intervals, and then only upon close inspection. And when it does reveal itself it often says as much, if not more, about the person doing the inspecting than about the intricacies of the weave.

The Dramatic

As some aspects of a context live in sentences, so too do some of them live as performances. The notion that communication between and among persons in organizations—whether engaged in decision-making groups or not—can be read as performance is neither new nor particularly novel. It appeared in the novels of Charles Dickens, Sinclair Lewis, and F. Scott Fitzgerald long before the "pioneering" work of Kenneth Burke, Erving Goffman, or William Whyte, Jr., and it lived on prime-time television series and in popular films long before it was created in sentences that are part of our evolving literature on organizations. But merely saying that organizational communication includes aspects of dramatic performance has not yet produced much in the way of heuristics beyond the obligatory endnotes that reify this statement as a fact of our scholarly passage.

This is not to say that Burke's pentad and ratios, or Goffman's analytical schema, or for that matter the wealth of critical studies that improve our understanding of these concepts are not important. They are more than important; they are the legends of our own collective myth-making mind. But they seem to pause at the concept rather than carry it to some sense of completion, leaving the reader intellectually wiser but often unable to invest that wisdom for profit in the everyday market. Bottom line: Nobody does a better Burkeian reading of a scene than does Kenneth Burke; ditto for Goffman.

So what, then, can be made of the presence of drama against the absence of a master dramatist? How does the drama of the everyday form aspects of context that reveal meanings deeper than the terministic screens (roles, scripts, actors, scenes, etc.) we employ to describe them?

Perhaps we should remember that dramatic performances begin with entrances, end with exits, and encompass everything in-between. In real life, however, it is possible that one particular past entrance or exit stands out despite other empirical evidence to the contrary, shaping an interpretation that is literally impossible to live down. Performances are guided by an unfolding plot that everyone has some stake in, and at least in life not everything is always worked out before the exits end.

Performances are likewise full of gestures—empty, full, half-felt, half-hearted, half-meant—that like their spoken counterparts are intended for the audience of fellow players rather than for an attendant audience of payers whose admission price is a bet on the quality of the performances.

What is dramatic here may not play very well on Broadway. This makes it neither less dramatic nor more meaningful than Broadway renditions of this or that sort of life. Nor should it suggest that the dramatic metaphor is less of an analogy because of its figurative rather than literal bases for comparison. It is, after all, the terms of the critique that supply the critical light, the making of sentences that spell out the performances as performances that make them so.

But there is something else. Call it the dramatic value of the performance, the interpreted whole of judgments that are rendered about the behavior of the actors against some standard of excellence for decision-making performances. This seems to me the aspect of the dramatic that nominates itself as a candidate for any definition of context. It is a summary that bodies forth a judgment:

We are again in the decision-making chamber. We are nearing the end of our quest. We are in the part of the process that demands that we settle for less, somewhere between an overt compromise and a furtherance of present ambiguities, a place the group has come to in its deliberations that requires a unifying perspective. Put another way, we simply want to get back to our offices and get on with our own work, and we are willing to buy into something, anything that will allow us to save face in the service of that goal.

The new chair suggests that what we have come down to is an appreciation of the fundamental differences that separate us. There are nods, grins, and a grunt. However, he continues, this may be the most productive finding of the group: for the first time these differences have been clearly and publicly articulated. Another grunt, no grins, a scowl. He leans forward and points his pen toward the chandelier. It is a small gesture, but everyone is fixed by it. So then, he continues, let us draft our final report in a way that capitalizes on what we have discovered rather than dwells on our disagreements. No one speaks. He looks around the table, sees what he perceives to be agreement—however slight—and brings down the pen, twice, on the pad before him. If there is no further comment, we stand adjourned, he says quietly. I'll draft the report and send it to you prior to the next—let us say final—meeting.

Every context demands a focus, and in this one the focus is on the full performance of the chair. I say "full" because it completes for the group their own disparate experiences while gaining control (and power) over the decision making. As such it serves as a summary and as a judgment, a performance center stage, a strategy of redefinition that is capable, for whatever reason, of uniting a divided house toward some common purpose. The pen, however trivial my sentence about it makes it appear, is an important part of the performance. It serves as a kind of wand, and its movement as a gesture, that imbues its actor with a sense of the moment. And it is that sense of the moment, the seizing of it, that defines the performance as laudable, worthy of the group's attention, consideration, and, ultimately, consensus.

This is but one small example of the dramatic in the everyday operations of this decision-making group. I use it to advantage, of course, evidence for my claim about the summary impact of dramatic performances, and there may be some doubt about how well or poorly other performances fit this rather narrow definition. I would even go for that. Truth lies within a context that asks questions about the dramatic among the performances; the images that stand out are defined more by actions read over presumed intentions, presences read over possibilities of absences, moments seized when they didn't have to be.

So the context is never merely dramatic, despite performances to the contrary. To read the drama in the context of decision-making performances is to seek the light among the shadows in dark places that cry out for light while a lot of other things are going on. Once the light is bright the context changes, perhaps defined anew by the sudden and spectacular wash of illumination, perhaps better defined by its absence when in comfortable shadows the truer measure was only the need, as yet unarticulated, for a light. To watch a play for its drama is to do exactly that.

The Hierarchical

Every decision can be read as a movement from problem to solution, and as such every decision is bound by a hierarchical imperative: to improve a position, to move forward into new territory, to gain control over a situation—ultimately, to scale the symbolic hill and capture the symbolic flag. So too our language about decisions is rife with hierarchy: What is the best solution? Is this better than what we now have? If we do that, what will we gain?

There is a sense in which all decisions are bound by the language used to describe their outcomes. It is the context, perhaps the ultimate one, that we play for in a world where the most dominant symbols are ones born of the master tropes of winning, progress, ownership, and control. The language of decisions, then, can be read—like a musical score—as the movement from something to something, where the "from something" defines hierarchical desire and the "to something" defines hierarchical satisfaction of that desire. Within this context the language becomes the technology of achievement (or anarchy), an arrangement of words settling into places that the actors can identify with, orchestrated to some antecedent, emergent, or consequent theme.

This process of language-induced hierarchical action is often expressed in plainer terminology: finding the right words, making sure the report will meet the approval of the boss, getting everything important in it, leaving out nothing that will help us make a convincing case. Expressed these ways, each of the hierarchy-seeking words—"right," "approval of the boss," "important," and "convincing"—provides a unique sense of context, where context is interpreted as "purpose." It is as if the whole of the decision-making process has been aimed at this final objective, at once a satisfaction of both the form and the content of the assignment.

All along the journey to this transcendent place there have been clues suggesting that this is the context's end, the time and place for the discovery to be made that purpose is the ultimate definer of all contexts, the pattern made out of the weave of everything. Early on, decisions were made that shaped this objective, decisions about the locus of talk, the frames for viewing the validity and appropriateness of arguments, even whose advice would be sought out in an attempt to relieve various disputes. Later, as facts were gathered, decisions regarding their utility were made on the basis of some sense of purpose, but purpose perhaps misread then as bias, perspective, turf, or simple self-interest or desire for control. But as these discussions moved forward (an intriguing term, considering the various possible feelings associated with the discussions) toward some destination, all the influences of the physical, the economic, and the dramatic coalesced (or perhaps collapsed) into one final hierarchical thrust. Like this:

The new chair reads aloud from the draft of the final report. Its language is vague; its intentions can be read differently by each member of the group—indeed, by anyone looking into the document for evidence for or against a particular point of view. Each phrase selected seems to have its own history within this group, but outside of the group it may lead a life of its own. You consider, for example, the central passage: "Strategic planning decisions must be derived from the mission of the University, which this committee believes to encompass educational, research, and service to the region objectives. Because these objectives are currently not subject to a common definition, the committee recommends that further study be directed toward resolving these issues." What this means is that the committee could not agree on a common definition; what it says is that further study is needed. What is present is the conclusion; what is absent is the context— the various contexts—that produced it. What is present, then, is the language of purpose, albeit unfulfilled. What is absent are all the reasons why.

SUMMING UP: CONTEXT AS PERSPECTIVE, PERSPECTIVE AS CONTEXT

A context lives between the perceptual filters that respond to certain cues and ignore, or resist, others. As part of the process created by and constituted in communication it unfolds within the discourse, and what is not articulated does not cease to exist but exists rather as the presence of an absence, while what is articulated becomes another sort of presence, part verbal construction and part consciousness of something else— physicality, economics, dramatic event, hierarchy, purpose. What it becomes depends on the words put into it and left out of it, the "it" being the articulated, purposeful surround of perspectival reality known as context.

In this reading we have considered some of the ways in which sentences about context can shape meanings about how contexts are woven into the fabric of discussion. Like its subject, this essay contains both presence and presence of absence, where what has been left out may be as meaningful as what has been duly considered. This is not to say that I have labored to be obscure; instead, this contradictory formulation represents two opposite but equal characteristics of any context—its utter and absolute dependence upon words to mean anything, and its freedom to mean anything that words can represent.

For example, some sources of context have not been discussed in this essay because they did not occur within the emergent realm of the sample discussion used for the analysis. Consider race. Or religion. Or ethnic heritage. These are but three of the unarticulated possibilities that were absent from our discussion, yet very much present as framers of meaning for other kinds of decisions. Consider regional or national stereotypes, a family's decision to have (or not to have) children, the meaning of peace or war. And so on.

A context is perhaps the most situationally relevant construct in any theory of communication. It is a response we make, individually, perspectivally, to the presence and absence of possible aspects of reality. Sometimes we offer those observations as statements, sometimes we don't, and sometimes they find their way into the how, rather than the what, of our discourse. As such, that which constitutes a particular context for any individual is as capable of gaining assent as it is of sparking criticism, a rhetorical display with an equipotential to unite or to divide the listeners. Considered this way, there is no such entity as a purely empirical context, only statements and questions that attempt to define it or that respond to it as if its definition was either commonly held or commonly misunderstood.

Given this grounding, itself existing only in sentences, a context—and particularly the ability to engender or articulate it—is a master strategy, the master strategy, for any decision-making endeavor. For everything that counts exists within it, can be understood by it, has purpose and meaning because of it. Odd, isn't it, that what starts out in every discussion as a thread equal to any other ends up being the pattern that is what has, up until that point, only been.

5

The Case of "Meaningful Orders of Persons and Things" in an Organization's Culture: A Tale Told in a Participant's Voice

The nature of this environment is set by the meaning that the
objects composing it have for those human beings. Individuals, also
groups, occupying or living in the same spatial location may have,
accordingly, very different environments; as we say, people may be
living side by side yet be living in different worlds. . . . It is the
world of their objects with which people have to deal and toward
which they develop their actions. It follows that in order to
understand the action of people it is necessary to identify their world
of objects.

—Herbert Blumer

A human act is a potential text and can be understood only in the
dialogic context of its time.

—Mikhail Bakhtin

Motives are shorthand terms for situations.

—Kenneth Burke

The semiotics of organizational displays has seldom received more than casual lip service from scholars. Perhaps this is because the most obvious aspects of any culture tend to be the most overlooked. Everyday artifacts suffer similar fates; they are seldom preserved by a culture and therefore become "rare finds," years hence, for archaeologists.

Ian Mangham and Michael Overington (1987) suggest that the theatrical model for organizational analysis requires textual consideration of the role played by sets and properties. The point of their analysis is not to focus on a typology of organizational staging, settings, costumes, properties, and cues, but instead to show how these elements of dramatic performance "inhibit, facilitate, or function as a catalyst for actions . . . serv[ing] to predict and prescribe it" (119). This sort of dramaturgical

79

analysis, then, establishes the cultural bases for cues to organizational action and reveals how settings function as "more than physical adjuncts to scenes" (202), signifying subtle and nuanced agents of meanings that contribute to cultural codes for communication in organizations.

Studies of organizational cultures tend to ignore settings, costumes, and properties as meaningful cultural codes. In life, however, we regularly take our interpretive cues for action from the types of structures we are entering (banks, churches, shopping malls), the costumes worn by its inhabitants (uniforms, fashionable garb, work clothes), the symbols and signs present in the environment (name tags, security badges, posters, office adornments), and the ways in which people use these props to suggest meanings that work with or against the ongoing script.

Cultural studies focus either on enacted, behavioral communication (rites, rituals, jokes, gossip, stories) that are generally devoid of a feeling for the set against which these scenes are enacted, or on physical artifacts that leave out the role of the set and properties in the unfolding drama. In either case, organizational scholars often leave an incomplete record of the organization's culture.

For me, the maddeningly abstract term "organizational culture" and the studies that are done in its "tradition" are perhaps best understood within the broad scope of Sahlins's (1976) reader-based definition: cultures should be approached as "meaningful orders of persons and things." The task, then, of the organizational culture analyst should be the discovery of that meaningful ordering and the processes that sustain it (Smircich 1983). To try to accomplish this interpretive understanding without taking into account the sets and properties is to suggest two things, both of which are problems. First, it denies the importance of certain aspects of culture despite the fact that in everyday life we use them to guide our choices and judgments (Sennett 1977). Second, and perhaps more important, it suggests that the sense of culture created by those meaningful orderings of behavior and artifacts do not necessarily differ from organization to organization. Clearly this is inappropriate to the task at hand. Cultural analyst Sonja Sackmann (1987) argues:

> The mere recording of the presence of . . . artifacts does, therefore, not give much insight into the culture if the specific meanings that are attributed to them in a particular setting are not known. What is needed is an understanding of these culture-specific meanings. This requires an understanding of the ideational aspect of culture—the underlying cognitive constructions or the

cultural knowledge which exists in a particular organization and which is used to attribute meaning to things and events. (1)

To display the meaningful orderings that make possible the unique cultural contexts of organizational lives should mean to examine attributions of significance to everyday scenes of organizational experience. What is named "culture" by the scholar should be that which shapes or gives particular meaning to the ordinary and extraordinary experiences that emerge from episodes of communication played out against sets and with uses of properties natural to those experiences. The scholar's task, regardless of the study's microfocus, is to find the "meaningful ordering of persons and things" within scenes; to discover how and why meanings are attributed to them; and to convey to the reader, with a sense of verisimilitude, the results of the investigation.

DISCOVERING MEANINGFUL ORDERS OF PERSONS AND THINGS

An organizational scholar who enters an organization for the first time suffers the fate of a newcomer entering the same organization, a fate best summed up by Meryl Louis's (1980) phrase "surprise and sensemaking" (1980, 23). Out of the great delirium in which one's senses are assaulted by movement without ascribable purpose, talk without clearly understood references, and a veritable bombardment of signs, symbols, and messages all vying for immediate attention, the scholar, like a theatergoer who has not yet read the play, must be willing to consort with the ambiguity and attempt, through whatever means possible, to reduce it (Weick 1979).

When one goes to the theater, one generally examines the set for initial clues. Of course, this is best done when the lights are still up and the actors have yet to perform. For this reason I believe that one of the most essential analyses of an organization's culture should be performed at night, after hours, or on the weekends. The objective is to have free rein over the exterior and interior of the set, an opportunity to record (with notes and diagrams, or better, when permissible, with videotape or photographs) the naturally occurring traffic of the available signs and symbols.

This is the time for doing what a theatergoer does: looking at the set for clues to the themes, motifs, ironies, contrasts, or other evocations of meaning present in the ordering of things that, during working hours, surround the players and contribute to their unique sense of place. Performing this sort of elementary but necessary analysis of sets and props has two strategic advantages. First, the analyst can document the existence and placement of objects for further study and for later evidence of evolutionary modifications or changes. This is important because longitudinal studies of cultures are rare, and changes in sets and properties can be as important as (because they may correspond to) changes in management, policies, or employee attitudes. Second, the analyst can learn how individuals and groups differentiate themselves, establish their own organizational or personal identities, and express their inner voices through displays of art, photographs, posters, and other memorabilia. This close examination of individual workspaces and group territories can establish premises for the orders of things (including hierarchical or status orders) that can later be connected to premises about the orders of persons gotten from observations, interviews, questionnaires, and casual talk.

To discover the orders of persons and things exhibited within an organization's culture requires an appreciation for interpretive possibilities that are not reflected in our literature (see Calas and Smircich 1987). Our literature is, after all, the manufactured product of *our* academic culture, in particular a subculture devoted to interpretive cultural studies of organizations. To assume that our grammar, our perspectives, or our language is appropriate to the study of organizations is to commit an intentional fallacy under the guise of an elitist scholarship. Worse, it is to assume that *our* culture is the one against which all other cultures should be measured or understood.

To discover the ordering of persons and things requires two conscious decisions on the part of the scholar who will ultimately write about them. First, and most important, is the decision to record details of the set and properties (and their uses) in any account of an organization's culture. Second is the decision to write the account in a way that reveals how these signs and symbols contributed to the interpretation.

ORIENTATION TO THE CONTEXT OF B-BCSC'S CULTURE

My study of the culture of a Boston-based computer software company (B-BCSC) whose regional office is located in Huntsville, Alabama, took place from May 1984 through September 1988. This was a unique and important time in the history of the company because it marked the entrance of a new corporate vice president to oversee the Human Resources (HR) Business Unit, which is the basis of all of Huntsville's operations. It was also important because during this time plans were made and carried out to move from one leased building to a new office structure specially designed for B-BCSC. Previous work on B-BCSC's culture, and on the broader milieu of Huntsville, Alabama, appears elsewhere (Goodall 1989a), and references from that lengthy work are included in the present study to reflect some of the changes that took place. That study focused on the evolution of cultural rituals, stories, and legends under the influence of an "evangelical" new leader; this one focuses on the roles played by sets, costumes, and properties in the everyday formation of cultural consciousness.

In the account that follows, what I am after is rather simple: the association of choices of cars and their colors with cultural understandings and the representation of individual and group identities by displays of office art and memorabilia. Their depiction is rendered in a way that suggests the impact these taken-for-granted set pieces and properties have on my reading of the culture, which is itself a microcosm of a broader corporate culture within this geographic region. Also, by comparing the same organizational culture after a major change in location accompanied by changes in policies affecting individual and group displays, I try to show the importance of sets and properties as evolutionary signifiers, as emblems of outward, mandated change that reflect inner attitudes and sentiments. The result is admittedly a little off-putting within the context of the literature of an academic culture because it does not fit the format, use the voice, or make use of the familiar icons of that genre. The voice of the narrator, like the voice of any author working in any genre, including the academic press, must address the sympathies of the audience, even though in this case the goal is to challenge them. But it does, I found, represent the meaningful ordering of persons and things within the context of B-BCSC.

Geertz (1980) explains that what is going on here is a "blurring of the genres," a blending of perspectives. As Pacanowsky (1984) rightly points out, interpretive scholars seem to be missing the point of Geertz's critique. The term "genre" has less to do with ways of thinking about scholarship than with how scholarship is written. For my purposes here, the theatrical genre includes appropriate considerations of sets, costumes, properties, and so forth, and the result should be a writing style that incorporates them, ripe with interpretive possibilities, within the naturally occurring contexts of a dramatic organizational story.

Individuation and Group Identities

Theatergoers appreciate the subtleties and nuances of costumes, accessories, and colors that in some cases are used to represent or body forth an image or identity, and in other cases are used to suggest the absence or contrast of those effects. Rarely do we encounter descriptions of clothing, accessories, physique, movement, gesture, or manipulations of objects within office or manufacturing environments in scholarly studies (a notable exception is Miles and Leathers 1984). It is as if we are reticent to discuss them; they represent a source of academic taboo.

This omission is particularly unfortunate for cultural studies of organizations where, in my experience, a good deal of informal talk and most of the gossip focuses on what people wear, how they look, what kind of car they drive, where to go to buy objects to decorate an office or home, how to lose weight or to become physically fit to enhance one's appearance and health, what's wrong with someone's outfits or performances in them, and so forth. If the signs and symbols of nonverbal properties figure into the talk, it is hardly unreasonable to assume that it should appear, at least in a cameo role, in our literature.

My experience with B-BCSC revealed one major use of properties within the cultural context of this organization. That use was for the purpose of displaying sources of individuation and group identification, as shown in the themes and motifs of office art and posters, photographs, and the like. But within this culture the meanings people had for their individual displays was more important—and subtler—than the previous sentence conveys. Their approach and affection for the displays was more akin to what the novelist Tom Robbins calls "the romance of objects" (1980), an affective enjoinment and enjoyment of persons for things.

It is also important to point out that when the scene changed and the new building was occupied, the employees who wanted to carry over previous expressions of self and group were disappointed to learn of the new policy limiting their freedom of expression. During this transition period a subculture of underground terrorists who refused to go along with the new policy found subtle ways to express their concerns, in much the same way as the rebels of an earlier historical period expressed theirs (Gregg 1971). Clearly, individual and group egos were using a particular policy complaint as a rhetorical shield to protect their desires for self-expression.

Conveying the Culture, with Verisimilitude, to the Reader

A major task for the organizational cultures analyst is the writing of the final report (see Clifford and Marcus 1986; Geertz 1988). The writing itself is a dramatic performance (Goodall 1989a) that should be guided by an appreciation and artful use of narrative techniques such as voice, dialogue, episodes, tension, conflict, and a devotion to the craft of the word capable of reflecting a total immersion in the scene.

What I try to do in the episodes that follow is to display the organization by juxtaposing three different tales (see Van Maanen 1988). In two representations I give you a company tour that begins in the streets leading into the building, spends a little time reflecting on the vehicles in the parking lot, and then brings you inside. However, the particular twist to this seemingly natural progression is in the attempt to build into the description the views, both individual and collective, of the employees, so that the result is sort of an informed show-and-tell that attempts to capture (and condense) the experiences, sentiments, and thoughts of a variety of people into a singular, occasionally naive if seemingly omniscient narrator. The third tale is drawn from my own participation in the organization as a member of its summer softball team, an experience that revealed itself to be a microcosm of the changes evident in the earlier evolution of the organization's culture. The three are intertwined to create a dramatic organizational story.

I

I am an organizational detective. This is a story about how I read the clues to a culture while observing and participating in it. Everything here is important.

There are some natural limitations.

I am not a video camera and I am never neutral.

I use words to capture experiences that words have no ability to fully capture, and I have readers to please.

The human frailties of this cultural investigator no doubt influence what I see, think about, and write.

Mine is a method based as much on opportunity as motive; a desire to get out of the office and play some ball is at least as important as the desire to make a scholarly contribution. I admit to the necessity of basically hanging around, talking with the subjects of my study in much the same way that you might talk with a friend over dinner about the meaning of life.

Truth is that I just went out there and played the game, immersed myself in its metaphor and experienced, firsthand, at least some of its drama.

2

You will want to know something about me. How else could you trust my judgment?

I am the only son of a spy and a nurse, perfect environmental influences for my current work as a college professor. Secretly, I am still hoping for my break into the major leagues as a relief pitcher for the Yankees. In my youth I started writing novels and short stories, the best ones always about baseball, writing, and love; now I write articles for our professional literature about the same things, only on an analogic, interpretive level.

I was married to a woman who was a manager at B-BCSC, and it was through her that I first began these cultural investigations. When we threw parties we invited people over who liked rock n roll, sports, literature, and humor, and who still believed in the American dream.

There is another part of the American dream, however, the part they don't show you in the movies and the part you don't recognize until you are living in it. It's the part where something is gone and you think you missed it, and something else is ahead of you but it looks too much like today feels. So you open yourself up to possibilities that a year ago would have seemed absurd. This is the part of the American dream where you wake up wondering what that dream was all about; then you look out the window, and it is already mid-afternoon.

3

The spring of this story I was called up by B-BCSC's new team forming in the industrial league. It's lower than the minors, a sort of D level with no bus and you have to pay for your own uniform, but it's a chance to play again, so I do.

My then-wife has not fully bought into, but has nevertheless fully repeated, some of the lies of my fabled baseball hero youth to the team's management, who in turn expect me to show up a gloved wonder capable at least of pitching them into the play-offs, if not onto a spot on national television. During the first practice session out behind the new B-BCSC building, I catch a line drive in the teeth; spitting blood and refusing to leave the field, I personally take this incident as metaphorical justice being doled out by a vengeful God, who at this point in my life clearly sides with my wife and is out to teach me lesson. Or it could be a sign that what they are seeing is precisely what they are getting.

The next practice is held at an elementary school playground. This is a sign, reader, that you should not fail to read as a symbol.

4

This is a mixed league, women and men mingling together on sand diamonds, and the game is played slow-pitch. There are some interesting basic rules.

The game is played on a regulation field which varies considerably in size depending on who marks off the distances between bases. Teams play for no more than seventy-five minutes or six complete innings, whichever occurs first or is likely to draw the least amount of complaints from the coaches. To make it fair, the ballplayers are not allowed to wear watches and must hustle on and off the field to show good faith in their intention to move the game along or at least not to delay it.

What this means to the game it also reflects in the culture. At B-BCSC the scheduled work hours are from 8:30 to 5:00, but the unwritten rule is you work until the project is completed. Clock-watchers are not allowed to work for the Huntsville office of B-BCSC, which has a reputation for getting the job done regardless of what time it is. So it is that to get to work before 8:30 and not to leave until after 5:00—to hustle on and off the playing field—is a sign of having the proper attitude.

There are other rules. For example, this is a "mixed" league, which means that women and men must play together. However, to field a team for regulation play means that you need to field only two women for every eight men. There is an ugly assumption at work here. Furthermore, if the person batting ahead of a woman is walked by the opposing pitcher, the upcoming woman can automatically walk without ever stepping up to the plate. Usually she is encouraged to do so. Draw your own conclusions.

But remember, these are league rules, not necessarily B-BCSC rules, but B-BCSC must play by them too.

Finally, this is a game of slow-pitch softball. It gives the team at bat a decided advantage, an advantage that is best realized by aiming for a steady accumulation of singles instead of long balls that more often than not turn into long fly balls easily caught by the opposing outfielders. What this rule suggests about the workplace is that rewards belong to those steady players who avoid trying to stand out too much, who know how to fit in and play the game, who are ultimately members of a team.

When the team wins, you win too. But when you strike out, pop out, or fly out in a dazzling display of pumped-up glory seeking, you may stand out but the whole team goes down with you.

5

This is a game in which attitude is very important.

This is an era at the end of the twentieth century in which attitude is defined in the popular mind by its outward appearance. Contrary to the work of some cognitive psychologists, here attitude is an expression dressed out as behavior. And the behaviors that best reflect an attitude are looks, clothes, cars, actions, and colors, individually and collectively functioning as symbols to induce meanings in people through manipulation of appearances and accumulations of things.

This is an America addicted to images, craving the surface satisfaction of the desire to be consumed. This is an America where you can buy what you want as well as what you want to be. This is an America where how well you play the game is in part understood by how good you look, and how well you act, and what you have consumed before, during, and after the game.

It all adds up to attitude.

If Erving Goffman were still alive, perhaps he would see it as the next evolutionary move from presentation of self (1959) in which saving face is the central issue, to presentation of attitude in which the values of a culture are embodied and displayed. Something to wear; something to do; somebody to be.

6

You walk inside the new B-BCSC building and there is evidence of a new B-BCSC attitude. This is, and is not, how it used to be.

In the old days, up until the move to the new building in Research

Park, B-BCSC was housed in a rented structure on Sparkman Drive, across the street from The University of Alabama in Huntsville and next to Executive Plaza. In 1986 I wrote in my field notes about getting to it:

> You cross a sewer drainpipe to get there.
>
> Lately, the ditch where the sewer water runs has been the final resting place of a rusted Winn-Dixie shopping cart, an artifact no doubt stolen from the nearby Winn-Dixie Plaza, which features (in addition to the Winn-Dixie) an Emergency Clinic, a Buy Wise discount drug store, a Radio Shack, a Buy Rite discount shoe store, a European Tanning Spa, a Hills' discount department store, and one of those afternoon saloons without windows, the kind of purely functional dive that might, if you walk into it, change forever your views on the nature of things. . . .
>
> Ninety people, their vehicles, their artifacts, assorted groups of customers in for training on the company's products, and the company's products are crammed into a space intended for half that population. There are people and things crowded in the narrow hallways. Privacy is difficult.
>
> There is one bathroom.

Out of this environment and its people grew a powerful corporate culture, a sense of shared meanings in organizational identification and membership (Cheney 1983). In part, it was shaped by an evangelical leader named Henry who reorganized persons and things into a new meaningful order; in part, it was influenced by the drive of individuals in the company to preserve their individuality in response to that new order; and in part, it was the development of hiring and retention practices that sought out what would later come to be known as "a B-BCSC person."

Also, it was probably none of these things and something else entirely, a curious, mysterious, unnameable, magical "it" that was the traffic of meaningful symbols and attributions of significance to them during a particular time, in a particular place, among particular people.

In other words, it may have been a glorious accident. But as any postmodern observer knows, no matter where you go, there you are. Persons and things. Meaningful orders. Things to figure out.

7

I am bringing you into the architecture of the new B-BCSC building, although we have not yet left the old one.

We are talking about attitude, of which culture is its nature and set pieces, props, and costumes are its outward manifestations. Consider a ball team, by analogy. Its attitude is identifiable by its ways, its habits, its style of play, an aspect of which is the meanings we attribute to its artifacts, its uniforms, the stadium in which the performances are carried out. Maybe it has one voice, maybe it has many. When times are good, the magical "it" of it stands out, is named, is argued about, and nothing changes on the bet that if anything changes the good times will change too. But when times are bad, changes are made and the magical "it" loses its charm.

Look at what I said about the old building in relation to an "accidental" change in costumes that became an aspect of the B-BCSC culture back in 1986:

> From the parking lot you enter the building, which is one of those ordinary beige boxes with a pillared facade that suggests anything the sign on the door wants it to suggest, and you see two more significant symbols. The first is the company logo, which consists only of its name—B-BCSC—interesting because when undisguised it includes the names of the founders (as in Smith & Jones) and because one of them—let's say Smith—left the company over a year ago and for a long time everyone thought the company would become "& Jones" but it didn't, and because the founder who remained behind to run the company, a man fond of using lyrics from Dire Straits to explain company policies, a man who jogs every day and drives a silver Porsche 928, is not the kind of regular Joe you would expect to hang something as simple as his last name on a high-tech computer software company whose major product is "Z-Two." But he did.
>
> This is also the man—let's call him Elliot Jones—who walked into the office one day in blue jeans and inspired a revolution. The blue jeans, he said, were his way of rewarding himself for a hard week of work. In corporate America, it is the simple slogans that seem to move the soul, and so it was with this statement. The idea was that B-BCSC pays its employees every two weeks, and paydays should be special, so why not have a company policy that encourages wearing blue jeans to the office on payday?
>
> The policy went into effect immediately, and received the sort of tentative, let-me-see-yours-before-you-see-mine kind of reception that one might expect from a radical shift of tradition. Clothes, after all, are coverings of our personalities as much as our bodies, and the sight of a moderately overweight middle-aged man who sits at a desk for a living wearing Calvins is not necessarily inspiring. Such a man might, if pressed as a senior executive in Huntsville was pressed, buy what amounted to his first ever pair of blue jeans, not the soft, prewashed kind, but the superstiff starched variety, and, not knowing any better, turn them up at the cuffs and snap them into place with red suspenders, giving all the world and particularly the local customers the impression of a farmer on first Saturday at the county fair.
>
> It was not the costume, but the calculated effects of the costume on the customers that prompted the strongest criticism. Salespeople in Alabama and Georgia objected to looking too much like where they came from, especially when talking business to someone from San Francisco or Boston. One person in the company took offense to the policy this way: "I'm an adult and I don't

need to be told what to wear." As the weeks passed, Elliot Jones relented a bit in deference to his sales force and modified the policy to encourage "those individuals who did not deal directly with customers" on paydays to wear blue jeans, etc. The revolution was well underway, and its later influences on the culture could not yet be imagined. (1989a, 20–21)

Persons and things must be read together.

8

In the old building everyone contributed to the making of a culture. In the new building a culture was given to them.

What is the relationship between buildings and cultures? How does a change in one lead to an alteration in the other? Territories, how we mark them and how we understand them, are the issues here (see Ardrey 1967, 1970).

The old building was small, ugly, and cramped, but what went on inside of it was bold and new. In 1986 I described it this way:

As you leave the receptionist's area you move through a maze of adjoining corridors, temporary walls, and meaningful symbols.

The building has a closed-in atmosphere that is made unnerving by the generally cramped quarters, but is made more bearable by the presence of interesting, colorful artifacts. . . .

One significant aspect of the B-BCSC culture is nonverbally clear: There is a strong tradition of individualizing one's office area or workspace. So clear is this tradition that certain motifs become apparent. The motifs include some ordinary and expected symbols: symbols of family and families with pets, symbols of academic and professional achievement, symbols of recognition and reward. These are the positive, traditional symbols that you find in American offices from sea to shining sea, symbols that suggest ordinary values, or, if looked at differently, symbols that suggest exceptional continuities.

A second motif concerns symbols that are inner pathways to a mindscape of petty fears, rages, senses of humor, and bellicose warnings that coalesce into a collage of general and specific corporate psyches and that oddly enough correspond to the individual positive symbols of home, and learning, and achievement.

For example, "Shit Happens" is an emblem, a sort of badge really, that is laced through the building next to degrees and family snapshots, a common source of strategically ambiguous identification with an anonymous but ever-present enemy. "Is This Fun?" and "Are We Having Fun Yet?" also permeate the nonverbal atmosphere, particularly at eye level. The urge for self-preservation and recognition can be seen in the variety of "Me" buttons that tell their own stories: "God, I'm Good!" "Me First," "I'm Wonderful in Bed," "I'm Getting over This," and "I'm Not Crazy" are some examples. . . .

A third motif suggests identification with things corporate, such as "User's

Conference" posters, memorabilia from company picnics, Christmas parties, and the like. One characteristic of this motif is the absence of symbols drawn from previous places of employment, despite the fact that virtually everyone at B-BCSC held at least one job somewhere else prior to joining the B-BCSC team. This characteristic is easily understood as a show of corporate loyalty or as the nonverbal desire to make blank the past, but it is singularly at odds with other nonverbal symbols that strongly suggest a pride in past associations, schools, achievements, and times. It is also at odds with the talk exchanged between or among employees in which stories of past companies are routine. Perhaps this means that we guard our nonverbal communication more carefully than our verbal communication, or perhaps it is a broader reflection of a cultural value: To fit in means to make an opening in the symbols of one's life, an opening that represents a space reserved for the present, a space dominated by the visual channels of thought, where how we see or need to be seen can play a major role in demonstrating how we choose to fit in. (1989a, 25–28)

The new building, by stark contrast, strives to be bold and new and ends up being large, odd, open, and strangely ambiguous, and what goes on inside strains to be the same, only somehow better, and manages to be neither and so is misunderstood.

In 1987 the new building was voted one of the ten ugliest by the Architectural Society of Huntsville. Inside the new building some people interpreted these results as entirely political and not at all true. Others agreed. But with whom?

When you look at the new B-BCSC structure, what do you see?

I see McDonald's golden arches, or perhaps a Baptist church facade from which jut two sides of the same ambiguous question: What? At sunrise it reflects the sunrise; when the moon is high and full it gives back a high and full moon, perhaps suggesting that it is user-friendly in an adaptive, cosmic way.

Walk around the structure and you discover that the back is the same as the front, an oddly unsettling realization otherwise unknown in nature. Grass struggles for life all around it, but this has been a drought summer and you can't blame the architect for that.

Move out into the L-shaped parking lot and what do you see? Not the same cars as at the old B-BCSC. Something here has changed dramatically. Consider these paragraphs, written by me about the old U-shaped lot on Sparkman three years ago:

You can learn to ask questions about the culture of an organization by examining the contents of its parking lot.

This is particularly true if the organization in question is actively concerned with building an image or is making a serious attempt to develop a culture. We have known for some time now that nonverbal communication predates and precedes other forms, and it is reasonable to assume that in organizations where culture is the issue, this may also be true.

The cars you pass in the B-BCSC lot are artifacts of the interchange of traffics public and private, and they do, both singularly and collectively, suggest realities whose appearances are of primary cultural importance: Honda, Chevrolet, Buick, Toyota, another Honda, another Honda, another Buick, a Fiat, and a small Ford truck. And so on. Nothing is very much older than a forty-eight month note could purchase, and there are no motorcycles, bicycles, or multicolored Volkswagen microbuses.

These are the cars and light trucks of aspiring, mostly boom-generation professionals who derive a way of knowing and being from the office that often follows them home. In an older generation this might have been called an identity, separated into its corporate and individual components, analyzed for its dependence on the status of work or the prestige of the firm. But for this generation *identity* is too large and too stable a term to describe the movement of roles we enact and functions we carry out, the intricate interplays of working and living, the changes in attitude or values that circumstances adapt us to. Ways of knowing, ways of being, ways of doing, ways of seeing contribute to purposes more fluid than identities can catch.

Perhaps this is why a parking lot with only three red vehicles in it, and nothing vaguely exotic, not even a four-wheel drive, attracts attention, appeals to the sense of mystery that any cultural investigation begins with. There is much strategic ambiguity passing for beiges and light blue and off-white on cars that are uniformly protected by optional side moldings. They rest just on either side of the B-BCSC building, straight rows of muted colors suggesting some sort of pattern. (1989a, 17–18)

Persons and things.

What we see at the new building is a different sort of vehicle population. There are far fewer boom-generation Hondas and Toyotas. They have been replaced by Trooper IIs and big black Ford 4×4's and Supercabs leading a gaggle of lesser light trucks. Of the three original red vehicles, only one remains and that in the hands a new owner. But now there are many red vehicles, and in general the B-BCSC lot is filled with far more aggressive color choices.

What can all of this mean for the culture of B-BCSC-Huntsville? Does the move from smaller to larger, from cramped to open, from car to truck, from muted to aggressive colors, from an active, internally defined culture to a more passive, externally prescribed one, from then to now, correspond to something, or is it just a coincidence?

The difference isn't in the persons. The persons are mostly the same. In fact, less than a handful of the persons who worked here in 1986 no longer do, and there have been few new hires. The differences are evident, at this point, only in the things.

Persons and things. Something is being suggested here.

9

Our team has no name. We do have blue and white uniforms with numbers on them, however.

It was suggested by one of our coaches that we should call ourselves the B-BCSCers. There was a round of polite laughter. It was suggested again, a week later. This time nothing happened.

So we have no name. This, I think, is significant. Did you ever play for a team that didn't have a name? Did you ever work for a firm that didn't have a logo? A mascot? Some significant symbol? What is the meaning of this absence of common definition? This reticent stop in a flow of cultural ambiguity?

During spring training we are awkward but enthusiastic as a team. Our managers, Jim and Anthony, are stern taskmasters who run us through infield and outfield drills and batting practice, giving fair but fairly harsh criticism when our play fails to meet their standards. Every day we are reminded how tough a league this is, how strong the competition will be.

We learn a lot about each other and slowly begin to play together as a team. Positions are chosen, tried out for, changed around. Nicknames emerge. We have about twenty players, including one B-BCSC intern who was talked into joining the team after it was discovered that he had considerable athletic talent.

On the day of the first regular-season game an announcement goes out within the new B-BCSC building asking everyone to come out and support their team. Players wear their uniforms to work and are the envy of their colleagues. There is a lot of talk about victory, rumors about the other team.

We are defeated 38–7. I manage to give up fourteen runs in the first inning, but do partially make up for it by hitting a solid home run during my first at bat, driving in three big ones. Our eight fans chant "Babe!" but to no avail. We shake hands with the other team at the end of it, walk over to the assistant coach's truck and drink a few beers while our coaches admonish us for the ugliness with which we played.

We promise to do better next time. Jack, on his own initiative, begins documenting our team's efforts and sending out memos to the HR Business Unit ("Bullstaff"—not a reference to the current movie hit *Bull Durham* but an indication that most of what is displayed here is bullshit) on the company's internal network. It is an effort at communication that becomes, as the season progresses, a highly valued activity, one of those magical and spontaneous innovations that emerges from inside a culture that is—at least for now—happy with itself despite the heavy odds against its winning.

1 0

Come inside the new B-BCSC building.

You *are* in another world. It is a glass house in which the dominant colors are maroon and gray; there are well-tended plants and a consistent sense of a submerged feeling that defines the attitude of medium cool.

You are in the center of something, that much is certain. The floor is marbled, there are low-backed couches and love seats and chairs around a coffee table upon which are placed recent copies of *Fortune, Newsweek,* and *Software News.* There is no Muzak. You face a large mirrored pillar that houses the elevators, but there is never an elevator sound while those who go up go up and those who come down come down. To the left is the receptionist's area, and her name is Mary.

Mary is an alert, attractive woman who exudes a businesslike but reserved attitude and is very fond of California. She manages a desk neatly laid out with technologies of communication—a complex telephone connecting system, intercoms, and paging devices—and a noticeable absence of anything personal. When Mary isn't on duty, this space belongs to Anne, another attractive, alert woman who also exudes an attitude of distant professionalism.

At odds with the medium-cool, high-tech message suggested by these meaningful orders of persons and things is a sign-in book usually to the left of a visitor, atop a small wall that separates you from the receptionist. In 1986, back in the old building, I found the same sign-in book but read into it a very different sense of place. Then it was a source of humor, evidence of a motif of good-hearted fun and occasional wickedness that was laced throughout the building, a book in which visitors, spouses, and delivery personnel would take pride in outdoing the previous entry. For example:

Joe Blow   11 or so.   Looking for one good woman with whom to share lunch and sexual favors.
Large Bear   12:01.   To see smaller bear. No bear there. No honey either.
Dr. Strangelove   Zero Hour.   Desperately seeking Susan.

Now there is no humor in the receptionist's book. None.

What can this mean? Is it a sign of change? Maybe. It is true that the "old" receptionist was Ellen, who now works in the telephone support room. But I think there is more to it. In the old building humor was addressed to a public, a Chaim Perelmanian "universal audience," and served as a way of communicating the value of laughter to some of the meanings of work that contributed, daily, to a unique sense of place. Like graffiti, items of humorous display—whether in the receptionist's book or on the Gary Larson cartoons that were strategically placed by the coffee machine—invited meaningful contributions from others whose identities were otherwise unknown. Thus humor built a sense of community in which the act of participating was valued, and the quality of the participative performance was the stuff corporate stories and even legends were made of.

Now the humor has lost its edge, perhaps in part because it has lost its sense of public display. Cartoons for public display are "not allowed" under existing policy. The receptionist's book is a place for names and dates and company affiliations, not fun. Examine the House Rules again. Notice how many times the word "professional" shows up? This is further evidence that, at B-BCSC as in America, to be a professional is to lose what is personal and passionate. It is to mask the genuine sources of your identity.

Identity is further masked by a new program called "My Secret Pal," in which "special" gifts arrive at your workspace on birthdays, anniversaries, etc., from unknown company donors. How special can that be? Wouldn't you like to be able to communicate your thanks to someone who did something *special* for you? Are we having fun yet?

I I

It is mid-season and we have yet to win a game.

We are down to three or four fans. As a team we are down to about twelve players who regularly show up, two of them new: a female second baseperson named Terri and a male ex-hockey star intern from The University of Alabama in Huntsville named Blim. In an effort to find the winning combination, positions continue to be shuffled, a further sign of the desire to do well in an environment that believes in the value of rearranging the meaningful orders of persons and things. Jack's last internal memo read like this:

Howdy y'all:
  Well we lost again, but we have not given up the ship. Last night's game had some very interesting plays. There was a catch followed by an Indian rain dance by Slugger "The Scoop" Brown, a diving slide into third for no apparent reason by oo, and a collision/catch in the outfield by Hop-along and Buckwheat which resulted in a kind of funky double-play. The high lite of the evening was the finishing of the Milwaukee's Best Beer. It shall Lite from now on. Our games are so comical that they deserve a look by anybody who has a need to laugh and have a good time.
  Our next game is on Monday, June 13 at 5:30 PM at the Redstone Field. Come on out and support your team. (By the way, the score was 15–5).
  Ouch!!!
  Jack

Jack's next memo reveals another part of the unfolding story:

Howdy y'all:
  It went down to the wire. We were in it until the last swing of the game. But in the end the score was B-BCSC 11, CAS 15. Game highlites include a body block by "Goose" Gordon on oo (the "Goz" must think softball is a contact sport) and a spectacular out made by Tim "The Stitch" Ledbedder when he tried to catch an infield fly with his nose (we can laugh about it now, but at the time it was serious). We went down swinging with the tying run at bat. All in all it was a fun time for everybody, though for some reason our refreshment consumption after the game was down.
  Next game: Wednesday, June 15, 6:45 PM, Chrysler Field. Be there to support your team.
  Aloha
  Jack

The next game is with Teledyne-Brown Engineering, on the Chrysler Field. This is one of those Alabama mid-summer evenings when the temperature hovers around ninety along with the humidity; there is distant thunder and dry lightning that promises no rain in a summer already wet with humid drought. Everyone sweats a lot. Not a pretty sight. But we are charged with enthusiasm, want to win so badly that we outplay ourselves and our imaginations against a team that clearly expected far less from us. At game's end we win 14–13!

There is general cheering all around as the cold beer and soft drinks are handed out. Our coaches tell us that winning feels better than losing, doesn't it? We should remember this feeling, they say, let it guide us through our remaining games. This is the method-acting approach: remember the feeling and perform it again.

What I notice is that everyone stays around to party. Someone turns on rock n roll music from a truck stereo, leaves both doors wide open to fill the surrounding air with sound. On the really good tunes we all join in. When we lose, this is not the case. People wander back into their own smaller worlds. There is a need to keep the borders intact. We retreat to personal spaces reserved for remembering who we are when we have lost something outside of ourselves while in the presence of others. We may turn on the music, but our doors are closed and we don't sing along.

This is how a community turns entropic, where the center does not hold. Most notable tonight is that we worked hard, played hard, and won together, and nobody wanders away. There is contrast in this scene, a social construction of reality that hangs in the air like a single intoxicating breath: *Remember this feeling.*

There is a center here, a rush of warm emotion, laughter, victory, and camaraderie, and at least on this one night before the gathering of a distant storm, it is in fact *holding.* Consider Jack's memo from the next day:

Howdy sports fans:

The thrill of victory . . . how sweet it is. Your team won last night, putting to bed once and for all rumors that we were going to give Baltimore a run for their latest record. It was an exciting game filled with much controversy. In fact, we won after having filed an official protest with the umpire. MVP for the game was unquestionably none other than Big Jim "Oh What a Stroke" Banks, with Jimmie "The Zipper" Deal running a close 2nd. Winning pitcher was Kathy "#0" Keller with Dr. Buddy finishing them off with some killer pitching. Everybody deserves a big hand, especially Coach Smith and Coach Henson. Congratulations are in order. The final score was 14–13.

Next game: Monday, June 20th, 6:45 PM, Teledyne-Brown field against Hilton Systems. Come on out to the ball game and cheer your team on. Let's extend this winning streak.

Oh what a feeling

#00

And for a while, a glorious while, we won and did nothing other than continue to win.

I 2

There are four separate work areas in the new building.

On the first floor, behind the receptionist's area, is the Curriculum Development/Employee Services complex, which includes a large computer room and a modern weight room and sauna. Also on the first floor is the Customer Training Area, which includes a customer lounge consistently referred to as "the bordello" by B-BCSCers because of its soft, dim lighting and general ambience. Don't get the wrong idea; nothing like that goes on at B-BCSC.

On the second floor, the work area above Curriculum Development/ Employee Services is laid out for Support/Marketing/Maintenance/Administration. Also on the second floor, above the Customer Training area, is Development/Quality Assurance/Testing.

There you have it. The whole layout of the set.

You are a theatergoer. What does this set suggest to you?

First, what we have here is clearly an "open office" concept (Klein 1982) realized by the use of large open stages upon which sit individualized work stations known internally as "cubes"; the cubes are fashioned out of richly textured maroon and gray fabric panels designed to absorb sound and provide visual continuity throughout the office. This concept was first introduced in America in 1968 by Robert Propst of the Herman Miller Company, working from earlier models provided by the German-based Quickborner Team, and has in its brief history been responsible for roughly 50 percent of the redesign efforts of American organizations (see Klein 1982, 37).

Since its inception, the open office system has attracted both praise and blame. Originally intended as an improved management technique, many workers still feel that it robs them of privacy and status, a view echoed by many employees of B-BCSC when they moved into the new building: only senior-level managers and the corporate vice president have offices with walls, while everyone else occupies a cubicle.

The new building also has six separate restrooms. The old building had one. Common sense suggested that the increase in restroom facilities within the new building would be better, but at what cost? According to Henry Peppertree (the Huntsville branch corporate vice president), one cost has been a sense of shared community and communication. People simply no longer talk to each other while waiting for a pit stop; also, they move into each other's work areas less frequently and therefore have fewer informal exchanges than they did in the old structure.

The concern for a lack of communication is voiced by a number of other employees who attribute part of the problem to the layout of the new building. Divided into four quadrants, each with a special mission and specialized clientele, the new office impedes cross-company talk and encourages a more insular view of who one's colleagues are. Hence, persons who work in Development are viewed as different sorts of individuals from those who work in Support, and because they spend less informal time speaking with each other there has been a deeper division in expressed attitudes toward the other's contributions.

For example, there are constant references to the "support" versus the "development" side of the "house," evidence of a segregation of mental space reserved for what used to be union, a suggestion that there is a pervasive "us" versus "them" where there used to be a "we." I am being overly polite here. This is a very touchy situation at B-BCSC, one that fires the emotions of employees faster than anything else.

But you, reader, can probably see the pattern without my help. I think anyone could.

This pattern reminds us of both of our initial and pressing questions: Does the stage affect the way in which the actors interpret the scene? Does the arrangement of set pieces (such as cubicles) and props (such as decorations of work stations) influence how meanings are attributed to persons and things? Have these become rhetorical questions?

The deeper issue is one of interpretation. How, specifically, do these set pieces and props contribute to the meanings this culture holds for its participants? As I have just suggested, one way into this issue is through the use of language by B-BCSC employees and the various embedded sensitivities that are contained in those expressions. On the inside there is a striking awareness of what persons and things mean, together.

13

There is significance and magic in numbers.

Consider a team that began the season with a surplus of players, that at mid-season was down to a critical level, and that at season's end was worried it wouldn't have enough to field a team in the play-offs. What are the implications of this? What does it mean?

This was an up-and-down summer, a long season of trying to find the right combination to win, a time when "Oh What a Stroke" Banks continually asked the question: "Are we trying to win or are we just out here to have fun and hope to win?" It was a question that was never really answered. Frustration was evident, player turnout for practices dwindled, and there were barely enough of us to field a team for the last few games.

Among the players, factions developed; things were said. The humor disappeared and with it vanished some pride.

The numbers were down and against us.

You could say that although we won three more games, that wasn't enough to inspire confidence. You could say that. You could say that the play-offs were held in early September, on the same weekend as the beginning of dove-hunting season, and think you had said something important. But you wouldn't have. Or you could look at the numbers as signs of something else in the broader concerns of culture, as signs of magic (or in this case its absence) within the general mystery.

Let's back up. There is more going on here than numbers alone can account for.

Late in the season there is a team party. Everyone is invited, but only a core of players and their spouses come. "Where is so-and-so?" is a question that has no necessary or sufficient answer. During the celebration, awards are presented for "most improved player" (Elizabeth "Slugger Brown" Hardy-Brown), "fastest baserunner" (Dr. Buddy, which, if you know me, says something other than what the words normally mean), "best swing" (Lauri Deal, who is absent), and "most valuable player" (Jimmie "The Zipper" Deal, who is also absent).

There is significance in all of these awards, both at the time they are given and later. For instance, the MVP award was an issue that found its way into the conversations of several B-BCSCers, even those who did not play on the team or ever go to a single game. The odds-on favorite was Jim "Oh What a Stroke" Banks, easily our best athlete, but who was also the subject of a controversy among some of the players because he "left" an internship at B-BCSC for a paying job at Intergraph but continued to play on our team. Some people believed he didn't get the award because he didn't work for B-BCSC. But then somebody else remembered that neither did The Zipper; in fact, he also worked for Intergraph. The controversy deepened when the MVP showed up late for the team awards party and didn't show up at all for any of our play-off games. Oh What a Stroke did, to his credit.

The "fun" awards for fastest baserunner and best swing were reminiscent of a B-BCSC tradition for giving "gag" awards at public ceremonies that serve two important cultural purposes. First, they "honor" a characteristic that is designed as a corrective to a situation: the fastest baserunner wasn't, the best swing was a miss. Second, the award symbolizes acceptance within the culture despite the award winner's obvious flaws. So in a way, the winning of a "fun" award is a mixed message that serves as a transcendent rite of passage. Within the broader cultural context of B-BCSC these awards have included the infamous "Pig" award to male chauvinist of the year and the "Bitch" award for top nag. It has also included, recently and within the stage setting of the new building, a thinly disguised award for "Informed Leadership" to the company's vice president, combined with a "gag" video production which showed he wasn't sure who worked there or what work was being done.

He did not respond favorably; as an indirect result of the gag award, each side of the "house" now sponsors its own corporate parties and gives out its own awards. These days, gag awards may not be issued at corporate-sponsored public events. Do symbols of division evident in a vocabulary ultimately lead to real divisions down on the playing field? Is this one way in which subcultures are formed?

And what about the leader, the evangelist who put something larger than himself in motion when he used his rhetorical powers to inspire, to cajole, to fire up, to define? What happens when said leader fails to see the flaws in himself, refuses to laugh at some admittedly cruel but culturally acceptable shows of affection, and decides to leave immediately after the ceremony and further separate himself from the situation that produced the need for the symbol? Something is definitely wrong. Ditto for the MVP and best swinger who didn't show up for the play-offs.

There were silences and gestures in these moments that I can't capture in words. Correspondences in evolutions. And they stole the whole show.

Persons and things.

This was a losing season. All the numbers, and some of the magic, were against us.

WHAT MEANINGFUL ORDERS OF PERSONS AND THINGS SUGGESTED TO ME ABOUT THE EVOLUTION OF CULTURE AT B-BCSC

This is where my voice changes. This is where I put up my glove, put on the old school tie, and begin the formal, academic analysis.

In retrospect, there seem to be three key ways in which the subtle, nuanced displays of organizational sets, costumes, and properties interacted with the actors to influence communication and establish some aspects of the culture of B-BCSC-Huntsville.

Theatrical Frameworks for Cultural Depictions of Organizational Personalities

Just as every organization reveals a unique sense of culture, it may be said that every organization also displays a unique "personality." The term "personality" requires scrutiny that evokes a cultural connection. To draw on the writings of Ernest Becker, in a tradition that includes Harry Stack Sullivan, George Herbert Mead, and Karen Horney, the concept of "personality" represents a "locus of sentiments within a phenomenal field" (Becker 1962, 160). It is the narrative given to what is expressed by an actor within a given context over a period of time. It is a story turned out about the reading given to a story within.

"Personality," then, lives in sentences spoken by actors who are themselves caught up in the scene. Like interpretations of observable behavior or physical artifacts, evaluations of "personality" reflect an engagement of a particular pattern of meaningful orderings by an analyst trained to find, and to locate meaning in, those patterns (see, for example, Lacan 1968; Laing 1965). By analogy, this is akin to an interpretive reading of a multilingual organizational text from the perspective of a reader capable of responding to only one language. Viewed this way, Geertz's (1973) use of Max Weber's description of culture as "webs of significance spun by ourselves" applies equally well to the narratives we have created about "personality" and "culture."

As cultural narratives, patterns are meaningful orderings to which significance and meaning is attributed. Such attributions are made differently by different readers, a pattern that may not change over time but whose attributions of significance and meaning often do. "Personality" within organizations is most often a story told about someone else by someone else, a story that is often repeated but in whose repeatings certain words, meanings, or symbols are altered to reflect the character of the storyteller more than the character of the subject of the story.

Given these conditions, what struck me in my study of B-BCSC was the presence of the term "personality" in sentences that connected judgments of persons with judgments of cultural fit. "Personality" was—and still is—a term that defines a person's relationship to the organization's culture, as in the statements "She doesn't have the right personality, she just isn't going to fit in here" and "We knew we would hire her. She's a B-BCSC person." It is as if culture and personality are integrally related, mirror images of each other, a theater of motives in which the dramatic appearance and performances of the players are pitched against an immovable set (set of values?) and whose properties are nonverbal displays of what is never clearly articulated. Cultural "fit" then, is how a player is defined within a space—a stage setting—already filled with significance and significations.

This suggests that our approach to communication studies of how newcomers "fit" into organizational cultures may be missing an important point. What we have done is to share the perspective of the newcomer, in which "surprise and sense making" seem to wed themselves to a transcendent vision of acceptance if only the newcomer can learn how to "read" the cues, make sense of the sentences spoken by the players, and blend into the surroundings as if camouflaged.

However, what this study suggests is just the opposite. Cultural fit may not be determined so much by making sense out of one's environment, learning "the ropes to skip and the ropes to know" (Ritti and Funkhauser 1977) or the other attributes of strategic organizational competence, as it is by *already having what it takes in terms of appearance, costumes, accessories, and uses of set pieces*. Cultural fit, put starkly, may have more to do with theatrical continuity than with strategic competence. From a theatergoer's vantage, cultural fit may be best appreciated as *casting,* a notion which would give a more dramatic reading to the professional literature on why fit and loyalty are more important than job competence.

Consider, for example, some of the casting continuities reflected in the story I have constructed about settings, props, and costumes relevant to the culture of B-BCSC. The cars in the parking lot have changed, but collectively they reveal a common motif, one that is subtly different from other firms in town. The influence of clothing as costume, both at work and when the workers are at play, suggests that fitting into the culture of B-BCSC requires attention to appearances that mark an individual as a "B-BCSCer." Decorations of office space, and particularly decorations that fit the existing pattern, are important sources of a message about who you are and how you fit in. Collectively, talk is exchanged on the basis of vehicles, clothing, artifacts, and work tasks by persons who have stories to tell, stories that fit into the existing traffic of symbols. Perhaps this is one of the reasons why new hires are increasingly products of an internship experience. It is their corporate "tryout," a time to see whether or not they fit into the image B-BCSC has of itself and its employees. The idea is not merely to educate or to train them in the tasks relevant to their work, but to share space with them, take them to lunch, invite them to company functions, sell them on playing for the softball team. The summary judgment of their personality is not one of "Will they make it?" so much as "Are they the right kind of person to work here?"

Within the broader contexts of "personality" and "culture" this alternative view of cultural fit has a strong, if somewhat peculiar, appeal. If a culture is, as my oft-repeated Sahlins definition has it, "meaningful orders of persons and things," and if "personality" is, as Becker defines it, "a locus of sentiments within a phenomenal field . . . [representing] a vocabulary of motives" (1962, 22), then it is neither competence nor learning ability that characterizes the ability to fit into a culture, but a personality that already fits the established meaningful orders of persons and things. The judgment of cultural fit is a blend of B-BCSC human personality and B-BCSC physical culture, a sense in which the actor and the set are interdependent. Although the art of the B-BCSC performance is far more than the sum of its set pieces and artifacts—as is any good drama from the perspective of the reader/viewer—it certainly wouldn't be, couldn't be, the same without them.

The Use of Signs and Symbols as Interpretive Bases for Character, Interests, and Flaws

If personality and culture are mirror images of each other in determinations of scenic fit, then it seems reasonable to give deeper significance to how "the locus of sentiments within a phenomenal field" and the "meaningful orders of persons and things" coalesce in and contribute to the readings given to dramatic performances. To do this at B-BCSC requires attention to how meanings are attributed to the various signs and symbols that are used to describe character, interests, and flaws.

What this suggests about our understanding of organizational cultures is subtle, but I hope persuasive. Just as ground gives meaning to figure and vice versa, so too do properties, costumes, and artifacts give and share in the meanings attributed to the words and actions of the players. Scenes are played out in environments where meaningful symbols derive their powers from culturally shared understandings of character, interests, and flaws.

Because I was trained in the field of rhetoric, I cannot help but read into the elements of character, interests, and flaws a modified version of an older text (see Aristotle 1954), in which *ethos, logos,* and *pathos* suggest that these elements of the dramatic performance of B-BCSC are best understood as *appeals*. They are inducements to know, to be, and to do (or not to do), a sort of rhetorical spell cast upon an audience with a message that can be read this way because the audience draws its vocabulary from a similarly defined field of cultural motives. Perhaps this is why, if the goal is to write about a specific culture, it is better to live with the natives and go to their plays rather than simply to examine their artifacts in your office or generalize about the meanings of corporate behavior among colleagues. The things to examine may be the same everywhere, but their meanings are likely to be very different according to the settings in which they are found. It is not the things or the persons, but the ways in which meaningful orders of persons and things are put together that ultimately matters.

How Grammar and Vocabulary Distinguish among Classes of Employees, Determine Degrees of Cultural Fit, and Induce an Observer to See Connections among Persons and Things and Culture

One of the questions that guided this study was "What do we talk about when we talk about an organization's culture?" Another one was "What do B-BCSC people talk about when they talk about their organization and the people that work there?" I had hoped for answers that held a certain correspondence, and there was one. Our literature acquainted me with the vocabulary of cultural study; my study of B-BCSC's culture showed me how to make a specific grammar from that vocabulary.

When we talk about the culture of an organization, we talk about its stories, its rituals and rites, its hierarchies, its power structure and politics, and, among categories of knowledge, its artifacts. As Stephen Tyler (1988) argues, we continue our Western, Platonic tradition of creating words to measure reality, of creating definitions and categories to contain knowledge about that verbal representation, and of creating modes of reasoning about those words, definitions, and categories that place a heavy emphasis on the *what* rather than the *how* of persons and things. Ours is a knowledge of vocabulary more often than it is a vocabulary of knowledge.

To get to a vocabulary of knowledge requires more than simply immersing oneself in a culture and letting something happen on the categorical assumption that this is the way it happens so when I name it this will be what it is. It is to immerse oneself in a culture, let something happen, and look for clues. There is a subtle but very important difference at work here. At one end you are happy to describe what you think it means; at the other end you describe the meaning of the experience, and *that* makes you happy.

The issue is one of rhetorical appeal and a necessary dialectic between the observer and what is observed and recorded, an issue that involves the effects of symbols and performances on us that in turn have us responding to them with the vocabulary we are caught up in. Oddly enough, this response is precisely the same sort of grammatical learning that is always taking place among the actors and within the scene. It is a grammar of motives played out in a theater of motives where everything counts and nothing is ever neutral.

For these reasons it is not the *what* of cultural terminology that intrigues me about B-BCSC. It is *how,* within that theater, I was induced to respond to clues about the meaningful orders of persons and things and culture that encouraged me to distinguish between and to make connections, and to believe that what I was distinguishing and connecting had similar meanings for the persons within that culture.

There is a blending of personal and professional concerns that says something unique about B-BCSC when it is read as a figure against a ground of historical and evolutionary understandings and values that also combine professional and personal concerns. Similarly, as I have tried to display, there is a consistent interplay of persons and things that somehow stands out at B-BCSC. This is a workplace rich with symbols and signs that encourage connections to be made between them and their uses and the persons who create and constitute their meanings.

One final observation on my own observations. As I pointed out earlier in this essay, I am never neutral. So it is with a sense of selectivity that I responded to the various and changing cues reported within this study. My experiences as a softball player, for example, added up to something more than they might have had I not also been involved in studying the culture of this organization. Then there is the overriding issue of language. My chosen metaphor and way of life is drawn from the vocabulary and style of the image of the organizational detective I have, admittedly mimetically, created. As Gareth Morgan (1986) has demonstrated, change the metaphor and you change the frame; change the frame and you alter what you see and how you describe it; change what you describe and you change what it is that you are appreciating or understanding. And, finally, there is no doubt in my mind that my study of this organization's culture was influenced by my then-wife's position within the company, her friends' attitudes toward what persons and things represented and meant, the experiences of our university's interns at B-BCSC, and the fact that when I was there, things seemed to happen that may have happened differently, or not at all, when I wasn't there.

Call these limitations on my study, due to the music of me, and mystery, and metaphor. Tell me I'm only reading the surfaces of persons and things. So be it. No argument. But then, please, read as my summary on the issue of context, within the context of this study, this final paragraph:

A culture—any culture—is like an ocean. There are many wonderful things and creatures in it that we may never understand; they change and so do we, regardless of the depth or perspective of our study. But the ocean is also made out of waves that are as regular as the cycles of the moon, and just as mysteriously musical, powerful, and enchanting. The top millimeter of the ocean is a world unto itself, and a vital one, in which the broader secrets of biological and evolutionary life itself are contained. But even their meanings must be read in a vocabulary that is separate and distant from it. So it is that within that millimeter, among those waves, we find clear and recurring themes. Like the great questions about culture that we pursue, these themes are always with us and not yet fully understood.

PART THREE Writing the Autobiographical Mystery: The Detection and Manifestations of Self

Autobiography, Style, and Dialogic Authenticity: The Detective's Mystery as Mystery of Self

Instead of being merely an organism that responds to the play of factors on or through it, the human being is seen as an organism that has to deal with what it notes. It meets what it so notes by engaging in a process of self-indication in which it makes an object of what it notes, gives it meaning, and uses the meaning as the basis for directing its action. Its behavior with regard to what it notes is not a response called forth by the presentation of what it notes but instead is an action that arises out of the interpretation made through the process of self-indication.

—Herbert Blumer

Self-consciousness, as the artistic dominant in the structure of a character's image, presupposes a radically new authorial position with regard to the represented person. . . . A man never coincides with himself. One cannot apply to him the formula of identity $A = A$.
. . . the genuine life of the personality takes place at the point of non-coincidence between a man and himself, at his point of departure beyond the limits of all that he is as a material being, a being that can be spied on, defined, predicted apart from its own will, "at second hand." The genuine life of the personality is made available only through a dialogic penetration of that personality, during which it freely and reciprocally reveals itself.

—Mikhail Bakhtin

Man is the symbol-using (symbol-making, symbol-misusing) animal inventor of the negative (or moralized by the negative) separated from his natural condition by instruments of his own making goaded by a spirit of hierarchy (or moved by the sense of order) and rotten with perfection.

—Kenneth Burke

In this essay I want to explore the writing of autobiography as a natural theme in texts devoted to the practice of interpretive ethnography.

This chapter, then, will serve as a transition from studies of contexts to studies of self within contexts. It is a setup, if you will, in which the detective does the setting prior to the commission of what will at first appear to be a crime. In this case we are concerned with investigations of self, an act of writing often thought to be a crime among the social sciences, a crime of supreme self-indulgence or worse—irrelevant to the pursuit of scholarly inquiry. But the detective's task is to establish grounds for a serious questioning of that assumption, and to show, in fact, that what at first appears to be mere self-indulgence is actually—well . . . you'll see.

To make this work, I must use the familiar "professional" voice again. I do so because the contexts in which we must immerse ourselves involve current literary discussions about the descriptive and analytical adequacies of traditional rhetorics of cultural display (Clifford 1988; Geertz 1988; Goodall 1989a; Rosaldo 1989; Rose 1989; Tyler 1987; Van Maanen 1988) as well as the role of self and Other in autobiographical writing (Anderson 1987; Eakin 1985; Egan 1984; Gunn 1982; Olney 1972; Siebenschuh 1983; Stoller and Olkes 1987; G. O. Taylor 1983).

I do this also because the place for the use of this voice, indeed this genre of writing, seems most appropriate for investigations of what William James termed "knowledge about" (theoretical arguments *about* the world) rather than "acquaintance with" (immersion *in* the world). For me, then, this voice is appropriate for "knowledge about" arguments that exist primarily in the professional discourse of the field.

To begin this exploration requires locating ethnography within the larger framework of writing cultural critique. Cultural critique, in turn, relies on an appreciation of the relationship between the various sites of cultural production and institutionalized forms of knowledge used to represent them (see Connor 1989; Fish 1980; McHale 1987). First, I will provide a reading of the texts involved in both the production and representation of ethnographic and literary knowledge. This reading will show how these texts and their rhetorics have induced my own particular response. Then I will offer an argument for restructuring the rhetorical nature of *ethos* from a concern with the ethical character of the speaker/ author to a narrative display of the dialogic character of relationship between the speaker/author and the reader/other. I offer this argument because, as I will attempt to show, such a move is inherent to judgments concerning the textual authenticity of descriptive rhetorics.

READING AT THE BORDERS OF
INTERPENETRATING TEXTS:
THE CRITICAL SITE FOR THEORIES OF
AUTOBIOGRAPHY AND STYLE

Ethnography is a form of cultural critique (see Marcus and Fischer 1986). Viewed this way, ethnography has been shifting its theoretical interests from understanding—through intensive fieldwork—the various symbolic dimensions of the everyday life exhibited by exotic peoples and their environments, to a mediating concern for how such an acquired understanding can or should be written and for how various rhetorical strategies may be employed toward that end. As Clifford Geertz phrases it:

> "Being There" authorially, palpably on the page, is in any case as difficult a trick to bring off as "being there" personally, which after all demands at the minimum hardly more than a travel booking and permission to land; a willingness to endure a certain amount of loneliness, invasion of privacy, and physical discomfort; a relaxed way with odd growths and unexplained fevers; a capacity to stand still for artistic insults, and the sort of patience that can support an endless search for invisible needles in infinite haystacks. And the authorial sort of being there is getting more difficult all the time. The advantage of shifting at least part of our attention from the fascinations of field work, which have held us so long in thrall, to those of writing is not only that this difficulty will become more clearly understood, but also that we shall learn to read with a more percipient eye. A hundred and fifteen years (if we date our profession, as conventionally, from Tylor) of asseverational prose and literary innocence is long enough. (1988, 23–24)

Given Geertz's long list of ills that befall the ethnographer, his sense of a shift of interest from fieldwork to deskwork, from acting *in situ* to recreating said *in situ* as text, from scientific validity to literary quality—all this, like his insistence that writing is "getting more difficult all the time," should be read at least as much as a challenge as an invitation. However, as soon as that sentiment is aired it quickly becomes problematic: Certainly his rhetorical stance should be read as a challenge, but as a challenge to what?

In this section of the essay I forward the argument that the challenge here has at least as much to do with issues of style and autobiography as it has to do with the available means of representing situations and Others. To do this, I think, requires invoking a metaphor, because this particular argument requires simultaneous travel to distant destinations that always correspond but have not yet been shaped that way. The metaphor, then, is one of a visit to an everyday place—a neighbor's house—that will change, unexpectedly and perhaps forever, our views on the nature of the work we do in our own homes.

Let us, then, leave the comfortable disarray of our own house, within the convenient context of this sentence, and simply walk across the lawn to visit the next-door neighbor, to go there perhaps to derive (borrow) something or better yet to recover (in the sense that means to get something back). We go there unaware that something is happening in that house, for our arrival has not been preceded by a phone call. This is why when we arrive we enter what is obviously a very busy kitchen where we suddenly realize that we are in the presence of a lively conversation in literary studies concerning how style functions as argument in contemporary nonfiction.

Is that Jimi Hendrix in the background?

STYLE AND AUTOBIOGRAPHY AS ETHNOGRAPHIC TERRITORIES

Why should autobiography, much less the style through which it is committed as text, be of concern to the practice of ethnography? After all, ethnographers have always been "in the texts" they have created, whether their presence has been relatively active (e.g., Lévi-Strauss 1955; Malinowski 1922, 1935; Conquergood 1985, 1987; or Goodall 1989a, 1989c) or relatively passive (e.g. Ardrey 1967; Carbaugh 1988; Katriel and Philipsen 1981; Van Maanen 1981), and whether the texts they perform are dedicated to understanding Others (Bateson 1936; Mead 1928; Rosaldo 1989; Trujillo and Dionisopoulos 1987) or devoted to furthering understanding of the concerns of the field (Clifford 1988; Clifford and Marcus 1986; Goodall 1989b; Pacanowsky 1988; Philipsen 1977) or the nature of doing fieldwork (Fetterman 1989; Van Maanen 1988).

The issue here is not, however, whether authors are present, but *how their presence is manifested in prose* and what the nature of those manifestations should suggest to us about the scope and limitations of their arguments. As Geertz has it, "Getting themselves into their text [that is, representationally into their text] may be as difficult for ethnographers as getting themselves into the culture [that is, imaginatively into the culture]" (1988, 17).

This problem is easy enough to state and relatively straightforward in its implications: the issue here is one first of the explicit symbolic capacities of language to induce understanding (Burke 1969; Gregg 1984) through the proverbial "shedding of light on a subject," and second of the implicit symbolic baggage carried by any use of language that casts into the shadows everything not directly in the path of the light. So it would seem that language is not merely an issue and not only the nature of the problem; language is also the only way to approach the issue and the only code available to cipher some solution to the problem (if a solution is the necessary outcome, which I will show later is hardly the case).

Furthermore, language is itself too broad a category to be very useful as a map or territory for this linguistic dilemma, for language holds all of the known world as its domain, all of the universes of discourse and deportment as its legitimate work, and all known metaphors as its cosmic (used here in the Latin sense of "universal") vehicle for the doing of that work. No, language *qua* language won't help because it won't do, and yet we can't do anything here without it.

However, one of the uses of language, if not its principle use, is to make rhetoric. One of the slier characteristics of rhetoric is its ability— within the body of the appropriate magician and much to the dismay of philosophers since Socrates—to cast spells, to work magic on a subject. When the issue is language, this trick is very much like the strategy of chasing one's tail with one's head in the vain hope of wearing the tail out before the head gives out, and being able at some point to sneak up on the tail and observe it firsthand while it is napping and unaware.[1] As incredible as it seems this strategy often works, at least in sentences that say it works, which is what this sentence now does. What we have done here, courtesy of the rhetoric employed to make the previous sentence, is to wear out the wagging *tail* of language, for once examining it not as a tail that holds us hostage to its wagging, but as a *tale* that is told in the voice of some actor.

We are, therefore, reclaiming for the head its rightful place before the tale. When we do so we come back to the voice of the actor who lives in and through the tale, and we get there by recovering, through and for rhetoric, the interdependence of self and style as the naturally occurring, evocative, metaphorical comet that, in its spin across any given universe

---

1. This rhetorical illusion is derived from an original treatment by James Olney (1972).

of discourse, leaves behind, in the telling evidence of the tail (tale) of its passage, traces of brilliance and magic and stardust that induce all of those who may read the stars to find in their meanings a renewed human intensity, a renewed appreciation for the value of the individual experience as the shaper of all that is, or that can be, known and made known to others.

We are concerned, suddenly, for the *how* of the human voice that makes the tale through intricate weavings of words, that has lived the life that finds itself in the midst of the weaving process, and that must make sense out of—as well as make sensible—both the experience of the words and the words of the experience. We find ourselves embarked on a journey into the deeper reaches of self, Other, and context that form the inner and outer borders of an exotic and uncharted territory, a territory that coexists within us in the everyday as well as in one of the mythical dimensions of a forgotten chapter in the histories of rhetoric and knowing. We find ourselves, then, present at a site, a critical site known in literary and cultural studies as the intersection of autobiography and style.

THREE APPROACHES TO THIS CONVERSATION

There seem to be three general positions, three approaches to this conversation about style and autobiography, that suggest three ways to work out the experience and role of style in the writing of autobiography (see Eakin 1985, 181–278). My use of these three positions is *not* meant to imply that there are only three ways of working out this relationship, merely that this is the way the conversation in literary studies is, from my reading, currently being constituted.

First Position: Autobiography as Metaphor for Self

The first position is a historically informed tradition for seeing autobiography as a *metaphor of self* (see especially Olney 1972). Viewed from this perspective, the ontological status of autobiography reveals a text as the site of individual identity and the making of a text as an exercise in translating one's life experiences, personality, and character into a narrative form.

James Clifford's observations about the narrative problems inherent to ethnobiography seem equally applicable here, particularly his two formulaic but eerily prescient questions: "Where, in short, does a person begin? Where does he or she end?" (see Clifford, quoted in Aaron 1978, 41–42). Between those questions, and the prose decisions the author commits to print in an effort to resolve them, lies an even stranger series of inner penetrations that, as Olney observes, "shift[s] attention from *bios* to *autos*—from the life to the self" (Olney 1980, 19).

Viewing autobiography as a metaphor for self, then, carries with it a necessary rhetorical bifurcation—what Louis Renza calls "writing's law of gravity" (1980, 279)—that forces the author to choose between third- and first-person carriers of the metaphor.[2] Each choice brings with it an array of possible assembly tactics, uses of language, and images of self, but the most important characteristic of this dilemma is the way in which it governs how the author positions him or herself in the text as either the *object* or *subject* of his or her own life. To become an "author," when authorship itself is viewed as the position one takes towards one's own experiences and the voice one uses to re-create it, is to reserve (or perhaps, *preserve*) for the self a poetics of space in which the poet becomes the poem. Viewed this way, one's life is experienced either as an ordered composition in which the "Name" stands out as the performer in the there-and-then of experience, or as a composition ordered from elsewhere, usually the narrow perspectival moment and motives of the language of here-and-now as rendered in the first person, in which the performance appears fated or destined or shaped by forces outside of the immediate arena of the self.

This position, the one historically represented by autobiographical voices from Augustine to Rousseau on the one hand to Henry Adams and Norman Mailer on the other, provides more than information about available rhetorical strategies and tactics of representation. This position speaks directly to the way in which the self is viewed by the self, which has obvious effects on issues greater than style.

Imagine, if you will, how each of these positions influences the writing of an ethnography. The question "Who are you?" usually directed at the Other in the ethnographer's quest comes back around to be asked this way: "Who am I when I study You?" Do I see myself as an actor engaging

---

2. Second-person autobiography assumes a different problematic—the appropriation of the experience of the Other as equivalent to the experience of one's self. One effect of this voice choice is to beg identification with the character of the narrator; another may be to alienate the reader.

the scenes I encounter, the signifier of the signified, or am I merely the recipient of these performances, a person enmeshed in the webs of signification that are happening in this curious surround that I call "culture" when I run out of rhetorical room or when all else that helps me make sense either does not work or breaks down?

But these are merely the broad strokes of a much finer set of implications to be drawn from this initial question on positioning in the text. Consider, beyond the voice of "I am" that is and that acts upon, the mind-set of its owner. Here we encounter a tension that is very real and very difficult to resolve. I am speaking of the tension between "owning" the voice and the experiences of that voice as one's own (and therefore taking full responsibility for it) and avoiding the neocolonialism that tends to affect an individual who encounters a "Them" and tries to make sense of the experience by remaining an "Us." The experience may be my own, but it is also the Other's, and we have not yet reached a stage of linguistic evolution where these two opposing forces can comfortably rest in the same text without some conflict.

Or consider the finer weave of a text written from the voice of the participant fated by hegemonic forces beyond her or his control to be in this scene and to have to give it a reading of some sort. Here we confront a tension not of Buberian "I-Thou" proportions, but of trying to name those forces that you bring to this reading and at the same time trying desperately to avoid their influences on what you see and experience. This tension may be easier to work out because our discipline's history is one shaped by texts that increasingly absent the author and embed all real and potential insights, arguments, and meanings within extant literatures. Hence, "the literature" speaks only the language that "the literature" has been taught to speak, and those doing the teaching are forced to acquire their vocabulary and grammar from "the literature" (see Connor 1989; Goodall 1989b). It is a Catch–22 of immense proportions.

Either way you turn, the first position that defines autobiography as a metaphor for self includes strategies of textual representation that bear further scrutiny. Hayden White, for example, in his discussions of narrative, argues that "even in the simplest prose discourse, and even in one in which the object of representation is intended to be nothing but fact, the use of language itself projects a level of secondary meaning below or behind the phenomena being 'described.' This secondary meaning exists quite apart from the 'facts' themselves and any explicit argument that

might be offered in the extradescriptive, more purely analytical or interpretive, level of the text" (quoted in Siebenschuh 1983, 105).

The narrative itself reveals a subconscious, poetic level that is both the
product of the author's own subconscious, poetic, symbolic environment
and the subconscious, poetic, symbolic environment of the reader (Goodall 1983). Here again is White:

> This figurative level is produced by a constructive reader of the text more
> or less subconsciously to receive both the description of the facts and their
> explanation as plausible, on the one side, and as adequate to one another, on
> the other.
>   As thus envisaged, the historical discourse can be broken down into two
> levels of meaning. The facts and their formal explanation appear as the manifest
> or literal surface of the discourse, while the figurative language used to charac-
> terize the facts points to a deeper structural meaning. (Quoted in Siebenschuh
> 1983, 106)

Style, then, however plain or ornate, is not mere ornament but is a co-
conspirator to the metaphors of self. Just as there can be no neutral
language, no purely "objective" observation, neither can there be such a
thing as a "neutral style." For behind the style is always the person, behind
the narrative the author's self. And in standing just over there, in front
of them and across the street at this particular intersection, is the reader,
and the reader's self, also never neutral or objective.

Viewed as a metaphor for self, the voice of the narrator in autobiography
is always "the *displayed* self . . . who speaks, who lives in time" (Gunn
1982, 8, 9). Curiously, then, the language of self that is part author's
deep reach into the life of experience and part reader's deep reach into the
experience of the text, is a language of display, not distortion (see Gunn
1982 for further explication).[3] It is through the metaphors of language
that the metaphors of self are manifested, and it is through this manifesta-

3. Gunn's argument is better read in the original (1982), but for those readers
who may not be familiar with it I will attempt a brief recap. Essentially, she
argues for autobiography as a kind of cultural space for reading experience. As
such, autobiographical displays of style are part of the creation of that cultural
space as well as instructions (or inducements) to the reader about how to engage
those experiences. Without the display of style there would be no direct way
into the character of the author, and there would also be a denial of the legitimacy
of that cultural space.

tion that the self exists. Therefore, it is through the act of writing (and reading) autobiography, through the displays of language and metaphors, through the dialectical tensions of voices that create and experience the text, that the self is actually discovered. As Olney nicely sums up this position, "We do not see or touch the self, but we do see and touch its metaphors: and thus we 'know' the self, activity, or agent, represented in the metaphor and the metaphorizing" (1972, 31).

This first position makes a compelling case if and only if we accept the premise that a self exists and therefore may be discovered and experienced through the mediating presence of a text, a text authored by some sense of self. However, as Michael Sprinker argues, "The self is constituted in a discourse it never fully masters," because "the self can no more be the author of its own discourse than any producer of a text can be called the author—that is the originator—of his [sic] writing" (quoted in Olney 1980, 342, 325). This brings us, then, into contact with a different way of seeing this intersection, a new contributor to this kitchen conversation, a voice representing the literary, mostly French, left.

Second Position: Autobiography as Language of Privation and Death

The challenge to the idea that autobiography represents something other than metaphors of self is derived from poststructuralist, postmodern interpretations of the positioning of language in culture that call into question the positioning of the author in the text. Viewed from this perspective, language and culture are not resources for freedoms of expression and creation, but sources of institutional constraint, instruments of hegemonic distortion, that seriously call into question the possibility of an individualized self much less its representation (see Derrida 1976; de Man 1979).

There is a strong economic, neo-Marxist, critical theory flavor to this conversation. The voices involved in it see a text as a "production" and its writer not as a writer, but as a "producer." The overarching principle here is one of production and consumption, and what is produced is determined by what is demanded, needed, or co-opted for the engines of consumption. Hence, autobiography can be read as a demand made by a postmodern "panic" culture (Kroker, Kroker, and Cook 1989) that, suspended between the hyperemotional realities of public anxiety and private dread, privileges the possibility of unity over the fragmentation of personal experience.[4] This "fact" of postmodern life is reminiscent of this note from Albert Camus: "Nostalgia for other people's lives. This is because, seen from the outside, they form a whole. While our life, seen from the inside, is all bits and pieces. Once again, we run after an illusion of unity" (1964, 17).

When autobiography is thus reduced to a source of capitalistic critique, the self revealed in it does indeed die. Formal argument for this position is often found in Paul de Man's (1979) critique of William Wordworth's *Essays on Epitaphs,* in which de Man deconstructs the poet's attitude toward autobiography as self-restoration as revealing, paradoxically, "a language of deprivation" (Eakin 1985, 186). De Man argues:

> To the extent that language is figure (or metaphor, or prosopopeia) it is indeed not the thing itself but the representation, the picture of the thing and, as such, it is silent, mute as pictures are mute. . . . To the extent that, in writing, we are dependent on this language we all are, like the Dalesman in the *Excursion,* deaf and mute—not silent, which implies the possible manifestation of sound at our own will, but silent as a picture, that is to say eternally deprived of voice and condemned to muteness. (1979, 922–23)

All references to life, to knowing a life, outside the "pictures" of language are hereby—and ironically within sentences claiming their own muteness—reduced to mere illusions. As Eakin reads this text, "The deconstruction of autobiographical discourse is now complete; stripped of the illusion of reference, autobiography is reinscribed once more in the prison-house of language: 'Death is a displaced name for a linguistic predicament,

---

4. One critique of, and certainly another way to read this contextualization of the fragmentation of personal experience, is that postmodernists did not "discover" the problem of fragmented selves. For example, Friedrich Schiller, at the turn of the eighteenth century, lamented a similar problem in his essay "On the Aesthetic Education of Man." This is certainly true, as Augustine's *Confessions* also offers evidence of fragmented experience through autobiographical expression, but it is too narrow a reading of what postmodernism is about. The fragmentation of postmodernists is not a discovery of a problem of self in culture, but a critique of the determinations, the modes of production, reproduction, and consumption, that contribute to it in contemporary cultural life. Here again we find evidence of the tensions between the experience of culture and its institutionalized forms of representation. That is, for me at least, an important and distinguishing aspect of the postmodern condition, and one that speaks directly to the role of autobiography and style in ethnography. To wit: How does one display the fragmentation within "legitimized" styles of discourse that only allow for its naming?

and the restoration of mortality by autobiography (the prosopopeia of the voice and the name) deprives and disfigures to the precise extent that it restores' " (Eakin 1985, 186–87).

Autobiography, then, is not an experience of self but the production of a convenient fiction. It is a commodity produced in an illusion of self by a victim of language and culture, and it is produced for consumers who are themselves victimized through consumption by the very act of its production. Autobiography serves as a cultural sedative, not a powerful metaphor for self but merely a metaphorical Valium that depresses consciousness by insisting that life, any life, is but an illusion of self, that writing is an illusion of creation and discovery, and that any pretense that autobiography may have to the capture, experience, or understanding of self, context, and Other is just that—pretense. There is no self, no subject, no use to the first-person "I." The world is a fated, overdetermined, lost paradise of language in which third-person estrangement and distance must pass for the experience of life.

Admittedly, this is a political reading of a political tract; but de Man's was a political life. In de Man's critique are the residues of a history he lived that, as events have shown, he would rather have not had chronicled. It is possible, therefore, to read into his sentences the desire to "forget" by way of justifying, insisting, that all attempts to recapture a past and to use such a vehicle for self-exploration are futile, distorted, controlled. Within his critique, then, lies quite another text, an autobiographical text, that reveals a desire to deny that figures of language, or pictures, can speak (for explication of this perspective, see especially Neumann 1988a). What de Man finds in muteness can be read as a desire for forgetting, for who among us can so easily agree with a position that denies voice(s), historical accuracy, or representational truth to the death-camp pictures of Auschwitz, or that would deny to autobiography the testimony to personal discovery found in a text such as Paul Frielander's *When Memory Comes?*

This is not to suggest that de Man, or for that matter other critics of culture and language who draw premises from the political left, should be discounted. Their awareness of the limitations of language to represent perceived reality—and their contribution to understanding, with Lacan for instance, that our construction of self is a tap into the linguistic unconscious structures that are deeply embedded in mind and culture (1966)—provides complementary evidence, albeit "left-handed," as well as complementary testimony, albeit ironic, for the weave of the argument being constructed here.

Nor would I suggest that de Man's views of language are to be discarded wholesale, merely that their retail price is too high. He effectively deconstructs the "how" of autobiographical metaphors and places the whole notion of language in sync with a postmodern questioning of the possibility of representational truth. In so doing, he contributes to a position that is in accord with another set of voices in the autobiographical dialogue, voices that trace their own heritage to a profound concern for the impossibility of any one-to-one equation between language and reality. It is to these voices that the kitchen crowd now turns.

Third Position: Autobiography as Mysterious Reality,
Self as Mystery

Robert Elbaz, in his essay "Autobiography, Ideology, and Genre Theory" (1987), suggests an entry point for a third position in our ongoing conversation: "Behind this preoccupation with referentiality is the problem of differentiation between fiction and nonfiction" (8). He goes on to argue that in the tensions found between and among the arguments of Emile Benveniste and Philippe Lejeune there is an opening in the discourse on autobiography for recovering the self through manifestations of the first-person singular. This view, however—founded as it is on an existential phenomenology of experience and a dramatistic view of how an interplay of language and voice constructs texts of self and identity—seeks to collapse the traditionally regarded, canonized, modernist categories of "genre" into a postmodern crisis of interpretation.

To review the history of this discussion requires more space than I have in this essay, but to summarize through Elbaz: Benveniste's thesis is that "a speaker's being depends upon the audience and the nature of the discourse he [sic] directs at it, his performance, his role within the social whole. And it is precisely this role that defines the I" (Elbaz 1987, 6). Lejeune, then, applies this thesis to the name inscribed on the autobiographical text and suggests that "the declaration by the author on the first page of his [*sic*] autobiography that indeed this is the 'true' story of his life, and his signature to that effect, sends the reader back to the existence of a 'real person' . . . on which the reader can check" (Elbaz 1987, 7).

The tension here, according to Elbaz, is in the misreading that Philip Lejeune provides of Emile Benveniste's intention, and the opening is there precisely because of it. Referentiality is a futile pursuit, both for the "extratextual . . . social and material conditions that make for the possibility of discourse [as well as for] the individual author who generates it" (Elbaz 1987, 8). The text, any text, does not try to mediate the "true conditions" of history, science, or one's own life; instead, it is a positioned performance that connects an author and a reader through a dynamic, communicative encounter. Elbaz concludes: "History, science, or for that matter any meaningful statement, in no way duplicate reality; they construct it. For language is functional to the ideological position of the speaking subject, and 'reality' is the creation of this same subject. One does not report, duplicate, or verify the truth: one makes it" (8–9).

Chris Anderson's study of style as argument in the work of Tom Wolfe, Joan Didion, Truman Capote, and Norman Mailer deepens the value of this perspective by situating "the principal theme of contemporary nonfiction [in] its own rhetorical dilemma" (1987, 5). Anderson then suggests that the writing, always autobiographical, of these authors is "profoundly metadiscursive, concerned with the problems of style and expression and language in America, and in this way it provides all the terms we need for understanding its internal workings and its cultural value" (5).

Viewing the work of these authors as emblematic of similar endeavors at the borders of rapidly disappearing genres, Anderson reveals a countercultural stance emerging in the rhetorical performance of the words themselves. Anderson's notion of style becomes at one with the ways the words themselves weave self into context, context into Other and even other back into the self, a rhetorical feast in which serious display and serious self-indulgence come to grips with issues that go beyond representation of experience to the experience of representation.

Within the realms of this experience, each author in his or her own way confronts a situation, a story, that is essentially "wordless," and each author, in her or his own way, must find a way not *out* of the problem, but *into* its mystery, and through that quest "circumvent the inevitable limits of language" (Anderson 1987, 180). Summing up his accomplishment, Anderson finds a powerful counterargument to the politics of language that rely on the death of a subject and the impossibility of self:

Contemporary American prose is not finally about wordlessness, not about failure, but about the rhetorical power of words at a time when language is

constantly being threatened. For every impulse toward silence there is a linguistic impulse, a rhetorical impulse, underneath. For every acknowledgment
of failure there is a new form which gains strength and cogency from that
failure. The story of contemporary American prose . . . is not about the
rupturing or the collapsing of the envelope of language, the death of the
membrane. It is about the expansion of the membrane to accommodate new
realms of experience. . . . This is what makes it important for American
culture. (180)

What are these new realms of experience? To get at this is to get at the
core of the interpenetrations of culture and writing, which is to suggest
that it is to get at the heart of autobiography, style, and interpretive
ethnography. The way in, however, lies not in finding a new method or
countering an ideology but in the ways in which language allows us to
define what it is that we are seeing and doing with words, and equally
important, what the words we use are doing to us.

I briefly introduced the work of Gabriel Marcel in the Preface. To recap:
Marcel (1949a, 1949b, 1950) suggests that there is a profound difference
between defining a situation as a "problem" and defining it as a "mystery."
As a "problem," we tend to divide "objects" from participation in human
experience, narrowing our focus to see our way from some thorn in the
here-and-now to its removal in the there-and-then. Problems invoke
science, and science invokes the need for a method of moving from problems to solutions. Moreover, problems invite us to separate the world into
categories of persons and things and to believe that problems are either
object-residents of self or object-residents of Others, and not that self and
Other can share in or jointly participate in them. By dividing the world
into categories, into persons and things, form and content, logic and
rhetoric, fiction and nonfiction, reason and emotion, and so forth, and by
further inducing in us a deeper division between our experience of and
participation in the world, the realm of problems encourages distance,
boundaries, monologue, method, and authority.

Mystery, on the other hand, suggests something else, something far
more complex and involving. There may be a thorn, but who placed it
there? If we remove it, what else is likely to befall us? What "mystery"
does is to encourage us to see and to define situations by their unique
human and spiritual poetic, the interpenetrations of self, Other, and
context, by our complexity and interdependence rather than by some
simpler linear or causal logic. Mystery is a "question in which what is
given cannot be regarded as detached from the self" (quoted in Gallagher
1975, 32). And perhaps for this reason, as Busch points out, "Scarcely

could Gabriel Marcel write a chapter of a book, an article or deliver a paper without becoming autobiographical" (1987, xi).

For Marcel there is a natural correlation between being and creation: "as soon as there is creation, in whatever degree, we are in the realm of being. But the converse is equally true: that is to say, there is doubtless no sense in using the word 'being' except where creation, in some form or other, is in view" (quoted in Gallagher 1975, vii). As evidenced by his life and work as a dramatist, pianist, philosopher, and man, "creation" refers to artistic involvement with the always autobiographical experience of being-in-life, which is to say being aware of the rapture of being alive: "My life is not a succession of images at which I am a spectator. . . . The reality of the self lies beyond its finite and material expression" (quoted in Gallagher 1975, 63). However, it is in the dramatic tension of the experience of one's own being-in-life, and in the realization that the reality of self is beyond that experience, that artistic creation becomes the mediator between the reality of self and the material and finite limits of being. And it is awareness of the possibility of participation in that creation that brings us to confront the experiences of life as mystery and to want, therefore, to enter them, participate in them, be involved in that creative process. Once we own that awareness, not only do we own a vision of the autobiographical self as a questing, experiential phenomenon, but we also learn to see that our quest, our experiences, while necessarily our own, are also connected to, intertwined with, the mysteries and quests and experiences of Others.

In his treatment of the role of language in the construction of self, P. J. Eakin first defines the positions we have elaborated here, then, not surprisingly, sugggests that the experience of writing autobiography places "the self finally as a mysterious reality, mysterious in its nature and origins and not necessarily consubstantial with the fictions we use to express it" (1985, 277). With Anderson, following Marcel, and in accord with both the proponents of the first position—who offer an experience of self, albeit necessarily fictional, as the autobiographical quest—and the critics of the second position—who offer the possibility of a quest not for self, but out of the prison-house of language and the politics of hypercapitalism—we find in the positing of *mystery* a new and common ground.

Trying to define the experience of mystery is difficult because mystery lies at the borders and crossroads of self, Other, and context as well as at the intersections of time, space, and the cosmos. However, I believe we can get a sense of mystery by examining a variety of autobiographical texts, each one—to appropriate Joan Didion's powerful emblem—"slouching towards [its own] Bethlehem" in a style, voice, and self of its own making. Particularly close to my own experience of autobiographical and ethnographic writing are the following words from Michael Herr's *Dispatches,* and though the excerpt is taken from a section that deals with the experience of war I read in it a curious, resonant wisdom about the experience of writing self:

> Finding it [the place war makes for you] was like listening to esoteric music, you didn't hear it in any essential way through all the repetitions until your own breath had entered it and become another instrument, and by then it wasn't just music anymore, it was experience. . . . [It was] a complete process if you got to complete it, a distinct path to travel, but dark and hard, not any easier if you knew that you'd put your foot on it yourself, deliberately and—most roughly speaking—consciously. Some people took a few steps along it and turned back, wised up, with and without regrets. Many walked on and just got blown off it. . . . And some kept going until they reached the place where an inversion of the expected order happened, a fabulous warp where you took the journey first and then you made your departure. (1977; quoted in G. O. Taylor 1983, 127)

In Herr's passionate account we feel the borders of self, Other, and context blur into a reading of experience that occurs *after* the experience has created the reading; at the same time we see the impact of style on how we are persuaded to read the text—to hear its "polyphonic" qualities in the various ways others dealt with the same experiential contexts—and are yet induced through the movement of words through space to arrive at a beginning where an ending "ought" to be. It seems to me that these strategic turns of context are intentional, but that their tactical subtexts, like the experience of self in war that Herr is trying to display for us, exist simultaneously as different polyphonic reads on different planes of experience available to those who come to the words from different angles of approach.

Herr does not define for us the way to read the war; instead, he provides ways into it that liberate our experience of the reading via our own level of engagement of the text, which is to say, via our own engagement of self with the Other through a shared context—in this case, Herr and the words of his text. What he sets up for us through his personally stylized writing is a framework for dialogic engagement, a site for an autobiographical reading of self (his, ours) into the contexts of Others (ourselves as readers of his text, him as the narrative partner to our own).

The time has come for us to leave our neighbor's house. The music is still playing—Steve Morse's fine "High Tension Wires"—but we have to go. We thank everyone for everything and do so sincerely, and walk back across our shared lawn to our own discipline's particular if now seemingly invisible border, arriving home with time to reflect on how this experience, this experience of self, Other, and context, has changed us and may contribute to our understanding.

CHARACTER AS STYLE, STYLE AS DIALOGIC ETHOS

For Mikhail Bakhtin, "language is all" (see Wayne Booth's introduction to *Problems of Dostoevsky's Poetics,* 1984a, xiv). Read one way this means language is, essentially, the "being" of a text, the "being" through which form blends into content and becomes indistinguishable as form, and in which meanings can be discovered, appreciated, interpreted, and evaluated. "Being," in this sense, is not located in the monologue of an author who addresses a silent, passive reader, but in the connections that become possible between author and reader when language invites a complex "artistic visualization of the world" (11).

This "artistic visualization" is carried out through language, obviously, but more to my interests here, a language which posits "style" as equivalent to "character." We come to know a character by the style used to portray her or him, and it is through differentiations of style that differentiations of character become possible. Perhaps more important, differentiations in style seem to acknowledge more than character distinction and development. For style, as Anderson (1987) has demonstrated, is neither mere affectation nor ornament; it is the figure of argument. Style is the manifestation of an argument the author has with the ability (or inability) of language to represent adequately the territories of self, Other, and context; it provides evidence not of a failure to accomplish that, but instead demonstrates an awareness of the complexity of the task, of the mystery that lies at the heart of it, and of the folding of autobiography into all texts and contexts, and especially into all invitations to know the Other.

If style is character, then it seems to me that one way to approach its value to a reader is as a source of *ethos. Ethos* is used here as referring simultaneously to its Aristotelian sense of "the character of the speaker as revealed in the speech" as well as to its added Ciceronian dimension concerning artistic, autobiographical representations of the "true nature of the soul." Read together within the context of this essay, *ethos* has at least as much to do with the mystery of self as it does with bodying forth in the discourse some immediate sense of the public good.[5]

We do not, however, live in the same historical period or share the same contextual referents for *ethos* as did our Greek and Roman counterparts. This does not in any way discount the relevance of their contributions in rhetorical theory to our understanding of critique, but it does suggest a need for revisions, as well as additions, to their original notions. In so doing, it seems likely that we may recover for rhetoric both a sense of heritage as well as a renewed presence in postmodern dialogic critiques.

The ancients viewed the rhetorical canon of style not as disconnected from text, but as a powerful source of embellishment to be added to the text's essential reasonableness. Style's power was derived from the artful uses of language that made possible both identification and pleasure; its limitation, at least for Aristotle and certainly for Plato, was its ability to play upon the audience's emotions, particularly when such play was not directed toward the power of the case but was deflected to merely stirring the passions. In other words, Plato disapproved of those tactical uses of language designed "to make the worse seem the better case" (*Phaedrus*).

In one way, this sentiment privileges the rhetoric of the speaker over the intelligence of the audience and denies the ability of the text to inspire multiple readings. This is odd, given that throughout the dialogues of Plato we have precisely this sort of strategy in place and that both Aristotle and Cicero make it plain that they have provided just such an intelligent, alternative read to the speeches of their colleagues. This sentiment also divides *logos* from *ethos* by suggesting that the reasonableness of a case is somehow distinct from the character of the speaker, and positions *pathos* both above and below the text and somehow in front of and behind the speaker.

---

5. Some explication is necessary here or else my appropriation of Marcel's approach to mystery would seem entirely misplaced. For the ancient Greek and Roman rhetorical theorists, *ethos* was an "objective" evaluation of the character of the speaker as revealed in the speech. This would seem to be at odds with Marcel's rejection of the dualism of participation/objectification and is not my intention. When I use the term *ethos*, I am suggesting that we need to expand its referential territory, to relocate it to a more appropriate historical site that is both dialogic and participative rather than merely reserved for the objective evaluation of a monologue of self.

This may make—has made—for interesting categorical criticism in the neoclassical sense, but it does not make sense in a world no longer divided by, or appreciative of, such distinctions. Our worlds are different despite our common planet. This is perhaps given additional force by the fact that it is only in the *Phaedo* that we have any autobiographical account of Socrates, and nowhere in the public work of Aristotle is there any real sense of a private character. We know a little more about Cicero, mostly through fragments found in his *Letters to Brutus,* but the march of rhetoric and time seems to acquire, with the occasional rare exception such as Augustine's *Confessions,* autobiographical necessity only with the advent of philosophical notions of self realized through everyday language exchanged with Others (rather than, or in addition to, prayers directed toward a God) and with the literary creation of narrative texts that existed as texts and seemed to be true but were "not true," and therefore came to be known as "fictions."

As I have tried to show in this analysis, these romantic and then modernist bifurcations of fiction and nonfiction no longer work from any of the three positions articulated earlier. Georges Gusdorf, in his fine analysis of the "scripture of self" that marks existential autobiographical quests, expresses it this way:

> Proving oneself to oneself—crossing inner borders—is richly replenishing to a wandering consciousness that pays this price to discover the true center.
>
> Self-knowledge, existential questioning, cannot be reduced to the dimensions of a psychological problematic, in which the states of the soul would each refer to each other according to circuits of some natural intelligibility with, when all is said and done, a typology, characterology and a psychotherapy, backed up by prescription of a few tranquilizers if necessary. Still less is it possible to transfer the anxiety of existing to a sociological plane, devoted to demonstrating various conditionings linked to the system of production or to nothing at all, or even devoted like others to enclosing itself within the universe of some rhetoric's discourse, with ready-made formulas meant to entrap anyone believing he can speak the meaning of his life in words that are his own, whereas he speaks like everybody, that is to say like nobody (since man, just as easily, does not exist). In this case, moreover, the one who boxes up other people's discourses exists no more than they, and speaks in order to say nothing. (1986, 280–81)

What moves to the forefront is an appreciation for style in autobiography as *a reflection of the artistic struggle for meaning through the experience of language which is the experience of mystery,* and for the experience of mystery in the quest for language of one's own self. It is, then, on this new frontier that I now want to recover and to reshape the classical idea of *ethos* as the interpretation and evaluation of the experience of self as it is stylistically negotiated through a constant dialogic encounter between reader and author with—and within—the text. In so doing, I want to conclude this chapter not with any postmodern nostalgia for *ethos,* but instead with a place for it in the swirl of side-by-side modern and postmodern experience as it can be fully represented in interpretive ethnography.

STYLE, AUTHENTICITY, AND CHARACTER

It is through words and actions—the engagements of self and Other in contexts—that we come into knowing, being, and doing. It is also how we do the work of interpretive ethnography. There is a correlation between the ability to write about experience and the ability to observe it in detail that brings to our interpenetrating texts the *sursum corda* mix that is the complexity of living. Therefore, it is through our own experience of the words and actions of Others that we learn to read a textual pattern of motives, moves, and mystery into our personal evaluations of who and what we and they are. That read is informed by judgments of character, which is to say it is gotten at by the attitude we adopt on behalf of that judgment toward style. That read also always works both ways— from us to them and back again.

Style in interpretive ethnography is made and rendered in a coded language, and ciphering that code is necessarily a part—and for some a large part—of how one reads the autobiographical quest into the quest of the Other, of context. Style, then, may be viewed as the ways in which we embody the argument of our own being and assert it in the general haggle of the world. It is not the experience of truth, perhaps, but the truth of my own experience. That is why we can reach through style, through its language, and find sources of mimesis as well as originality; it is how we understand the expressions of nostalgia, irony, and comedy in manner and in speech. But beyond even this level of reading there is a way that style allows us to access the *ethos* of the display, the language out of which it constructs its self—and their selves—and that induces in us some deeper, penetrating sense of its essential authenticity.

This sense of authenticity is necessarily always partial. However immersed we become in the language, however immersed that language is in the experience of self, Other, and context, however close we feel we get to a reading of style that means something, there will always be a distance, a mystery, between our experience of the language and the language's inability to grasp all that is experienced. So authenticity, like style, is a name we give to a penetrating but partial reading. It is the expression of a moment of language, of a moment in the experience of language, that sums up what is never full or complete and never can be.

Two projects seem to haunt as well as to inform interpretive ethnography. The first concerns the capture and expression of the previously ignored and perhaps ineffable "force of emotions" (Rosaldo 1989) that has been too often the invisible signature of rationalistic, self-denying, modernist ethnography. The second project concerns finding ways to include in ethnographic accounts those whose experiences have been marginalized, a project which, when viewed as a mystery of an impoverished language that precedes the more general problems of occupying privileged territories within a dominant culture, deeply involves the articulation of the never within the territory of the now.

Both of these projects seem related to the common issue of the role autobiography and style must assume if the projects are to be productively pursued. Both projects speak directly to the need to recover, for the rhetorics that may be used to shape such texts, an autobiographical resistance capable of opening up, if not liberating, such texts, and to redesign the dominant figures and forms of ethnographic experiences based upon a renewed conceptual acceptance of the stylistic values that shape the *dialogic ethos* of a text. For it is the character of the author as a questing presence in the textual search for the coterminous realm of self, mystery, and experience that shapes how we read the evolving story; and it is that dialogic presence that, finally, contributes an individual human signature to the always autobiographic/ethnographic destinations of our innermost, and outermost, journey.

7

The Truth of My Experience

The capacity of the human being to make indications to himself
gives a distinctive character to human action. It means that the
human individual confronts a world that he must interpret in order
to act instead of an environment to which he responds because of his
organization. He has to cope with the situations in which he is called
on to act, ascertaining the meaning of actions of others and mapping
out his own line of action in the light of such interpretation. He has
to construct and guide his action instead of merely releasing it in
response to factors playing on him or operating through him. He
may do a miserable job in constructing his action, but he has to
construct it.

—Herbert Blumer

Everything that pertains to me enters my consciousness, beginning
with my name, from the external world through the mouths of
others (my mother, and so forth), with their intonation, in their
emotional and value-assigning tonality. I realize myself initially
through others: from them I receive words, forms, and tonalities for
the formation of my initial idea of myself. . . . Just as the body is
formed initially in the mother's womb, a person's consciousness
awakens wrapped in another's consciousness.

—Mikhail Bakhtin

For a pattern of experience is an interpretation of life.

—Kenneth Burke

THE ART OF ASKING QUESTIONS

Who are you?

My father used to ask this one. There was low music on the radio and
it was always asked at dusk, when the inky edges of evening blurred
against the known borders of the day.

Information about my past was provided by many persons. Additional "Popeye"
stories can be found in the oral history collection at Georgetown University.
Inspiration and comfort for this examination was derived from Michael Leirus
(1984); Barry Hannah (1989) offered direction and perspective.

I think I shrugged. At least that's what I remember.

Where did you come from? What makes you tick?

He would light a cigarette and hand it to me. Buddy, he would say, these are difficult questions, and before you go out there making judgments about other people, you need to think seriously about them. Then he would light his cigarette, inhale deeply, blow out the blue smoke that would hang in the air over our common table, over our lives, mingling with his philosophy of difficult questions. You must learn the answers, he would say. He would smile. Then you must learn how to live a little bit above them.

My father was a quiet man, an excellent listener. Of course I would talk to him, it was easy. I would tell him everything. I didn't know then that my answers were part of the story he was trying to tell, that my voice was one he was trying to get back to, that his questions, his difficult questions, were exercises in self-interrogation at a point in his life when he was trying to discover who he was, who he had been. I was his Other. He was my father.

Now, in a way, I have become more than an extended him. Our names, the crazy patterns of our lives, the mysteries and music we participate in, the questions we ask and the way we ask the questions—so much that always seemed so separate now seems the same. The poet David Bottoms puts it this way: "What does it mean to own your father's name?"

Difficult question. Difficult because there is always more than one answer, and the voices I use to give the answers so often come from a timeless neighborhood of persons and things I carry around in my head and heart. Dad. Dad and Mom. Mom before Dad, and Dad before Mom. Popeye and Granny. Friends, cousins, teachers. Wife. Some of those voices come from the instant replay of movies, televisions, and radios that are always on in that neighborhood. So many shows, so many different people to be. Some come from characters in books from a bookstore I've always imagined on a broad intersection of ineffable wonder that forms a small, vital corner and within whose doors are stored the essential dramas of some of my most vivid dreams.

Who are you?

Where did you come from?

What makes you tick?

These questions are difficult also because the real answers are embedded in remembered lives and places, are socially constructed, live themselves in the instabilities of a history experienced, in the telling and retelling of stories that have coalesced to produce me. Difficult, too, because these stories express different perspectives on the whole of this thing I call the mystery. The stories do not always tell the most important parts, either, and they are always told only one at a time. Difficult because history—the experiencing of it—lives forever suspended in an immediate, permeable there and then, and beckons me back from any sense of suspended disbelief to the brightest and darkest parts of its narrative and its narrative quest, to the rush and force of emotions that live and move in that loud neighborhood, and that call into serious question any source of serious doubt.

Difficult questions because there are answers that can be articulated, and they too are difficult, partial, and suspect: This is how it *was* because this is how I lived it becomes this is how it *is*. Who would believe that? Who wouldn't? Who doesn't?

The sense of self in mystery is a tease that disappears at the moment of touch, that is lost even when it is found. Maybe that is why it is a mystery as well as why I always fall for the experience of self that lives in it. In the mystery of self there are presences in the absences and absences in the presences. There are ghosts in there that vanish before they can be explained, and there are people in there who themselves cannot be explained except as ghosts. The self I see in mystery does not look like me, does not wear a watch that wears out, and does not move ahead or behind but is always just with me. We share the here and now, a plural present of self and Other that is constituted out of the Other of self. It is not my mirror but my mystery; I own it but when I look into it I always see myself anew and somewhat differently. When I tell it I hear more than myself as I have known me, and yet I seem to speak a familiar poetry.

Who are *you?*

Where did *you* come from?

What makes *you* tick?

Difficult questions this time because in the enfolding and unfolding of the future that the mystery of self always imagines and fears, there are other stories as yet untold of what I hope to become, to experience, to discover, to learn, to be. That is why I do not want to repeat the past that my father handed me, not live the answers he gave me by example, but instead find my own way. The question he asked me, and the quest he set me—*Who are you?*—will always be with me, the central drama of that neighborhood I carry around inside of me and into which I must always go to find out who I am because of where and who I've been, and who I hope to become.

Welcome to the neighborhood and its many voices, the narrative of it that I know, the story of my life that is a quest for self and an exploration of the interpenetrations of self *as* other. It begins where the oldest story in me I know of begins, in America in the year 1900, along the mule trail beneath the shady banks of the C&O Canal as it ran from Cumberland, Maryland, to Washington, D.C.

POPEYE AND GRANNY

It is 1900, and my granddaddy (on what would become my mother's side of the family) is eight years old and already working.

His name is William Henry Saylor, the son of the late John Daniel Saylor and a woman whose name was never mentioned in my family but who died in childbirth eight years before. The late John Daniel Saylor himself met his maker the night before last when, drunk and extremely tired from pulling stubborn mules away from the muddy trench alongside the trail all day to keep the boats moving, he accidentally fell into the canal and drowned.

Someone woke Little Will up and told him his daddy was dead, and the boy, tall and gaunt even then, was so surprised and probably frightened that his eyes looked like they were going to pop right out of his head. So it was that he became known as Popeye Saylor. Later, much later, a cartoon character named Popeye the Sailor would appear in America, he too abandoned by his father to make his own way in the world, but there was no connection.

The next day he went to work, hired on with an X for a signature on the line where until yesterday his daddy's name was written, taking his daddy's place on that same line just above where an awkward line had been drawn through it. Such was his transcendence, at the stout age of eight, into adulthood.

Years passed. I can recall my granddaddy's face when I asked him about them: "So what happened, Popeye, between the time you went to work and the time you married Granny?"

His face turned hard. His words: "I worked."

"Did anything *neat* happen?" This from me, before I learned to refine my interviewing skills.

His face lit up. By this time, in his mid-eighties, he was nearly bald and had a high forehead, so when he grinned the expression took over his face, pushing his thick eyebrows up into the nether reaches of his hairline. "I met the president once." He winked.

"Really?" I am here recalling my conversational equipment circa age seventeen, which consisted mostly of one-worders like "Really?"

"Yes indeed. It was Sunday, and it had been raining all week long, so there was mud and ruts everywhere. I was sitting up along the hillside not too far from where you go to school now [Shepherd College], watching the rich people in their fancy machines on their Sunday drive. It was a beautiful day, as I recall, but the mud was terrible.

"Anyway, this big car veered off the towpath into the mud. I figured there was a dollar in it, so I hitched up my team of mules and went down there to lend a hand. I pulled the car out and three men stepped out of the shade to thank me. I was thinking maybe *three* dollars by then.

"First man steps up and shakes my hand like there was no tomorrow. You don't know me, he says, but I'm Harvey Firestone, and I made the tires on that car. Pleased to make your acquaintance, I said. No dollar, though.

"Second man steps up and shakes my hand. Hello, he says, you don't know me either, but my name is Henry Ford, and I built that car. By this time I could see there was no money going to change hands, so I just said *Uh-huh*.

"Third man steps up and says: You don't know me either, but I'm— and that's when I cut him off. No I don't know who you are, I said, but these other dern fools are such damn big liars I wouldn't be surprised if you told me you was the president of the United States of America!

"And it was."

"You didn't know who the *president* was?" I was having a hard time with the concept. After all, I had grown up with television. Everyone knew what the president looked like.

"No, Bud. I sure didn't. I wasn't old enough to vote so I guess I just didn't get around to it." He winked at me again. "But he was a *nice* fellow, and a good sport too. After the men all finished laughing he gave me ten dollars. I still didn't believe him, and said so, so he gave me ten more." He paused. "Twenty dollars that day. More money than I made in two, sometimes three weeks of working."

Popeye met Granny at a Sunday revival. Granny—Nellie Blanche Grimm—was reared to be a deeply religious woman, a fact of her life that would continue until her death, in 1982, of complications resulting from a paralyzing stroke and a long history of diabetes.

She was sixteen when they got married, he was twenty-three. He had told her he was only twenty, and it wasn't until he applied for a Social Security card some years later that the truth came out.

Of her life prior to Popeye I know almost nothing. She too was brought up on canal, her father and mother both worked for the C&O, so I assume Granny and Popeye must have known each other for some time before they said "I do." But to hear them speak of their long life together was to hear them pronounce its beginning precisely at the moment of their marriage in June 1915. In the family picture they look much older than their years, and genuinely afraid.

They proceeded to have two children, the first of whom was my uncle Jim and the last my mom. She was christened Naomi May Saylor on the day of her birth, February 17, 1917, and called *Naoma,* with great stress on the last syllable, all of her life. She was born at home in Frog Hollow, Maryland, a place just east of Sharpsburg that was known as the home of moonshiners, whores, evangelists, and canal workers. She never talked about it.

When Popeye was twenty-eight the owners closed down the C&O Canal operation. He had already put in twenty years and had built up a small pension that would get him started in another line of work.

He decided to move across the Potomac into the fertile valleys of the panhandle of West Virginia to become a farmer. He decided this, apparently, without speaking to Nellie about it, and in fact had already purchased the farm when he decided it was time to inform the family.

Imagine what mystery lies buried in that family conversation.

Furthermore, he had decided to farm turkeys, about which he knew almost nothing. So one day not long after he had purchased said turkeys, one thousand of them, with what was left of his pension and small savings, he left the turkeys out in the barnyard while he and Nellie went into Charles Town for some groceries. A thundercloud broke over the farm, and it rained hard for all of about fifteen minutes. Now turkeys, being dumb as, well, *turkeys,* turned their scrawny collective necks skyward to see what was happening, opened their collective beaks to the rain, and collectively drowned.

Granny and Popeye returned from shopping to see one thousand dead turkeys in the barnyard and the ruin of his dream evaporating into the grey mist. Imagine that.

The next day he found work as a dynamite mechanic in a local rock quarry, claiming expertise in a field he had just recently heard about. He learned quickly, though, and for a year or so everything was all right. But eventually he expressed the belief that by tying together a bundle of sticks and blowing up with great force the side of a particularly stubborn limestone wall, he could guarantee saving some labor.

His men did not voice disagreement, they collectively being about as wise in matters relating to the physics of dynamite as he was. None of them knew or probably had ever heard of the rule about the sum total of exploded energy being greater than the sum total of its individual components. And all of them were interested in saving their backs and hands the labor, so they all watched with great interest as my granddaddy tried his first scientific experiment. The wall blew, all right: not only did it scatter the stone far and wide, which would make for additional labor, but it also burned the clothes off most of the witnesses, including the clothes on my grandfather.

Blackened, naked men stood in awe of what had transpired. All of them were apparently a little shaken and not at all certain about what to do, so one by one they all walked to their respective homes to clean up and find clothing. Popeye, who was standing a little closer to the blast than were the rest of the men, on account of it was his baby, had been knocked a couple of hundred yards in the air by the explosion, and so returned to consciousness black and naked in an adjoining corn field.

He assumed he was dead. He simply began walking. First he hummed, then he sang. He expected a gate, and a worried St. Peter to welcome him, perhaps a symphony of angels singing. Instead of finding St. Peter he turned the bend and found only home, and, recognizing his house but still thinking perhaps that this was how it would be in heaven, yelled, "Here I am!" He was at that moment greeted by Granny with a cocked shotgun, who had taken him for a beggar or maybe a thief or maybe just crazy and, thus surprised, she heard him blurt, "Don't shoot, ma'am, I'm Will Saylor, your relative." Then he collapsed onto the front porch.

Imagine what Granny must have thought. Imagine life, at this point, from her point of view.

Then there was the family story about the time Popeye came home from the quarry Christmas party, after his men had gotten him drunk.

This was my mother's senior year in high school, 1933–34.

Granny always kept Christmas as a special holiday, partly because it celebrated the birth of her beloved Jesus and partly because it was a festive break in an otherwise hard and enduring life. She saved for it all year long, put away pennies from sewing she did for other people, and made a big fuss over trimming the Christmas tree, which was always tall and perfect. And it was a family tradition to do the trimming on Christmas Eve.

My granddaddy was also a religious man, but somewhat further down on the scale of holiness from Granny. He was, at best, a pragmatic Christian, a man who went to church on Sundays mostly to trade talk with his friends and to escape from the drudgery of six days of backbreaking labor. His God definitely had a sense of humor, and it was for a sense of humor that Popeye was also everywhere known.

Now my granddaddy liked his liquor, especially gin, and his ciggies, especially unfiltered Camels, and so even though none of this was ever exactly allowed in the house, there was a sort of tolerance that centered on matters of breath and behavior, and so long as no harm was done nothing much was ever said. I can still remember going down to the basement with Popeye to sneak a smoke from a pack that was always hidden in the same spot behind the freezer. Later, when he thought I was old enough for the sin, secrecy, and knowing that is an inevitable part of growing into a man, he would show me his secret storehouse of pint bottles of lime-flavored gin, just behind the jars of canned food Granny had stored.

So it was that I learned from my granddaddy about the pleasures of smoking and drinking, and the even greater pleasures of doing it all on the sly, with a wink and a nod as he used to perform it when we were jointly about to embark on an afternoon of pure sin. He also taught me something about the opposite sex by taking me on long drives back to Frog Hollow in his flashy Studebaker to see, as he put it, "the lonely widow-women." Those days I would go along, find myself instructed to remain on the front porch of some house hidden in the thicket and reeking of neglect, while he "had a word with the women inside." In my mind I imagined all kinds of things, and this occurred long before I actually knew what "things" were all about, which was also before I learned that Granddaddy was in there doing what I was imagining, which, if I had known it at the time, would have caused me to abandon my place on the porch in favor of at least one trip inside, just to make sure.

Always the ethnographer.

When Popeye died, while mowing his front yard at the age of eighty-five, this time for real from an implosion in his heart rather than an explosion in the mine, this deacon in the Church of God, this man who had lived a thoroughly explored life despite his never learning to read and write, this paragon of near-virtue that I dearly loved and admired, had his last will and testament challenged in court by three of those widow-women, two of whom claimed he had "certain responsibilities" given that he had fathered children with them while still apparently spry and in his late seventies.

Quite a guy.

Granny never spoke of the outcome of those hearings. Nor did she ever admonish him for the shame it obviously caused her among her friends. My mother, of course, was shocked and appalled, mostly for Granny's sake, and told me privately that she knew all along. I believe it was my father who actually intervened in court and saw to it that Popeye's obligations were paid, something my father, I would later learn, had a history of doing.

But I am ahead of my story. I still haven't explained Christmas.

The men at the quarry loved my granddaddy. They loved him for his fairness, for his hard work, and for his contagious sense of humor. But they also feared him, because he was a ferocious joker, a practical joker of absolutely the first rank, a man who would go a long way out of his way for a laugh, particularly at their expense and in public. And this had been a year, apparently, when he had repeatedly gone far out of his way on numerous occasions, and in numerous public places, and so it was time for the men to square their accounts with him, to level their fears and to regain some of the strange sense of male equity in friendship and work relations that includes as part of its natural regimen some very sincere pain.

Put simply, they got him drunk. And then they sent him home.

Aware of his condition, certainly, and aware of the consequences should it be discovered by Granny, particularly on Christmas Eve, Popeye showed up at home just in time to help decorate the prized Jesus tree, stewed in gin's most indelible juices, convinced, in that way that only gin can truly produce, that he was all right if he only moved slowly and that his drunkenness would not be detected if only he remembered how to behave himself.

All went well for a while. But as is the case with gin (I have learned this myself from serious scientific experimentation) the well that you can temporarily tap through application of will eventually runs out, leaving you back in the depths of your drunkenness, a prisoner of awkward flailing and slurred speech that, in that tiny part of the brain reserved by God for insidious comedy, still makes you believe that you are perfectly all right despite all other claims to the contrary. So it was at this unfortunate juncture, when his will had run out and absolute gin-drunkenness had regained its spirited claim over him and his actions, that he was called upon by the ever-tolerant Granny, still in the rapture of Christmas that overcame her particularly on the supposed eve of sweet Jesus' birth, to stand on the chair and place the angel on the very top of the perfectly decorated tree.

No task in the history of the human race ever seemed so important to him, or so far from his reach. He searched the room for an alternative, but Mother and Jim were already in bed and the only person tall enough for the job (Granny never grew past 4' 11") was him. He drew in a deep breath, gathered his courage, appealed sincerely in his heart to God to come to the aid of this sinner one last time, stepped up onto the chair, and fell immediately face-forward into the tree, causing the tree to crash against the floor with an authoritative collapse.

He lay there, splayed out in an alcoholic stupor, surrounded by broken ornaments, mumbling apologies to the angel he still held in his right hand. Mother and Jim rushed into the room to find Granny beating him with the only weapon she could find, a hickory broom. And although they tried to stop her she was a feisty little woman and would not be stopped until she was tired; then she made them beat him with the same hickory broom throughout the longest Chistmas Eve on record, taking turns to keep up the pace and veracity of the thrashing.

He came to early the next morning, hung over, repentant, and very sore. Granny did not speak to him again until well into the new year, which more or less ruined the holiday for everybody, and firmed up a particular resolve in my mother's mind, something she had been working up to for a long, long time.

MOM, BEFORE DAD

Naomi was a beautiful woman, easily the most beautiful woman in her high school graduating class.

She possessed a fine face remarkably akin to the actress Jean Crain's, with high handsome cheekbones and deep brown eyes, a sort of matter-of-factness about who and what she was—all 5'2" of her—and a figure that was lean, curvaceous, and strong. I should interject here that it was not until I escorted Mom to her forty-fifth high school reunion that I witnessed in the admiring eyes of men, as well as in their syrupy words, the effect she still held over them. I can remember thinking, "Hey, this is my *mom* you're talking about!"

She remained a good-looking woman all of her life. So possessed of good looks was she, so outspoken and daring, and so embarrassed by her poor lot in life—she complained of actually making and wearing feed-sack dresses to school, and of having to roller-skate the seven miles to get there—that she invented a better life for herself, beginning that Christmas Eve when her daddy fell into the tree.

She began with the claim that she was "from Virginia." In her mind this erased the unhappy accident of Frog Hollow and gave her license to a certain pose of Southernness that soon infected everything from her manner to her speech. This accomplished, she moved to higher ground. Remember, reader, we are now in the depths of the Great Depression, and this is West Virginia. We are remembering a woman way ahead of her time. What she did was to run away from home into a brand-new life as the wife of the president of the senior class, and she did it on the night of her senior prom.

His name was Harley, Harley Earle Alexander. From what I can gather he was the only son of a relatively middle-class scion of real estate and small business in Charles Town, West Virginia. He was tall, drove a flashy Model A, and used multiple palmfuls of Brylcreem on his shiny black hair. What he saw in the young woman who would later become my mom I will never know because, in fact, I did not know my mom had been married before she married my dad until that night at the high school reunion, and by then Harley Earle was long dead. This was another part of the inventing of her life, but I am getting ahead of the story.

What I imagine he saw is what I saw reflected in the fond eyes of those old guys at the reunion. As one of them put it: "Naomi, I've always loved you, ever since third grade, and the only reason I didn't go out with you is because Harley got to you first." His eyes were alive with the memory, the deep smoldering fire of pure love and impure desire, and the dance of a remembrance that had stopped time and blinded him forever to the possibilities that otherwise would have made his life. Mom smiled, patted this nameless, ageless lover on the hand as one would pat a fawning dog, and said, "That's nice, dear. Would you please get me some punch?"

I was going to have a word with him, but then thought, "What the hell? Who am I in this scenario? I wasn't even born yet." Besides, Mom never had any trouble dealing with men. I later learned that this particular suitor had never married, and in the center of the mantle over the hearth in his home he kept an old picture in a frame, a picture of three persons beneath a big oak tree. The three were himself, Harley Earle, and my mother.

Mom told me—only when pressed—that she had married Harley Earle to escape from the farm. She said that he had money and was nice to her. She married him that night because he wanted her to. They had lived together in Charles Town for five years until she decided to become a nurse, at which point she divorced him.

This would have been in 1939. Mom as a divorcee, in 1939. But why?

This is how she explained it: "Because I wanted to become a nurse, that's why. And in those days they didn't let you into nurse's training unless you were single. So Harley Earle and I divorced, I went into training, and we dated on weekends when I wasn't on duty." Imagine *that*.

But why did you want to become a nurse?

"Because I wanted a career. Being a housewife in Charles Town, West Virginia, was not my idea of life. Oh, Harley Earle was okay, but he had no ambition. He was content to work for his father, and he didn't like to travel or do new things. He wanted children, and I certainly didn't, not then anyway, and certainly not with him. So we lived like brother and sister. Not very attractive, I'm afraid." This is all I ever got out of her on the subject.

So she entered nurse's training in Winchester, Virginia, and graduated an R.N. The program should have been completed in two years, but something happened to her while she was in training that would not only delay her certification but also would forever change her appearance and her views on life. The story I heard about what happened to her in nurses's training was short: "I was brushing my teeth one morning in the dorm, and I had the door locked. My bathrobe was too close to the gas heater and it caught on fire. I couldn't get out."

Mom didn't say anything else about it. From other family members I eventually discovered that she had over 75 percent of her body burned, had spent over a year in the hospital, had skin grafted from the bottoms of her feet to repair the damage on other areas of her body, and had survived primarily on peanut butter. At the time, her recovery was considered a miracle.

She never locked a bathroom door again.

She could not stand to see, hear about, or be near fire.

She always got sick when she ate peanuts.

When I was very young, I remember seeing the scars on her back and thinking everyone must end up like that.

Naomi got a very good job at Johns Hopkins Hospital in Baltimore, got an apartment, and bought her first car.

About this time, from what I could piece together, she stopped seeing Harley Earle. Or maybe, fed up and disenchanted as I imagine he might have been by then, he stopped seeing her. She worked there until the war came and then tried to enlist but was denied entrance to any of the services on account of having flat feet.

I've never figured that one out.

Maybe it was because of the scars.

Disappointed because she wouldn't be part of the war effort, she resigned from Johns Hopkins and went to work at the Martinsburg, West Virginia, Veterans' Administration Hospital. At least here she could feel as though she was doing her duty. And, as fate would have it, she would meet not only the man who was to become my father, but also the man who would replace him.

DAD, BEFORE MOM

Of my father's side of the family I have been told exactly the following:

1. His father's nickname (I never knew his given name) was Oscar. Oscar was supposedly a Mississippi riverboat gambler and comedian. Oscar won his wife—a full-blooded Indian—in a poker game from her father when she was thirteen. Oscar kept the child until she was sixteen, then married her, retired from gambling and telling jokes, and moved to Huntington, West Virginia, to become someone new. I never knew her name.

2. Oscar fathered at least two children, a son and a daughter. Oscar named the son after his comic role model, Harold Lloyd, named the

daughter Donna for reasons I've never learned. There may have been another child, but I have not been able to verify this. The only record I have is my father's 1941 Huntington East-Hi yearbook, and in it there is child, in the sophomore home-room photograph, named R. M. Goodall. A relative, probably, maybe even an aunt. But he never spoke of another child, so this could be his cousin. There is another Goodall—H. G.— named in the yearbook, an older man who held the position of secretary-treasurer for the Civic Club that sponsored the building of the new high school, and this Goodall I assume must have been my father's well-to-do uncle, the one who owned the drugstore.

3. Oscar was not a healthy man. He suffered from sugar diabetes and died while my father was in training during the war. Oscar's last full-time job, according to my dad, was as the janitor in my father's high school. But I cannot find him pictured there. Maybe this is a fiction of my dad's making, or maybe pride kept Oscar from being photographed in the same issue with his kids. I'll never know. He was a man who led many lives and obviously kept many secrets. This would turn out to be something he passed on to my dad.

4. My dad was Handsome Mr. Everything in high school. Maybe he had to be, given that he would later claim that his father was the janitor. Who knows. In the yearbook he is a science major, president of the President's Club, a member of the Glee Club, Drama Club, Spanish Club, and January editor of the yearbook. He played the lead in the senior class play, *Guest House, Very Exclusive,* and his girlfriend was the beautiful Betty Walker, a Commerce graduate, president of the senior class, a member of the National Honor Society, assistant January editor of the yearbook, and also a member of the President's Club.

I wonder who he thought he was, then. In his senior class photo he has dark wavy hair that even today would be called fashionably cut, and his features are angular and clean. His eyes look like they know something you wish you knew, and on his full lips caught in a smile there is the hint of something almost sinister, something just above a sneer.

Who were you, Dad? You never told me.

Absent from this yearbook scenario is any mention of his athletic ability, which led him to try out in the spring of 1941 with the Cincinnati Redlegs, and supposedly to be signed by them and assigned to the minor leagues for the following spring season. This would have seen him that year in a very different sort of uniform from the one he would actually be wearing. This absence of sport on an otherwise full high school deck was due, according to him, to his need to work to help support the family, as a soda jerk in his uncle's downtown drugstore, which kept him from playing sports after school.

These days I'm not so sure I believe that, but I still want to.

5. Dad's younger sister, Donna, was, in the January edition of the yearbook, voted Miss East-Hi ("Stupendous! Terrific! Charming!" shouts the caption) by the entire student body on the basis of "personality, charm, and other outstanding features." Cheerleading was her major activity. She apparently married right out of high school and had a child. She apparently lived at home rearing the child during the war years.

6. When Oscar died, my father took over support of the family via his salary, first as a Naval Air Cadet and later as an Army Air Corps bombardier. According to his own account, he continued to support the family throughout the war.

7. When the war came dad joined the navy, was shipped to Pensacola, and discovered, along with his superiors, that he could not land a plane on an aircraft carrier. He was transferred to the Army Air Corps, took training in Texas, learned to be a gunner, operate the radio, drop bombs, and (much later, under combat conditions) fly the B–17. He was stationed in England with the 8th Air Force, 569th Bombardment Squadron, 390th Bombardment Group, where he survived various missions and won battle stars, oak-leaf clusters, and air medals before being shot down and taken prisoner by the Germans on August 1, 1944, near Tours, France.

He mentioned once that he had been shot down before that and that he and his crew spent eleven days getting back to Allied lines. The second time, however, he was the only survivor. According to his medical war records he suffered multiple penetrating wounds to his right thigh and left leg, with partial laceration of the right sciatic nerve, for which a debridement and suture of the sciatic nerve was performed which two months later resulted in traumatic paralysis. He would have frightening nightmares about falling out of the sky in a burning plane the rest of his life. I can still hear the screaming, remember running into his room and finding him on the floor, paralyzed and afraid.

No wonder he didn't want me to be a soldier.

8. He was captured and placed in a German-occupation hospital, where he remained until the place was liberated on September 4, 1944. He told my mom he was treated well because he spoke fluent Spanish and German, a testimony for him of the value of learning foreign languages in high school. He was paralyzed in both legs from the waist down, furloughed

for the rest of the war, told he would never walk again. In the convalescent hospital in St. Petersburg, Florida, a decision was made by the physicians not to remove a seventeen-inch piece of flak that would, as a result, lie for the rest of his life against his sciatic nerve.

He was honorably discharged May 3, 1945, and paid $165.60 as a final disbursement. His discharge letter, signed by Colonel R. C. Elvins, reads: "Today, brings to a close, your service in the Army of the United States. Your past performance in the service, has brought great credit upon yourself and family. It is with great pleasure that I extend to you on behalf of the Army Air Forces, best wishes in your new life as a civilian."

9. He returned home an American war hero, with a chest full of medals including a new Purple Heart. He arrived a war hero, all right, but a war hero confined to a wheelchair. The guy who wheeled him around was named Buddy, from whom I gained my permanent nickname. He returned home to Huntington happy to be alive, proud of his uniform, proud of his ribbons and many medals, proud to be home to the home he had fought for. He was twenty-three years old, had helped conquer the world, and believed that he could learn to walk again despite the doctors' admonition to the contrary. He was planning to enroll in the fall at Ohio State.

10. His mother and sister met him at the door. I can't imagine what they said. Here is the saddest story I know: they told him that since he was crippled they would prefer it if he wouldn't live with them, since "it wasn't right to raise a child in a home with a cripple." In addition, Donna, his sister, had been "real sick" and was just now recovering. This was in America, champion of the world, 1945.

11. Dad entered therapy and eventually, after another eight months of work and effort, regained the use of his legs. He walked, always in pain, on a sinew of courage and pure will. He entered the program at Ohio State on the Veteran's Accelerated Plan and eventually took a job with the Veterans' Administration Hospital in Martinsburg, West Virginia.

12. He never spoke to his mother or sister again, although my mom claimed he sent checks to them until the week of his death, from Legionnaire's Disease, in March 1977. By then he had been officially "retired" from government work since 1969, and was, at his death, all of fifty-four years old.

13. I talked to my grandmother on my father's side only once in my life, during a break in a debate tournament in Huntington, in 1973. All my life I had been forbidden to seek her out, to know anything about her.

So, in the height of my rebellion against Mom and Dad, I violated this rule too. I looked her up in the telephone book by last name only, because I never knew her first name, and when she answered the phone she wouldn't tell me. All I have of it is the first letter—S. When I spoke to her she seemed very much like anyone's granny, except for her last words to me, which were: "I guess Lloyd had his reasons for living the way he did. I never meant to hurt him, but it wasn't right, not then. Please don't tell him you talked to me; even though I love him and think of him often, it just wouldn't be right."

Of course, being the total asshole I was to my parents while I was in college I made the mistake of telling Dad I had spoken to his mother. I did it to piss him off, probably. He got angry with me, then got very drunk. It was the middle of the afternoon when I finally helped him into bed, and he was crying. Neither one of us ever made that mistake or broached that subject again.

MOM AND DAD

Having survived the war and transcended his family, Dad came down with an ugly case of tonsillitis. He checked into the V.A. Hospital for surgery.

Mom recalled how all the single nurses drew straws to see which one would "special" him. When she won she said it was the luckiest moment of her life.

Three months later they were married.

Maybe they were attracted to each other because of their scars.

There is, however, a twist in this story. It has to do with a man named Jerry Terlingo, who was a lieutenant in the Army stationed in Washington during the war. He had dated my mom for nearly five years, was in love with my mom, "worshiped," as he used to put it, "the goddamned ground she walked on." But in the summer of 1947 my mom, who had just turned thirty and who had also survived the war, wanted to remarry and have a family, her career now well underway. When she and Jerry discussed it he broke down and admitted to her that he was already married, had, in fact, a child, and could not get a divorce (he had already tried) because both he and his wife were Catholics, she apparently more devout than him.

Mom was shocked. Then she was furious. She abandoned Jerry on the side of the road just outside of Hagerstown, Maryland, and told him she never wanted to see him again. Then she drove her 1941 Ford back to Martinsburg, to the V.A. Hospital, and met the man who would become my father.

Jerry, to his credit, didn't give up easily. He called, he begged, he pleaded. He swore he would leave his wife and marry Mom. She told him simply to get lost. When he found out she was seeing someone new, he followed them on a date until they were at a dangerous place on the highway and tried to run them off the road. If he couldn't have her, by God, no one would! My mother, always a good driver, managed to control the vehicle and my Dad, always a good fighter, literally beat poor Jerry to a bloody pulp and left him, again, on the side of the road.

That bit of business out of the way, Mom and Dad proceeded to get married on December 22, 1947. In their wedding photograph they look smart and handsome together, Dad tall and lean and much older than his twenty-five years and Mom less happy than I would have expected. I've always wondered about that expression, but never thought to ask.

Then there was me.

At least, that is how the story was told for years. It wasn't until I had suffered through the New Math and knew something about dating that I realized five whole years had passed between their wedding and my birth.

So, Mom, what gives? What's the story?

"We both wanted a family. We tried very hard, and I had three miscarriages before you were born." She grinned. "Sometimes I think you were the fourth."

Good ol' Mom, always there with the irony and the humor.

So Dad, what gives? What's your side of the story?

"I worked for the V.A., studied for law school at night. I wanted to get ahead, do something with my life. After the war things were pretty boring. Then one day I was asked to take a test for the Foreign Service, and I did, and the next thing I knew it was New Year's Eve and we were throwing a party and I was tight. The phone rang and it was Washington, and I apparently agreed to take a job with the State Department. I woke up the next morning and couldn't remember where. So I called them back [notice, reader, how "them" is never clearly defined?] and found out they had changed their minds anyway—I was going to be sent initially to South America, but now it was going to be Rome—so I said what the hell and took it."

Good ol' Dad, always the patriot.

Notice how I am totally absent from his description of those years? I don't mean to sound whiney on this point, but wouldn't you prefer it if in your memory your dad had recounted the story somewhat differently— say, "I conquered the world, met your mother, got married, fathered you, and then launched my career"?

Remember, reader, I am an only child.

EUROPE

Family legend has it that we were greeted at the Rome airport by Clare Booth Luce, then ambassador to Italy and my father's new boss.

Family legend has it that Mrs. Luce asked Mom what my name was, and when Mom said, "Buddy," Ambassador Luce replied: "Dear, you must *never* use a nickname in public. From now on use his Christian name." Mom, to her credit, never did.

We lived in a large marble flat along the Via de Grasioli and had a very large, very Italian, maid/cook named Alfonsina. Mom, who had given up her career as a nurse on advice from the State Department, became a woman who had cocktail parties or attended them, and her life suddenly became precisely what she had always dreamed of from Frog Hollow on. But there is a point at which biology and history converge, and we call the result destiny or misfortune, depending on how things turn out. She struggled with the Italian language, she went to movies in the afternoon to learn snappy dialogue, she read the latest magazines and joined the Book-of-the-Month Club so she could be thought of as a reader.

Dad was almost never home. And he never talked about his job. I would come home from the Italian kindergarten and Mom would say, simply, "Dad's gone away for a while. I don't know when he'll be back." And then she would cry. It is from this time that I chart the beginning of my relationship with Mom as one of her personal confidant, the one who listened, who shared, and who, later, would counsel.

I want to insert something here that is out of sequence. It is about a role I played in my family, for my government. I was a child who was reared on the premise that "children should be seen, not heard." You've heard this line before, it was popular in the 1950s. There is another angle to the image evoked from that line, however. When you were a child in the State Department you were to be seen and not heard because you were always *listening*. My job at cocktail parties, every afternoon, was to circulate among the adults and to listen. When the children were ushered into another room, there too I was to listen to the stories of the other children. And then, after the parties were over, I was to report everything I remembered to Mom, Dad, or one of my "uncles," colleagues of my father who were always impressed by what I could recall. In retrospect this was my first communication course, and given the life I've ended up living, a very instructive one.

Now back to the story.

My memories of Rome, of Italy, are vague and seen through a sort of prism where light plays against images and then vanishes, only to turn up again in some other image that also then vanishes. I remember a park, it is summer, and I wander away from Mom and Dad. A beautiful woman kneels down in front of me; she is wearing dark glasses and has wine on her breath. Then there are voices, Mom and Dad show up, and there is more talk. After that I am with this beautiful woman on a regular basis, sitting for a portrait that makes all the papers. She is the famous actress Abbie Lane who is married to an even more famous band director, Xavier Cugat. I've never figured out her relationship with the portrait painter, one Leonard Creol. In the portrait, a large ornate oil, I am a little boy dressed in short pants and blue dinner jacket, seated like some indolent prince in a red velvet chair, playing with my little black dog, whose red nose, according to the papers, I painted as Mr. Creol guided my hand.

My eyes are huge and blue.

The next image is again summer and again in a park. This time I am riding my first bike. I take off, turn left, and end up going out of control down a hill that ends in a fountain. I remember the rush of air, I remember the sudden excitement of speed, I remember crashing into the small wall, flipping over the handlebars and splashing down in the cool waters of the fountain. I remember opening my eyes and seeing two nuns helping me out of the fountain, their garments soaking wet.

I remember laughing until Mom and Dad showed up, then crying.

The last image I have is of a road with tall pine trees towering over it, then I am seated next to Mom in an audience and on the platform Dad is giving a speech. Everywhere around us people are cheering, rising to their feet and cheering. This is my first memory of oratory, the first connection I can make between Dad as a powerful actor (something he had been since high school, something he did also in the theater of war) and my desire to be just like him.

Just like him.

Then we moved to London, this was in 1958, and Dad was even more important. For what I would never know until after his death, when I inherited his diaries. All I knew was that he was home more often, that we had more money, and that I had better be the best student in my class. "You are the image of the United States of America everywhere you go," I was told on countless occasions by Mom, Dad, tutors, Government People. "Tell us everything you know."

We lived in St. John's Wood, but there were times when we lived quite differently in Golder's Green. I thought every boy lived like that. There was an older couple, neighbors actually, in Golder's Green named Mr. and Mrs. Liddington who babysat me. I can still feel the cool damp mornings in their house, smell the coal fires roasting. I also remember Sundays in Hyde Park, hearing the corner speakers, watching Dad take notes.

Ours was a regimented life in London; even our meals seemed to follow a pattern. Saturdays were fun days because Dad would take me to the PX for a Mr. Goodbar and the comic book of my choice, which was usually *Sad Sack,* for reasons I still can't explain. I was in school from seven until five, there was dinner, and then my tutor from the State Department would show up for "lessons" which lasted until bedtime. I remember reading a lot.

I read tales of the Knights of the Round Table, which really paid off for me in a big way when I met Queen Elizabeth II. This was some stately affair, even I was dressed in a tuxedo, and my father was being honored again for something with a big plaque and applause all around. When I met the queen I spoke to her about the Knights of the Round Table, and, apparently impressed with the depth of my learning and my overall deportment as a Young Man, she actually knighted me in a ceremony that included a sword touching both of my shoulders, etc.

This is what queens do for fun, I guess. It was a big moment in my life, though, a moment of ineffable magic and one that I shall always cherish. Sir Harold, indeed!

I was in school at St. Dunstan's, a place that I couldn't recall until I saw films that featured private British boys' schools, with the pompous singing and uniforms and communal meals. I remember rote learning, oral recitation, foreign languages, soccer. I also remember the dunce cap, the public announcement of marks on homework assignments, and being beaten for not removing my cap when entering the school. For some reason

I also remember a dream I had then in which Mom, Dad, and I were waiting for the end of the world in a stone room with a large, open window. Bombs were falling around us; only Dad was cool.

One day I came out of school and was met by Mom and a Marine chauffeur—very unusual. "Come on, honey," she said, taking my hand, "our bags are packed and we're going home now." Home was the United States, a place I had no recollection of and yet, and yet, this was my country. I never asked why we were leaving so suddenly, never even thought to ask that question.

AMERICA

My first memories of America are of cartoons, Captain Kangaroo and Mr. Greenjeans. I watched them, learned about America from them, in our hotel room in Washington, D.C.

I believed everyone in America would be like these guys, that America would be sort of one large television show where everyone was having a good time either hamming it up, talking about the weather, or playing baseball. You had to worry only about mischievous animals: "Bunny Wabbit, stay away from those cawwots!" Eventually you were expected to join the army, fight in a war, marry your sweetheart, and raise kids who would keep on watching cartoons, Captain Kangaroo and Mr. Greenjeans, and the mischievous Bunny Wabbit.

Imagine my surprise, then, when for some reason we ended up living in Cheyenne, Wyoming. We arrived in the summer of 1962, the only people in this thriving three-mile-long metropolis of thirty thousand with diplomatic plates on our car and a son who spoke with a British accent. I never asked why, and no explanation was ever offered to me. All I knew was that here Dad worked for the V.A. Hospital, and that his job involved making and sailing paper airplanes across the expanse of his office and occasionally being gone for a week or so at a time, mostly without prior notice.

Mom returned to her career as a nurse, went to work in a white uniform for the Washington County Hospital, just up the street from our house at 2817 Henderson Drive. I went to a school where even the teachers asked me to "say something in English," meaning, of course, to make the most of my accent, which I very quickly learned to forget. I made friends with Mark Wingo, Charley Rowley, Jim Fru, Jim McCorgery and a host of others and spent my time learning the fine art of American sports.

Cheyenne was a good place to be a kid in, but this was a very difficult time for Mom and Dad. Though I did not know it at the time, Mom had become addicted to amphetamines in Europe (where they were over-the-counter medicines that did not require a prescription), and Dad, convinced that the rise of his career as a fair-haired boy had seen its last horizon, that he would be doomed to live out his days on "the vast plains of nothingness" that he called Wyoming, began seriously hitting the bottle. I played baseball and ate a lot of TV dinners.

Mom crashed one morning in the Safeway, hit her head while fainting against a shelf of soup and spent the next four months in the Washington County Hospital Psychiatric Ward getting off drugs. I was told only that she had taken a bad fall, slipped on something that she hadn't seen, and I wasn't allowed to see her in her "condition." Granny and Popeye came out West to live with us during this period, to take care of me and Dad. Dad proved to be quite a chore, his drinking now something he flaunted, even on the job, and his legs now requiring Librium to kill the pain. Still, all I remember is playing ball and eating dinner, thinking very clearly that this is how everyone lived and that I was no exception.

Mom recovered, I guess, but in the photographs of that period she looks blank. Gone is the seductiveness, the churlishness, the life that was once there. In its place is an even stare, her hair cut short, her skin puffy. Dad during this period is always wearing dark glasses and faking a smile. Me, I'm the tall, skinny blond kid with the crewcut and the Buddy Holly eyeglasses, always in the middle of them looking like I'm trying to figure things out.

In the summer of 1964 we drove across America to visit our relatives (on Mom's side, of course) in West Virginia. We stayed with Granny and Popeye in their new house on Van Metre Avenue in Martinsburg, West Virginia. Mom and Dad took a trip to D.C. "to see some friends," and on the way back Dad, who had as usual now been drinking, fell asleep at the wheel, ran off the road and smashed into someone's front porch in northern Virginia, throwing Mom through the windshield and breaking three of his ribs. The rest of the summer we spent at Granny and Popeye's, waiting for the car, Mom, and Dad to be repaired.

This was the summer I learned about the widow-women, incidentally. This was also the summer I got my first ride in an Austin Healey 3000, a memory that includes the brace of night air against my cheeks and my feeling of the infinity of freedom that was promised by the open road.

MY 1960S

We moved to Philadelphia in the middle of my freshman year in high school, which was 1967.

I went from playing sports in an all-white, middle-class environment to learning survival skills in a recently integrated (via busing), overly crowded public bathroom that passed as a high school. I didn't own the right clothes, much less the appropriate attitude. On my first day at Roxborough High I was nearly killed because my socks were blue. The only reason I wasn't is because I started laughing when the guy asked me if I was crazy.

Everyone dressed in black there, had long hair, and smoked. With these first cultural understandings I learned to fit in. Everyone also "hung out on a corner," a phrase that carried with it the support weight of a gang, something that was very important to survival in those times of violence and hatred. So I learned to hang out on the corner of Ridge and Summit, near the borders where Andora blurs into Roxborough, a tough neighborhood that kept an uneasy peace among Irish, Polish, and Italians. I remember spending my evenings there, smoking Marlboros, listening to rock n roll and soul on the radio, imagining women, cheesesteaks, and beer, waiting, always waiting for a fight.

Mom and Dad, where were you? You were on the skids, and my house was not a happy place. Dad was always in pain, trying to stay sober, seeing doctor after doctor after doctor to no avail. Mom was mostly a confused person, searching for something she could not name, having hysterectomies (three), going on diets, raging against life. So I stayed out a lot, in all kinds of weather, hung out on the corner with my little gang.

This is when I first started playing rock n roll. I played with the long-haired, the alienated, the dispossessed, the drug users. Rock n roll was not fun for the well-washed among us then; it was an escape for those who needed it, a way of getting out of the death of the world by disappearing into the life of the music. It was rebellion, a loud, often angry, fun musical hell that felt good even when it sounded bad, which was always. This was before quartz tuners and fancy digital sound boards and the rest of the high-tech surround that defines sound these days. We were seriously out of tune most of the time, but it didn't matter because the message of the music was in its anger and asserted supremacy, its raw pulsating power, not in its melodies, at least not in the streets where I lived.

I played with a bunch of guys, most of whom are dead now. We lost some to heavy drugs and some to Vietnam and some to themselves. We practiced in basements, in garages, and for a while in a church. There was Jimmy, who looked like George Harrison and played pretty well on Sears equipment. He was the closest one to normal among us, and was basically into the music for the women. There was Joe, a really fine bass guitarist who kept getting beat up by his father for having long hair, and who joined the army after one terrible night of it, and who never came back. The last I heard from him was when he sent me a picture from basic training: he was smiling, taking a shit, giving the peace sign. There was Glenn, a drummer with killer good looks who wound up getting a girl pregnant, dropping out of school to support her, giving up the band. There was Denny, who lived with his mom and who would play only the Who, and who later was nearly burned to death in an industrial accident that claimed both of his arms. There was Freddy, who claimed that he had written the lyrics to the Boxtops' hit "Neon Rainbow," and who was never doubted on that point because he was a good man to have when the inevitable fight broke out at the end of the night. And there was me, tall, blond, still wearing Buddy Holly glasses, playing what passed for rhythm, being what I thought was cool. We played in "Battles of the Bands" and usually lost, a few Polish weddings where the streets would be closed off and the party lasted three days, and some local parties. Some of us also worked summers at a bar called the Electric Factory downtown, setting up bands like Hendrix, Cream, Janis Joplin, pretending because we were that close to them that we were famous too.

Three years passed this way, and between the social herding that passed for education and the resistance that passed for rock n roll, I slowly stopped going to high school. Truth was, there was just too much violence there. A math teacher was thrown out of the third-story window when he failed half the class on an exam; a girl we all knew and whom I happened to be dating dropped dead in her oatmeal one morning from an overdose of black beauties that exploded in her heart. Then one day I was in an American history class and the door burst open, a kid ran in and murdered the guy in front of me, shot him in the face with a gun. I still see the brains on the blackboard, feel his warm blood on my face. Later I learned that it was over a girlfriend, and—this is the sad part—the shooter hit the wrong kid. It was all just a mistake.

I stopped going to school at all after that.

Mornings found me on the PTA bus with the leftover puking winos heading downtown for Rittenhouse Square. I showed up in school only to take tests. I just wanted to live through high school. Weekends I dated many different girls for the usual adolescent reasons, and almost died in fights over a couple of them.

Afternoons I worked as a janitor in an apartment complex, sweeping up, killing rats, doing the trash. Summers I worked cutting grass with the crew, a rare white guy among black men who essentially took pity on me, who taught me how to steal Kool cigarettes from machines with a coat hanger, how to fight with a knife, and who always made me go into restaurants first, just in case the owner wouldn't want to seat them. From them—Vince, Maynard, and Tubby—I learned a men's street language of women, learned verbal and physical techniques that made me far more knowledgeable back on the corner of Ridge and Summit than the other guys in my gang.

Then, one winter when the weather turned vicious and cold, I learned that Vince, Maynard, and Tubby had all joined the Marines, a choice between that and jail on a minor drug charge given to them by a white judge, and sometime in August of the following summer I heard they had all died, together, in a place called Ke Sahn. This was the beginning of my private Vietnam, the one war I never went to simply because nobody ever asked me to, unlike so many others, some of them friends, who never came back.

It was the following spring that I finally got kicked out of high school— asked, actually, to leave the state. I remember only giving a speech against the dress code, after which four thousand students walked out on my command. What I didn't count on was what would happen when you got four thousand heated adolescents, most of them in rival gangs, out on the streets in the middle of the day. What they did was riot, fight, turn over a police car and torch it, and stop traffic for miles. This, reader, ended up on Walter Cronkite's evening news, which Mom and Dad dutifully watched that night, catching a glimpse of their son as a "revolutionary."

Some revolutionary. This was just a mistake.

By some fortunate accident, Dad officially "retired" that June and we moved, as a family unit, to Hagerstown, Maryland, a cleaner and better-lit place. I took my guitar, my blacklight posters, my clothes, my walking-around cool, and my stereo out of the city and into suburban America. I was out of sports, didn't have a band, couldn't hang out on the corner. I ran away from home that summer, went back to Philadelphia and stayed at my girlfriend Jill McAllister's parents' place for ten days. Her father called my father and explained where I was and what was happening.

I went home and was officially grounded forever.

This was when I remember Dad beginning to ask me the difficult questions.

Who are you?

Where did you come from?

What makes you tick?

This was also the summer I began reading again. And liking it. My first real novel—a gift from dad, who gave it to me after one of our difficult question sessions—was F. Scott Fitzgerald's *The Great Gatsby*. Dad said it was important for me to read it, but he never told me why. From the opening sentence about Nick Carraway's father's advice to the last poetic passage about always being beaten back ceaselessly into the past I was spellbound.

In that reading I can recall very clearly that my life changed forever. It would be years before I would know how, or why. And it would be only now, in the writing of this line, that I would finally see the message in the patterns of that moment, that reading, that title, that story, the patterns that suggested something essential and true in that fiction not only about the difficult questions my father was asking, but also about what had been my father's life and what would become, almost as in some curious twist of history, of patterns, and of fate, my own.

I was beginning my senior year in high school; the year was 1969.

MY HIGH SCHOOL YEARBOOK

I graduated with the class of 1970 from South Hagerstown High School.

Our class song was "The Horse," a silly funky dance number, while our rival high school on the other side of town choose, more appropriately I thought, "Let It Be." Between these songs lies the world of difference that separated me and my friends from our peers at South High. To them we were "hippies"; to us they were simply wrong.

Look at the yearbook. In it I look like some sort of amateur pimp, a boy with long blond hair, still sporting those Buddy Holly black-framed glasses, wearing a blue suit with a blue shirt and a (you guessed it) blue tie. I was known for nothing (sorry, Dad) except having once lived in Philly, having once played in a rock n roll band, staying high most of the time, and driving a British-racing-green MGB. I didn't belong to any clubs, didn't play any sports, and was the editor of nothing.

In Maryland I was always out of place. And in my mind I was going to be a writer.

In mid-year I got into a program that allowed "academically talented" seniors to essentially skip the rest of their senior year and go right on to college. I was not "academically talented," so I assume I got in because the school officials didn't want me around. I had a bad reputation. So I went, on their orders, to Mount Saint Mary's College in Emmitsburg, Maryland, a private Catholic school, where I continued to nondistinguish myself and learned only that I didn't want to attend an all-male college.

Mom took me aside when my grades came in (I earned two C's) and told me, earnestly, that I wasn't "college material." She suggested I go to secretarial school, work on my typing and shorthand. Mom, by then, was totally out of touch with reality. Bless her heart, she wanted her son to at least have a job. Dad, on the other hand, who had just been admitted to one of those private country club sort of clinics that specialize in talking cures and drying out, suggested that I go to college for one year, until I turned eighteen, to see if I could do it.

He slipped me another copy of *Gatsby* while I was visiting him at the psychiatric hospital. He slipped it to me as if this was the one great secret between us. His lips were dry, parched from the drugs and the abstinence. "Shhh," he said when I started to say something, then, only: "I know who you are." Then he winked and broke down.

He was in there for a long time.

Somehow I won a four-year scholarship on some obscure veteran's program and entered Shepherd College that fall, just across the Potomac from where Popeye used to drive his mules. I chose Shepherd College, incidentally, because I was then dating the Dean of Student's lovely daughter, Tara, but she dropped me shortly thereafter.

I remember my resolve, that morning when I drove away from home, to make something of myself. I had no idea what. I took to college my past, my clothers, a typewriter, my two copies of *Gatsby,* and my electric guitar.

COLLEGE, ETC.

Shepherd College is a nice, well-tended, academically progressive institution for the state of West Virginia that rests, almost majestically, on a lush hillside overlooking the Potomac River.

I spent three years there and I remember them now far more fondly than I remember living through them then. Perhaps that is always the case. But then I was stoned a good deal of the time, and so my remembrances are always seen through a kind of warm, amberish marijuana haze, whereas these days I search for meanings that seem a lot clearer.

Oddly enough, my college record began resembling my Dad's high school yearbook. I graduated with honors in speech and English, starred in plays, worked on the student newspaper, and held offices in student government. I participated on the debate and individual events teams, won trophies all over the East, and generally had a wonderful time.

I was in love with a strikingly beautiful girl from Pittsburgh named Meagan Vickery, whom I ended up treating badly because I was a fool. I had some good friends there, Dave Bardsley, Tom Andrews, Ed Reebrook, Richard Hart, the Harper's Ferry twin brothers Dean and "Dew," and the New York brothers Fountaine. I worked at The Old South Mountain Inn, a national historical site and first-class restaurant where I was a waiter and learned how to cook seriously. I got elected to honor societies, ended up in *Who's Who*. I had some great teachers, too, particularly Mel Wyler (speech) and Charles Carter (English).

All in all, it was nice, very nice. I graduated in 1973 and felt the engines of my life just warming up. I remember thinking, on graduation day, that I didn't really know anything yet. I think now that was a good thing. I can't imagine how I would have turned out had I not had the wisdom to realize that I didn't know much and there was a lot I needed to learn. Dad and Mom, Granny and Popeye, the whole clan came to the ceremony, the only graduation I've ever attended. Dr. Joyce Brothers was the commencement speaker, and she talked to a group of mostly working-class West Virginians about the importance of good sex in their lives. I think she offended everybody. Afterwards we all ate at The Old South Mountain Inn and Dad invited me outside onto the warm patio for a smoke. As always, he lit a cigarette and handed it to me, asked the difficult questions. I just smiled and smoked. I told him I thought he was looking better. He said he felt like hell. Then he handed me a copy of *The Great Gatsby*.

"Don't say anything about this," he said.

I started to speak and he put his fingers to his lips. "Shhh," he said. "This is just between you and me."

Okay, Dad.

I went to The University of North Carolina at Chapel Hill after that, an intimidating place for an average guy from West Virginia. I learned that I had been admitted there because of a clerical error, which did not do much for my ego. Here is the place to become a scholar, I remember thinking, and so I tried my best to become one. I studied hard, partied hard, and engaged in endless debates about books I hadn't entirely read: that still is, to this day, what one image of being a scholar means to me, and why I prefer getting out of the office, participating in the mystery, and refraining from debates about books I haven't entirely read.

There I met my lifelong pal and colleague, Stew Auyash, who was in the Public Health School at the time and would later direct one of the nation's first child abuse programs. Good ol' Stewie, and his parents Marianne and Mo, and his sister too, they are all generous souls. Stewie and I lived in a trailer park outside of Carrboro, existed on assistantship monies totaling about $2,200 apiece per year, and had a great life driving back and forth in his sharp yellow Fiat Spyder.

We were totally cool.

Academically, my program of study was directed by Paul Dickerson Brandes and J. Robert Cox, Jr., and had some American historiography and comparative literature mixed into the communication courses, for which I am ever thankful. I wrote a thesis on "The Analogy in Rhetoric," which, for some reason which now escapes me, included a hand-drawn and colored-in-crayon geodesic dome and some fancy structuralist language that I no longer comprehend.

I went to the Southern Speech Convention in Richmond and landed a job coaching debate at Clemson for the fall. I completed the thesis by showing up every morning at 6:30 A.M. on Professor Brandes's front porch, where he would already be working. He would ask me to read aloud to him the sections I had revised the night before, and then he would ask me questions. This went on for three months before he was satisfied. I then had what I recall was a very weak thesis defense session, barely scraped by, but made it through that summer.

I was then in love with the Oklahoman Kitty Barkley, and she moved with me to Clemson to attend graduate school in city and regional planning. We didn't last long in Tiger City, but she ended up going on to be a city planner for Hong Kong and is now studying to become an actress in New York. On the trip down we smashed up my brand-new Audi when the U-Haul trailer unhitched itself from the rear bumper, throwing the car into an interstate spin that ended when the trailer crashed against a bridge.

Probably I should have read it as a sign.

Mom, incidentally, thought that a Master of Arts degree meant that I had learned to play the piano and paint; she never did fully comprehend that my degree was in speech. "What was that degree of yours in?" she asked repeatedly for the next several years. When I visited home, which was rare, she always made plans to take me to an art gallery or recital until I reminded her that my degree was in speech. Good ol' Mom, she always *tried*. By then I knew enough about her pain and disappointment on this planet to always speak to her gently, and to forgive her everything, including the actual curse she put on a TR–4 I bought in college; the car never, I swear, ran properly after that.

In Tiger City, where the streets are painted with big orange Tiger Paws, I stretched a one-year temporary appointment into a three-year teaching stint. Barbara Montgomery was there then, as a rhetoric person if you can believe it, and taught me the ropes and became my good friend. Barry Hannah, Mark Steadman, and Nick Guild were also there, all of them trying to become great writers; and all of them, each in his own way, succeeded.

Here's a story I have to tell. During my first year I was evaluated by the head of the English department, one M. A. Owings, a description of whom may be found in Barry's second novel, *Nightwatchmen*. Owings didn't like me and called me "bumptious" in my review, which, in retrospect, was probably true. But I was still young and didn't know any better, so I appealed to the dean to have that word removed from my review. The dean was merely amused; the word stayed. He told me that perhaps I wouldn't be as "bumptious" the following year.

I bitched and moaned about it in the faculty coffee lounge. I discovered that I was not alone. Barry had been advised to write "more serious novels," Nick had been told to abandon writing fiction altogether because he had no talent for it, and Barbara had been reviewed as if her "real" occupation was to be a wife and mother and this "role" she was playing was to be short-lived. Barry has since become a literary legend whose work has been honored by the American Academy of Arts and Letters, Nick has written several best-sellers, Barbara went on to quantitative fame, a chair at the University of New Hampshire and the presidency of the Eastern Communication Assocation; I, alas, am still "bumptious."

M. A., you were *wrong*, fella. Dead wrong. All you had was power.

I coached a great debate and individual speaking events team at Clemson, by the way. Jane and Squeaky, Lucy and Tom, Rufus and Cathy, Buddy Adams and his guitar, winners all. My roommate was Fred Mandel, a chemist from New York City and lover of classical music. We had a big time together but I never felt like I really got to know him. A couple of years ago I passed him on an interstate in Tennessee, waved furiously and could not get him to recognize me. Very strange.

It was at Clemson that I decided that I wanted to be a writer. I attended creative writing classes, hung out with writers, attended writing workshops, drank a lot. I wrote furiously every day, or at least thought about it. I wrote badly. Very badly. Only my poems were good, and even they were forgettable.

I left Clemson after Dad died. I was on a debate trip in North Carolina when the call came from my Uncle Jim: "Bud, your daddy died. You should come on home." My team saved me that night, walked with me out in the rain and dampness until I saw that all I was doing was walking and that wouldn't bring him back. All the way home on the plane I was thinking there were so many things left unsaid between us, so much unfinished business. The last time I had seen him was the previous Christmas vacation. He skipped the difficult questions that time, and I remember missing them. He walked with me to the car; he was in bad shape, down to about 120 pounds, but at least not drinking. He put his hand on my shoulder, smiled a little, and wished me luck. That was all, but now it had to be enough.

Good-bye, Dad.

He was buried in Sample's Manor Cemetery, on a pleasant hillside under a large, shady oak tree, in Granny and Popeye's family plot outside of Dargen, Maryland, near where Frog Hollow used to be. Somebody from the State Department had offered to have him buried in Arlington, in a hero's ceremony, but Mom couldn't handle it and I didn't care. So he rests now in relative anonymity, gently I hope, this brave and decent man who suffered a life I could not then imagine.

Among his documents in a safe-deposit box, which included a book of poems with a dedication to him from Ezra Pound and his own copy of *The Great Gatsby* with unintelligible notes, were the diaries he left to me. I opened them and read them straight through. It was as if I was reading about somebody else's dad, for his had been truly a double life and the half of it that I had known was nothing compared to the other half that existed for me now in his own words.

He had been, you see, a spy. This is my *dad* we are talking about. All those times he was away, he was doing the work of a field agent. The reason we left London so abruptly was that his cover had been blown. In 1956 he had handled the first evacuation during the first Middle East crisis; in 1959 he had been captured in East Berlin and tortured, and was finally rescued and airlifted out—and all I recall was him coming home with some broken ribs and bruises, claiming he fell down a flight of stairs when he slipped on some ice. *The Great Gatsby* was, it turned out, his code book. In its themes were messages that he had used to transfer and to receive intelligence. He saw himself, I learned, as Gatsby, for it was Gatsby's voice that permeated his notes, his messages. Nick Carraway was the field agent, the receiver of instructions and the gatherer of intelligence, and in one critical passage in which Gatsby asks Nick, "What do you think of me, sport?" he had penciled in my name.

And there was more. He had been married once before Mom, to a woman who claimed he fathered a child. This was just after the war, when he was still paralyzed. He had paid child support for years to a woman whose name I would never know for a child who was my blood relative.

I had a book full of answers to questions I had never raised. Now I knew it all, but what was it that I was actually knowing? I kept hearing his difficult questions vibrating in my ears, and behind them against my memory was only his face, with that last little smile.

Who were *you,* Dad?

I approached Mom with the big question: *Why?*

She looked at me. "He loved his country. He couldn't talk about his work, not even to me."

And the first marriage, the child?

"He thought it was better if you didn't know."

After that Mom became a wreck.

I became numb.

I moved home. I sold time. I went to work for one of the nation's first fully computerized 100,000 watt FM stations. I tried to make sense out of my life.

Who are you?

Where did you come from?

What makes you tick?

I became quiet and cynical about people, about me. I never got around to the answers. I always fell asleep. It was always raining and the radio was playing disco shit.

I began to hate and revere my father.

Two things happened that helped me out of this emotional pit, that reminded me that these were serious questions I had been given, and that if I was ever to become a whole person I needed to begin to answer them.

First, I learned I was not cut out for the radio business. Second, my uncle Jim arranged for Jerry Terlingo to reenter Mom's life.

I walked away from the radio business, literally. I just got out of bed one morning and decided I had to change my life for the better, so I packed a bag, grabbed my cat, and drove away from Hagerstown. I spent time in South Carolina visiting friends and finally ended up in Philipsburg, Pennsylvania.

I ended up in Philipsburg because of Jerry Terlingo and my Mom, who had gotten back together and were living in sin up there in the coal region. Jerry had retired from a company that had used him on the promise that they would take care of him, but when he retired they went bankrupt and all he could do was take what little money he had left and buy a diner in the coal region of Pennsylvania. He was there when the call came from my uncle about Mom.

One thing led to another.

Mom moved up to Philipsburg, worked in the diner with Jerry. They never got married because if they had, Mom's pension from Dad would have ended. This always bothered Mom, but Jerry never seemed to care about money. He had always been a gambler, but by then at least he was divorced. He bet large sums of the diner's operating monies on the Daily Number, and when he hit it, he and Mom would suddenly go on a big cruise down in the Bahamas, or fly out to Vegas for the weekend, or the like. I was for it only because Mom seemed happy.

I visited them in Philipsburg, worked in the restaurant, and struck a deal with Jerry. I would take over the operation of the place, he and Mom would move back into our old house in Hagerstown. I would apply to Penn State, and when I got in Jerry would sell the diner.

This is exactly what we did.

So I spent a winter and spring in Philipsburg running a coal miner's diner. I lived in Jerry's apartment just up the street, on the coal route. I got up every morning at 4:00 A.M. and walked down to the diner, fired up the stove, the oven, and the radio, and waited for something to happen. I cooked, ran the cash register, played air guitar, joked with the customers. I often defended the honor of my waitresses, which was usually more than they had done for themselves. Twice I had to throw a guy out on account of his behavior. During the afternoon slow periods I would play basketball at the local high school with released murderers and petty thieves who were just there hanging out. At night I would try try to write. In front of me, on the shelf above my typewriter, was *Gatsby*.

I got into Penn State the following summer. By then my pal Stew Auyash had quit his job in Carolina and decided to pursue his Ph.D. He decided on Penn State with a little help from me, and also because he was hired as an instructor to teach public health. So we became roomies again.

I received a fine doctoral education at Penn State and had, basically, a wonderful time there. Made friends, had lovers, read a lot, learned a lot, listened to a lot of music. Nothing bad happened. Gerald Phillips became my mentor, Stanley Weintraub taught me about research and writing biography and autobiography, Gerry Hauser and Herman Cohen and Dick Gregg taught me rhetoric and criticism, Doug Pedersen tolerated my semantics, and Phil Klass (alias William Tenn) helped my fiction along.

I still wanted to be a writer. I wrote every day, hung out with other people who wanted to be writers, read about the writing life, and even tried to look like a writer, whatever that means. I tell my students these days that I wanted to be a writer every day for thirteen years before I ever published anything except a few forgettable poems. Mostly that was because I confused wanting to be a writer with the act of writing, and was living a life based on the fiction of "having written" rather than the fact of writing fiction, or for that matter, the fiction of writing fact.

But I was hooked on it, the whole of it, wanting to be a writer and wanting to have written, and then, finally, on writing every day. I wrote term papers, short stories, even a couple of novels. I ended up writing a Burkeian dissertation on the courtship metaphor in the lives of Scott and Zelda Fitzgerald.

You can read a lot into that one. I know I do.

Professionally my life was coming together. I took a job at The University of Alabama in Huntsville in 1980, and the rest of that part of the story is chronicled in *Casing a Promised Land*.

That was when, and where, I began anew my interest in reading patterns, and reading into the patterns I observed the traces of other, older patterns, which were the patterns of self, others, and contexts deeply embedded in the stories that constituted my life.

THE PERSONAL MEANING OF PATTERNS

Mom died, of stomach cancer, on December 23, 1983, at the age of sixty-six. I had to make the decision to turn off the life-support systems. I did, the physician complied, I squeezed her hand for the last time and watched the machine slow to a halt.

Popeye had died in 1977. Granny in 1982.

Everyone, except me, is buried in Sample's Manor.

Everyone, that is, except Jerry Terlingo. He lived with Mom from 1977 until her death, and then died himself, of a broken heart, they said, three months later. All I inherited was a house and its contents, and sometime during the next year all the contents were taken from the house, without my knowledge or consent, including my father's diaries, supposedly by my uncle, who, after Mom died, turned inexplicably against me.

I could have gone after the stuff, I suppose. But for what?

Instead I vowed never to have anything to do with that side of my family again. I simply walked away from all of it. It didn't occur to me until much later, years later, that I was following the pattern my father had set, and when I realized that was true, I was shaken by it.

By then I was married to a woman named Donna Goodall, a former cheerleader, beautiful, full of charm and personality, who would, after nearly ten years of marriage and recovery from a serious illness, decide she didn't want to be married to me anymore. In the end, I would walk away from her, too, and we would agree that our marriage had been more a reunion of brother and sister than a union of husband and wife.

There's more. Mine also has been a double life. I am not a spy but instead call myself an organizational detective, and while I am not engaged in espionage, it is true that my work is generally done undercover. I use to advantage certain of the skills Dad taught me: interviewing, observation, reading for patterns, asking the difficult questions. I use what Mom taught me about gaining confidences, penetrating cocktail parties, listening for clues. I have learned how to receive inner truths, untangle webs of meanings in the ordinary, the everyday, tie in the small details to the larger picture that we make out of the nature of persons and things.

My favorite book is *The Great Gatsby*.

This has been my life, the story of my life. These are the words—the narratives—that have created me.

READING ME, READING WHAT I WRITE

Gerry Phillips once told me the story of the frog's eyeball. It goes like this:

> A frog is a simple creature, but probably believes himself to be very complex. Take, for example, his eating habits. Now as we all know, a frog eats insects. But you can take a very hungry frog, surround him with dead insects, and he will most definitely starve to death. Do you know why?
> No, I don't know why.
> The secret is in the frog's eyeball. You see, a frog can only see that which is in motion. Pick up one of those dead insects, flip it in front of him, and his tongue will reach out and capture the insect. He will eat it, and he will be happy. But dead insects? They simply don't exist in the world he sees; they are there to you and to me, but alas, not for the poor bullfrog.

The lesson, according to Professor Phillips, is that when we do research we act very much like the bullfrog. Our eyes may be wide open, but we cannot account for what they don't see. Our sophisticated methods cannot measure or deal with that which is beyond their power. We are human, after all, inherently flawed in matters of truth.

I like this story very much. For me it is a metaphor for doing interpretive ethnography and for writing the results. We cannot escape our limitations, and for humans, one of those limitations is personal history. We are, at any given moment, the sum total only of what we have become. Our past is always with us, our family dynamic always a source of what we see in relationships, what we believe to be true as much as any theory appeals to us only if, somehow, it fits into our experiences, helps us to explain what has happened and why.

We can overcome, certainly, but not until we take stock of who and what we are. We can look for patterns, I think, only when the conceptual presence of patterns has personal meaning in our lives. Flesh and blood matters; genetics and environment matter; language and culture are the parameters within which we all work.

Behind the description, the analysis, the insight, always is the genetic material, and especially the genetics of the eyeball. And, as my father so carefully taught me, when you consider other people you must always be aware of those difficult questions:

Who are you?
Where did you come from?
What makes you tick?

8

Free-Fallin' Through the Streets of Thirteen Dreams

Moreover, the scholar who lacks that firsthand familiarity is highly unlikely to recognize that he is missing anything. Not being aware of the knowledge that would come from firsthand acquaintance, he does not know that he is missing that knowledge. Since the sanctioned scheme of scientific inquiry is taken for granted as the correct means of treatment and analysis, he feels no need to be concerned with firsthand familiarity with that sphere of life. In this way, the established protocol of scientific inquiry becomes the unwitting substitute for direct examination of the empirical social world.

—Herbert Blumer

Carnival is the place for working out, in a concretely sensuous, half-real and half-play-acted form, a new mode of interrelationship between individuals, counterposed to the all-powerful socio-hierarchical relationships of noncarnival life. The behavior, gesture, and discourse of a person are freed from the authority of all hierarchical positions (social estate, rank, age, property) defining them totally in noncarnival life, and thus from the vantage point of noncarnival life become eccentric and inappropriate. Eccentricity is a special category of familiar contact; it permits—in concretely sensuous form—the latent sides of human nature to reveal and express themselves.

—Mikhail Bakhtin

Rhetoric is concerned with the state of Babel after the Fall.

—Kenneth Burke

I

I am on South Memorial Parkway, traveling fast. It is a red-and-white brick building on the left with a symbol for a name. The symbol says, only, TMT.

I notice nothing else.

Then I am gone.

2

Years pass.

I live in them, through them, come out of them only to pass into other years. Still there, over there on South Memorial Parkway, is the sign, the symbol. It never changes, although the building does: it becomes larger and always wears, or seems to wear, new white paint.

The problem, I am thinking as I write this, is how retrospective sense making brings to the forefront that which was only background. There is no convenient way to focus on a subject without focusing on a subject, no words for the simultaneous spontaneity of random thought and all the continuities it moves through and instantly recognizes, discards, attributes momentary significance to, and then moves on and/or is gone.

How do you show an attraction grow? It didn't happen in words so there can be none. It was like this: I was on the Parkway, South Memorial Parkway, and there was the building and its symbol on the left.

And that is all there was.

For years.

3

This guy comes out one night—this is in September and the year is now 1988—to play guitar, to try out for a role in WHITEDOG, which is a rock n roll band. This guy's name is Drew, Drew Thompson, and he carries a worn Gibson case with Muscle Shoals Sound emblems on it. We have been told that he played with Lynyrd Skynyrd, which, it turns out, is not true.

Now he is a broker, sells real estate, for TMT. Nothing went on inside my head when I heard that, although as an academic who would later want to write about TMT and rock n roll I wish I could say that it did. Instead, I remember thinking only that he looked friendly enough, a little nervous, and maybe even shy. He remembers thinking, he tells me later, much later, that you owned more luck and money than you did.

That night, however, in the shed behind my house where WHITEDOG got its humble start, Mr. Drew Thompson of TMT and not late of Lynyrd Skynyrd became the permanent lead guitarist. I remember this period of life fondly, like good sex or shared laughter. I remember nights under the starry skies of northern Alabama when I was learning songs, playing music, doing the male-bonding thing, eating together, drinking together, talking about women, pissing in the yard.

I do not remember thinking that my life, as I had known it, was over. I was living in a transition space where the boundaries were unsure.

Nor do I remember thinking about that little white-brick building with the TMT sign.

In fact, the things I don't remember seem far more important now than they ever did then, because then they coexisted in that ethereal space of the unspoken, the ineffable, and the mysterious, and occurred as empirical facts while I was elsewhere doing other things.

4

Months pass; everything except the band turns inexplicably colder. The sky is permanently gray and with it the wind is permanently bitter.

Everything came apart. What was surprising was how easy it was, and how safe. I just didn't talk about it, just let it go. I remember staring at the heavy gray skies low over the strange yellow stubblefields of that last December, feeling the personal sanction of the inevitable bitter winds that whipped out of the skies and cut across the fields, sucked the breath out of my mouth and chased it, raced with it, and then disappeared into that blue relief of the edge of evening that cautions us against the night. Strange how when my marriage was ending all I could remember is the weight and watch of weather.

But that was only how I felt it. For other people these days surely were bright and full of hope, held promise and were filled with the soft fluff of daydreams. According to the local paper, engagements before the Christmas season were at an all-time high, just as the volume of sales in retail outlets was also up. In November I remember there was an election and the country had a new president, the university also had a new president, and there was, amid the happy print that found its way into the newspapers, also new optimism about the Russians, cancer, and the homeless.

Increasingly, then, I played the guitar. To play rhythm guitar is to learn the bases for rock n roll. This is my life I am talking about.

5

Let's get to the point, connect all the dots that have thus far been left disconnected. Like this:

Drew Thompson's marriage ended on New Year's Day, 1989, ended in one complete sentence that fell away into a fragment, words that he spoke out loud and for the first time when his wife, Janey, suggested he do some thinking about their relationship. "I have," he said, "and I don't want to be married anymore. There just isn't . . ." And that is where the fragment fell away into the silence, and the silence gave way to the end. For a while he moved in upstairs in the big house in Ardmore, a house that already had upstairs in another room my then-wife's then-best friend who had, the month before that, gotten a divorce from her first husband who was then, and would be for a little while longer, the drummer in the WHITEDOG band. If this seems confusing, believe me you should have lived there, the comings and goings of people in retreat and needing repair, the long quiet conversations about women and men which were really about each other and the ones we knew or had been married to.

In the night there was rock n roll music. In the morning there was a day to get through. Drew and I took up smoking just to get out of the house where it wasn't allowed, stood bundled up in winter coats watching the wind chase the smoke of many Camel Lights out of our mouths, curl it into swirls that ran dead ahead in the nowhere that finds itself living, like I did, under the dual influences of the damned winter sun and the presence always, even in its absence, of a full, full moon.

My marriage ended the following month, on Valentine's Day, again in sentences that became fragments that became silence that became the end. The big house in Ardmore became a negative place, so much losing going on that even the dogs were unhappy. The woman who lived upstairs moved out; she said she couldn't be everybody's friend unless there was some distance, and right after that Drew and I decided to move in together, share expenses in a rented duplex well away from all that was Ardmore, survive all that was this by simply playing guitar.

The WHITEDOG band, suddenly, inexplicably, was hot, playing everywhere and all the time. When we weren't playing, we were either practicing new material or checking out other acts to see how we compared. With this schedule, and our regular daytime jobs, there wasn't much time left for any leftover emotions, the various and changing currents and swells of divorces, the obvious pity and hate of it all.

There were also other complications. Drew's failure to pay his taxes finally attracted the attention and then the hammer of the IRS. My failure to understand the unnameable crippling of a mysterious illness that later, much later, I would learn had all along been misdiagnosed cost me the aid and comfort of a close friend who thankfully wouldn't take sides in this ugly little divorce that everyone else was lining up to take sides for.

Everyone on my side hated my ex-wife even though I told them they shouldn't, everyone on her side hated me even though they were probably getting the same advice from her. It was increasingly difficult to be seen in public; it was increasingly difficult to see myself alone.

Then one day I accepted a new job in Utah, and that same day by some odd and positive twist of life's fates Drew began selling real estate like never before. WHITEDOG recorded its first single, there was talk of an album, we were running back and forth to Muscle Shoals Sound, and then suddenly there we were on stage before three thousand screaming, dancing people, surrounded by rockets and glitter and explosions into space. Everyone wanted an interview, everyone wanted a picture, everyone wanted me to return their calls, and my life moved comfortably into the fast lanes of conspicuous danger that is the full force of the life-form known colloquially as rock n roll.

It was during this time, a time full of contradictory emotions and difficult music, that I first entered the white building on the left of the Parkway with the sign out front that says only TMT.

6

Have you ever walked through a door that you thought was just a door and entered a room that made your skin tingle? Have you ever let go of the handle on that door and known that you let go on some essential part of yourself?

Then perhaps you have been here, or some place like this. The odd feeling you get is induced not by the empirical reality you confront—for, after all, this is clearly a real estate office— designer-decorated and highly inviting, somewhere in the mauve between of classy but low-key and comfortable but highbrow, and there are no angry voices or annoying artwork or even smells of leftover anything to tip you off in the usual way that tips are made of statements of fact and value and policy that typically are suggested by corporate walls and painted spaces.

There is nothing here to frighten or amuse you. In fact, there is nothing here that does anything to you, nothing to evoke within you any particular kind of response. Yet you instantly feel it, this vague sense of something gone that was once there, something absent that should be present, something you cannot name but can most certainly experience. There is, in fact, an absence of all emotions. It is precisely the sort of calm that makes almost every baby that enters here suddenly and without provocation cry.

There is something to learn from crying babies, the shrieks and torment they offer to us before they learn how to disguise them, cover them up, displace their passions with envy, jealousy, greed, drugs, sex, and the good life, and this is indicative of something basic, something that all too often, it seems, we have forgotten to notice that we need.

In this case, anyway, I believe this is true.

7

So it was that I was drawn into the mystery that was this study at precisely the time in my life when I needed it less than I needed anything. I was on my way out of Huntsville and was not prepared for this journey into one of the avenues of longing that define the human heart. I wanted the imagined open roads across America that would lead to the great adventure that I created in the breath of the single word *Utah,* not the openings for scholarship that came from uncomfortably enclosed and suspicious places inside a white building along the rush of traffic and rhetoric that I called merely "the Parkway."

And yet, in retrospect, this was exactly the sort of preparation I needed to understand the experience of TMT. There is a kinship between citizens who suffer within the same agonies; together they try to cover over what they try to live without. Even if their wreckages come from different parts of the heart or break up at different destinations, the light-speed meanings collapse for them against the tortured corners of the self, the sense of self that exists only and forever at the deep synapses of the mind. Here is the place where what cannot be seen may truly be known. Here, there is a necessary identification between researcher and subject that makes the intersubjective reality of a culture more than just a happy phrase, that allows for contact with the language within the meanings that language usage is intended to convey, and that ultimately privileges what is enacted there.

Perhaps this is what Renato Rosaldo (1989) means by "the force of emotion" that causes us to miss the experience of meaning because of what we are meaning to experience, which is ultimately the denial of self in the expression of the Other or the denial of the Other in the expression of self. In this case who you are as a researcher, or for that matter who they are as the subjects or Others, may be far less important than what you both experience in your lives that causes you to seek meanings together in the first place.

In other words, reader, the subject of this study may not be TMT at all. What it may be is the displacement of passion, a force of emotion that moves us to extremes in order to maintain a balance in how we live through the experience of who we are while we try to make a living and get on with our lives.

8

"Do you have the new Tom Petty?"

"Just a minute. It's here somewhere."

"What's on the list for today?"

"Thirteen dreams. Beginning in North Birmingham."

"Aw shit, really? Did you find that tape yet?"

"Yeah. Here it is. First song's killer. It's called 'Free Fallin'.' "

I am in a blue Volvo when the music starts. I am trying to observe the realtors of TMT on caravan, a weekly ritual of showing the new listings and singing praise songs to them. I am with Drew, Mary Frances, and Dave, whose blue Volvo this is and who is master to Jake, a famous local dog. Tom Petty's voice and lyrics begin the conversation:

She's a good girl, loves her mama
Loves Jesus, and America too
She's a good girl, crazy about Elvis
Loves horses, and her boyfriend too . . .

I look at Drew, Drew looks at me. We both look back up front into the free space between us and the stereo-god that is providing this message. Dave and Mary Frances are nodding their heads, tapping their fingers. North Birmingham is far, far away.

It's a long day, livin' in Receda
There's a freeway, runnin' through the yard
Now I'm a bad boy, cause I don't even miss her
I'm a bad boy, for breakin' her heart
And I'm freeeeeeeeee, freeee fallinnnn'
Yeah I'm freeeeeeeeee, freeee fallinn'.

"Wow," says Drew. He leans forward, lights a cigarette. Inside the blue Volvo, going down these streets of thirteen dreams, these words have spoken to us; they have mixed with the stuff of our lives and mean something. Later, I will learn that Drew saw images of his wife, his life, the street he used to live on in the city he used to live in where one night he stood outside and barbecued steaks and thought the poetics of life could not now be any more perfect and therefore could never change, an image that now simultaneously amuses and irritates him, reminds him of his innocence and stupidity and reminds him also that maybe, just maybe, if things could have stayed that way he would have been right.

I am thinking of air and light and horses, and of the odd absence of emotion that I feel in the absence of my first wife. I am thinking also that she does indeed love her mama, loves Jesus, and America too, that people think she's a good girl, that she is crazy about Elvis, and her horses, and— on this one I choke—her boyfriend too.

And I'm freeeeeee, freeee fallinnnn',
Yeah I'm freeeeeee, freeee fallinnn'.

Mary Frances is listening to the music, not the words particularly, giving the sway of it a nine out of ten, can dance to it, etc., wondering if her teenage daughter's new boyfriend wears rubbers, wondering if her husband's tax advantage will be lost if they can't claim the Mercedes as a business expense.

Dave is just driving, taking it all in. Serious about music, he appreciates this song, but it has not spoken to him yet and maybe never will. He passes a convenience store called Circle K and thinks about Vicki, then thinks about hot dogs as her flash smile fades into the hunger he creates out of blurred images of women and mustard and hot dogs and onions.

All the vampires, walkin' through the valley
Move west down Ventura Boulevard
And all the bad boys are standin' in the shadows
And the good girls are home with broken hearts.

I wanna glide down over Mulholland
I wanna ride through my name in the sky
I'm gonna free fall out into nothin'
Gonna leave this world for a while . . .

And I'm freeeeeeee, freeee fallinnnnn'
Yeah I'm freeeeeee, freeee fallinnn'.

The song lifts us into elsewhere, where it mixes with our convenient dreams and fades, fades out, fades out there somewhere into silence.

What the silence brings inside is the muted constant swishy whoooosh of Michelin tires against the melting pavement, against the melting pavement just north of North Birmingham. Somebody wants to hear the song again and says so, and somebody else rewinds the tape and makes it so.

I am outside of my body now, watching the somebodies, one of which is my own. I experience the peaceful fear and fearful peace of floating, freeeee fallinnn', the center of my being out over the valley, taking issue with the life I thought I'd left behind. Up here with me are these other souls, each one in her or his own unnameable orbit, spinning out memories of stories from the point of view of their own telling, playing all the right big roles and ignoring the rest: hero, loser, sinner, or saint. Up here there are only the great absolutes, no gray everydays or vague in-betweens. Self-definition is unnecessarily real; knowing the true selves and motives of others is just as unnecessary and real. From up here we all drive big impressive cars, make lots of money, have tons of talent, and make perfect wonderful love to lesser citizens who admire us for the simple kindness that is our heart.

All of this occurs in the silence between songs, and is, like prayer, a source of some communication that receives us as clearer, better, than we are.

9

"Now wasn't that something?"

This from Mary Frances, a big woman past thirty with big hair. She is a smoker, a mother, a wife, a realtor, and unimaginable other things. She turns to me, and I feel myself return to the backseat of the blue Volvo, hear the whooshing of Michelin and pavement and her words, which begin: "Hearing the right music on caravan is sometimes *better* than sex." She smiles as if she has just had me, just word-sex, though, because she is a Christian woman if occasionally a mild backslider, which she tells me later, when she adds that she is a married woman with standards, which she tells me carefully, as if without saying it I wouldn't otherwise know.

I wonder what it is about me that makes her need or want to say this. Hair? Teeth? Clothes? Recently divorced status, which I have learned marks me down like discounted meat at a supermarket, has become the main way to read me, the only important passage in the text that is my life. I examine the indentation where the ring was worn for the past nine years and I wonder whether the scar that was left behind will always show.

Is this dead passion I think I hide so well inside myself so obvious to everyone? Or just to some people, the ones who are themselves looking for it? How is it that some people can see right through me and others are only too willing to accept whatever I present to them?

I realize, right here in North Birmingham, in a blue Volvo whose passengers have been under the influence of rock n roll, that whatever read I give to this text, I am no longer its author.

1 0

North Birmingham lies about fifteen minutes south of the Tennessee River, the river that forms the southern boundary of Huntsville. The real North Birmingham is considerably farther, lying about ninety miles farther down from the up of here.

We are in rural Dixie when we are in the regions of this North Birmingham, which is not really North Birmingham but is called that just the same. We are in the rural Dixie of my imagination, or at least the parts of my imagination that have been informed by a particular, privileged reading of history, novels, hearsay, and films. This is a mythical, substandard land where Confederate flags still blazon the rear windows of dangerous pickups, pickups that proudly display gun racks upon which are mounted real guns, driven by thin, angry women who say to hell with the surgeon general and who bear military children for larger, less articulate, unkempt and hated men who say to hell with everything except you and me, and I ain't so sure about you. In my imagination those guns of theirs are always loaded, those women are always sucking the death out of red-box hard-pack Marlboros, and those men are always laid up half-drunk or just plain mean. Every one of them is in real and constant need. They live in houses that need paint, that need furniture, they have children who need clothing and education, wives who need consciousness and better hygiene, husbands who need understanding and a more liberal God.

There is no way that any of these needs will be met, so in my mind they just hate everybody and everything that cannot be generically reduced to their own rotten sameness or is not genetically related to them. In my mind all they do is drink, fuck, shoot, and hate, and in my mind they hate, most of all, just me. They hate me for what I am, and for what I'm not. I can feel their hatred in convenience stores, liquor stores, in the heat of their stares that dare me to cross over some unknown line in various American parking lots. I might as well be black, this might as well be fifty years ago.

But this is all in my mind.

The truth is much harder, and far more complex. My sense of hatred is partly projection derived from the nervous edges of fear, and partly from the guilt I feel, as Kenneth Burke puts it, from being "up" when others are "down." I am the one interpreting those houses, those women and children, and those stares. I am the one attributing significance and meaning to the unknown within of the Other, seeing myself as someone meaningful in the stuff of their lives, someone worthy of the deep hate that, in truth, is part of what I hope for. As if their hatred justifies me, my choices, my place in the commonweal, my mind. And in this privileged mental territory of my own cultural construction I grant no room for individuality, much less *bricolage,* to the Other; I fear the mere possibility of human connections between me and them based on the joke of a life that rushes us all too quickly to nowhere, regardless of our birth, looks, language, or money, and that requires us all to pay taxes along the way, taxes that are taken from wages that are never enough, wages that take time away from a life that is never enough, when what waits for us is the great trapdoor at the bottom end of the twentieth century that should mark our common generational tombstones thusly:

This citizen was born, reared, and educated,
Got a job in order to consume,
Consumed like hell,
Was famous, locally, for it
Realized that no matter how much was consumed it was
Never Enough,
Then retired,
Then died.

These are my thoughts as I pull off the main highway onto a two-lane blacktop that degenerates into a poor dirt road riddled with potholes, both real and imagined. We pass an old Ford that crashed into an oak tree and burned long before I was born and whose charred skeleton lives still by the side of the road. The air is dense and still. An old blue-tick hound ignores our passing, or maybe just ignores me, or maybe is just blind.

We come to a stop at the gate of Dream Number 1.

1 1

Dream Number 1 is a survivalist's community property: small brick homes organized for the end of the world in a place for which the world ended long ago. God is well-armed around here, inspiring a belief in instant guard dogs with bad gums who bare their teeth and barbed-wire fences upon which grow roses the color of blood.

"Jeeeeeesus Chrrrriiiiiiiiiist!" says Mary Frances, in a way definitely not intended to invoke the Lord.

"Price?" This from Drew.

Dave examines the handy fact sheet. "Seventy-two five for 1600 square and a single acre, additional acreage may be available."

Everyone considers the import of this. I am thinking, "Overpriced, and who the hell would want to live out here, and the extra acreage is available only if this intentional community approves of the depth of your ignorance and hatred." But this is merely a remnant of my white, middle-class prejudice that does not readily take into account those who survive on the margins of society. Actually, upon closer inspection the property is clean and well tended; in another setting—say, a suburb that renders invisible its own barbed-wire values—it would fit in nicely, a starter home for college-educated newlyweds oriented to want the two beautiful children and BMW like everyone else.

There are children here, too, but three of them, and all in a dressed-up, telling row along the narrow front porch. Each of them has a small sad face that defines, quietly, instantly, and obviously, the structure of this particular consumer narrative. "Divorce," says Dave. "One set of parents lives in the big house up on the hill."

"Yep," says Drew. " 'Owners anxious to sell' written all over this contract."

"How can you tell?" This from ethnographer me, still in the backseat.

"We'll show you," smiles Mary Frances, who also tells me to follow her into the house.

12

Before we go any further, I suppose I need to describe the vehicles, and their occupants, that make up the TMT caravan.

Up front is a new light-yellow Lincoln Continental, and out of it climbs a contingent of four blue-hairs, the well-heeled Society Ladies who do this job part-time to claim they "work outside the home," because their homes are tended still by colored (their word, not mine) maids; because they live in a historical era whose increasing demands on their learned self-definitions increasingly make them seem like monuments to a bygone time; because they, as human beings, as women, as distinct persons, strive to resist change. Mostly arthritic and always overdressed, these women of the thirties survey this improved cow pasture with old and uneasy eyes.

To them I am a "college professor," merely a member of a category, a stereotype, probably too smart for my own good. They are amazed that I would want to come along on a caravan and watch them work. They didn't know college professors did that sort of thing, and now that they do know it, they don't know what to make of it. So they smile and do not speak unless directly spoken to. I overhear one of them say, "He's *divorced,* you know," and another one responds, "Ohhh . . . ," and that's pretty much all of it.

Next in line is a recent beige Mercedes, driven by the recently divorced ex-wife of a well-to-do physician rumored to be on the mid-life skids, a woman who laughed when she told me that she bought this car not for its status, but because it would last. "You know," she teased, "like that girl on the Seiko commercials whose watch lasted longer than her husband did? Well, honey, I have a good old watch"—she turns up her wrist to reveal a platinum Rolex—"so I figured I needed a car that would stay with me."

I am tempted to tell her, out of plain meanness, that she could pay for a lot of repairs on a Chevrolet before she got to the price of a Mercedes, but I don't. Truth is I don't like this woman for the same reasons she probably doesn't care for me, the same reasons also that both of us use when we worry about who we have become in the world, and our views on the reasons for it.

This woman, incidentally, as I learn later from another woman who privately wishes she was this woman but isn't, is afraid of birds. It's more than that, really. She is *deathly* afraid of birds and also refuses to admit it. This is known to this other woman, as I find out later it is well known through TMT, because when a bird, any bird, not a particular bird, flies up in front of her while she is driving she covers her face with both hands, screams, "BIRDS!! BIRDS!!" and slams on the brakes. She has caused at least two accidents because of this behavior, and even though people who ride with her on caravan have learned to grab the wheel (if they are in the car) or follow her at a very safe distance (if they are behind her), she will pretend that these episodes simply never happen.

With her in the Mercedes today is Charlene, the woman and legend, a person in her late forties who carries herself with the practiced impatience of someone who has tried to be kind to one too many people in her lifetime and so has decided to never do it again. In an article about her in our local paper she admitted that even her children and husband have to schedule appointments with her, a fact which she read as evidence of her success but which I read as evidence of illness. I don't knock her success, though, for she is the pride of TMT, and at least for the period for which I was able to obtain information, she took home more money each year than did our two local Fortune 500 company CEOs together. That places her, reader, in a seven-digit category, which is two big and important digits to the left of the one writing this piece, which may say something about my perspective.

But there is more to it than digits can account for. Charlene also has cancer of the livable-within-the-limits-of-radium variety, and so does Mr. TMT himself, and neither of them will schedule treatments that interfere with their work or take off on account of pain. This says something that I think is important and not particularly pleasant about both of them, and it also helps explain part of the bond between them, which is close and yet wary, the sort of bond that counts as significant who gets to work first in the mornings because someday one of them won't get to work at all.

Out of the backseat of this beige engineering climbs, with some difficulty and no help, a beautiful woman named Debbie who wears a wooden leg and walks with the aid of a marvelously ornate cane. She is a widow whose husband died in the car wreck that also claimed her right leg, and although she does not need the money, she works for Mr. TMT because, as she puts it, she likes to. And that is all she says to me, period.

Next car in line is not a car, but a full-sized Chevy van, all decked out and trimmed up well into the thirty grand range by its owner, Rusty Wade Elson, former local high school football star and later a force in Auburn's defensive line who still looks, in his late thirties, like he works out regularly and whose three (and a half, as he phrases it, grinning about his impending divorce) ex-wives still call him up for dates. I see him, I swear to God, and I think of Rhett Butler. Out of his van climbs a cadre of younger swingers from TMT, and I can still hear the Doobie Brothers tape as Dave tells me that I should catch a ride with Rusty Wade if I want to hear great stories and do a lot of drinking.

It figures. And it figures that I don't.

Then there is us in the blue Volvo. Behind us are two more cars, poorer models of older Fords, both with new agents trying to take this whole thing very seriously and who obviously don't yet have many friends within the company. Last in line is an Audi driven by a recent college graduate son of a friend of a friend's of Mr. TMT, who, I learn from Drew, hasn't put a sale on the board yet and is just barely being tolerated. No one gets out of his car except him, and he does not appear to be enjoying this.

I wonder if the order of cars means anything. And then I think that perhaps only I would want it to. But everyday life in the real world of the real-at-stake isn't so easy or so neat.

13

Here are the unpublished but often clearly articulated rules for showing dreams on caravan:

1. All agents exit their respective vehicles and admire the property, issuing appropriate oohs and ahhs, gesturing toward the specific features that can be useful in making a sale.

2. The listing agent walks up to the front door and either enters it (if the door has been left unlocked) or rings the doorbell or knocks. Said listing agent then greets each Realtor as they march up and into the house in single file, look around, note all the bedrooms, baths, etc., that may be used to advantage when making the sale.

3. Rhetoric is constituted about the property, catchphrases are tried out in small groups, notes are taken. If the property is "just right" for a particular current client, a phone is used by an enthusiastic TMT agent to make the appropriate call right then and there. This tactic also has clear public relations value, particularly if the owner is present.

4. Agents exit the premises in single file, pausing once again to admire the property before reentering their respective vehicles and driving away slowly.

Here is what actually happens:

1. Cars line up in front of the house, and agents, in various states of health and with varying degrees of enthusiasm, stretch and complain about the ride, the music, and each other.

2. The listing agent knocks on the front door, opens it with a key, and yells "HELLLLLLLLOOOOOOOOOOOOOOO" into the general interior of the place, just in case they have caught someone inside half-naked or engaging in illegal or immoral activities, which occurs, according to the agents, more often than you might suppose.

3. The agents enter the house, look around, comment on the owners' taste or lack thereof, compare it unfavorably to their own listings, make small jokes about the conditions of sale, and leave as soon as possible.

4. Agents file back into their respective vehicles and check their respective watches, wondering how much time has passed since their last interesting life experience or perhaps just anticipating lunch break. When the cars are fully reoccupied, they leave.

14

As I walk through Dream Number 1 with Mary Frances as my personal guide, I am given clues to how these agents read the stories of lives that are part of what they offer for sale.

In the master bedroom I am told to notice that no men's clothing is hung in either of the closets, nor are any men's coats found in the coat closet just off the back porch. "Mrs. is still living here, husband has moved out or been shamed out, and the children will stay with the mother when the divorce is final and the property is sold."

Framed Polaroids are everywhere, showing a happy nuclear family that apparently is no more. We pause at the framed high school diplomas that hang on the center of a wall in what I imagine serves as a den, defined here as where you put things you can't put anywhere else, combined with an old sofa and a rocking chair. "They graduated together and got married"—she points to the wedding picture that shows the same basic age and hairstyle in the accompanying graduation photos—"had kids, and then something happened." Here Mary Frances grins. "My guess is that the Mr. stepped out on the Mrs. and got caught, probably more than once."

"How do you figure that?"

"Well, just look at these pictures. The Mr. ages considerably more handsomely than does the Mrs. Notice also"—she points to the certificates framed on the wall around the diplomas—"that the Mr. was promoted to sales manager in the chicken business while still fairly young. Money plus looks equals affairs. Money plus looks minus a wife who is not aging well and has three children equals more than one affair before the marriage ends."

I wonder at the way in which the metaphor of equations reaches into the experience of everyday life.

"Now notice the name on the mail left on the kitchen table," Mary Frances commands. You see "Carol Anne Green" on several of them, "Mrs. Robert Edward Green" on a few others.

"So?"

"So what was the name on the mailbox for the big house we passed on the way in here?" Her grin widens.

"Green," I say.

"The Mrs. is selling the house, plans to move in with her parents. The Mr. is on to what he thinks is a better thing, but she's probably just younger and has bigger tits." She grins awkwardly now, fingers the part of the dress in the most recent photograph that led to her conclusions about the tits. "Bitch never knew what hit her. Now she's got three small children, no education, and parents that will want her to find another man but quick."

This is the statement that ends our inspection of, and my education about, this particular American dream.

15

Drew has been noticeably quiet during this tour and seems a little distant in his business suit, staring out the window into the vanishing countryside. Maybe it's the Jimi Hendrix on the tape he is listening intently to, or maybe not.

What is odd about this whole episode is that we are seeing each other in the roles and costumes of our other lives, the lives we lead outside of the lives we have learned to live in as musicians, as roommates, as friends. It is hard to imagine him as the guitar-god of WHITEDOG, the man whose quick perfect licks and tricky slide work always awe the crowd. Here, in the backseat of a blue Volvo, even listening to the Jimi Hendrix he plays better, faster than the original, he is reduced to Mr. Salesperson Anonymous, a suit, a glad hand, polished shoes, a smile, and a tie.

No doubt I come off even worse. Gone is the "Doctor of Rhythm, Doctor of Style, the One and Only Dr. Bud," the me that is known by the fill that my good ol' '57 Strat provides; present and all too easily accounted for is Professor H. Lloyd Goodall, Jr., Pee Aitch Dee, whatever that means.

It occurs to me that this is how America lives because this is how America works. Most of us live half-lives in the black-and-white, going through days convinced of our own possible wholeness, a wholeness that exists full-blown and in technicolor stereo in some other space. This other space works very hard to induce our transcendence, pulls us away from our working selves, provides the extremes of our vision, our values, and our language.

Notice how I tend to generalize on the bad news?

In this blue Volvo are evidences of life-forms and their shadows that make all of this seem true, like the inescapable conclusion to a mystery that I am led to when I am led, in the course of the mystery's telling, to inescapable conclusions. But this is not yet Saturday. And no, the question is not who is doing the leading so much as how, exactly, am I being led?

1 6

Back into South Huntsville now, and we are accompanied by WHITEDOG, the promo tape, rock n roll of Dave and Mary Frances' choosing.

> There's a reddd house over yonderrr,
> And that's where my baby stays.

This is a WHITEDOG remake of the Hendrix version of an old blues classic, and is one of my personal favorites. I listen as Drew's lead inspires Dave to air-guitar an imitation of the man seated next me. Mike Fairbanks's vocals slide back in . . .

> There's a reddd house over yonderrr,
> And that's where my baby stays.

. . . I am thinking how it is that this song was first recorded, back in the big house in Ardmore with Mitch Rigel from Radio Tokyo, the Rossington Band, and Lynyrd Skynyrd on drums, and Rob Malone just back from L.A.'s Guitar Institute of Technology doing dual leads with Drew, and remembering how Traci Collins flew in from California just to hear us play and fell for Rob in my living room and was shy about it and nothing happened . . .

> Wait a minute, somethin's gone wrong here
> 'Cause my key don't unlock this door.

. . . I am thinking also how odd it feels to hear myself in stereo while driving up the Parkway, seeing other people imitate how I act on stage . . .

> Wait a minute, somethin' wrong here,
> 'Cause my key don't unlock this door.
> I got a bad, bad feelin'
> My baby don't love me no more . . .

. . . everybody joins in on the last line, Mary Frances dipping and tossing big hair, Dave leaning forward into the steering wheel, me and Drew just grinning through it all, until this last line, which is all Drew Thompson, just like in real life . . .

That's okay, I still got my guitar . . .

. . . and then the lead ride burns in, lifting us up and dropping us almost all the way down before lifting us up again, full of power, full of grace, never missing a note, just Drew Thompson being perfect, better than Jimi, *really* better than Jimi.

Dave cuts down the volume, says, "Sorry guys, but it's back to work now." We have pulled up to the new curb of a brand-new Dream, and our common transcendence vanishes like breath into daylight and we are left breathless and unready for the world we are about to reenter.

An American Airlines DC–10 filled to the max with humans roars over us; a red Speedster with a two o'clock blonde alone in it blows by.

17

This is a Dream in six figures, where the first digit on the left is a 3. It is large and square, its only source of charm, money.

This is a TMT listing and if it is also a TMT sale and the same realtor, in this case Charlene, both lists and sells the property, she stands to make a straight 6 percent commission. If an agent from a competing company sells the listing, then Charlene still gets 3 percent, so eventually she will bank somewhere between nine and eighteen thousand on this single transaction.

Not a bad day's pay.

The realtors are mostly quiet as they tour this one. It is a Chester West Home, which, in this town, is akin to a high-priced brand name product. It is Designer Americana all the way, complete with whirlpool bathtubs with the fashion handles for easier sex (this insight from Carl, one of the van riders), a master bedroom suite (pronounced with great French stress by Charlene) you could jog in, a dual-microwave kitchen, and a sunlit Florida room with a cedar hot tub overlooking the heavily shaded rear of the lot.

I wouldn't want to be the kind of person who would want to live here. But increasingly Huntsville is precisely this sort of market, and this large, unattractive, overpriced, and inconvenient yup neo-paradise will sell quickly. This news from Drew, who takes me aside and cautions me about letting my values get in the way of my research. "Dr. Bud," he begins, in his best good ol' boy voice, somewhere between a country cousin who has lost his patience and "I cain't *buhlieve* you don't know how the world works" millionaire, "this is the future of the real estate market. This is what most people want. This is what they have dreamed about, and worked for, and this home—it's not a house, it's a home—will be their reward. You've got to see it like they do."

"Yeah, but would you pay $300,000 for this?"

Mr. Thompson grins. This is not the rock n roll grin, but the business grin, and there is world of difference in the way it makes his face wrinkle. "Hell no. But I'd sure sell it to you."

"You're acting like a broker again."

"The IRS and Mr. TMT will be glad to hear that," he says.

"So how would you go about pitching this monster?"

"You want the sales talk?"

"Yeah, I do."

"Okay." He looks a little embarrassed, and a small crowd of realtors has now gathered around for this performance. They are wearing half-serious faces, faces that respect his past sales record and position as a broker in the company, faces that want to measure their skills against his in this little demonstration. I notice that Charlene and a couple of the old blue-hairs have returned to their cars and are pulling away.

"First, you have to explain to the buyer that you are legally representing the seller, even though you are working with the buyer. Then you ask them, point blank, if they would like to hire you and thereby make you their paid agent for this transaction."

"What do they do?"

"Usually they ask you if they can save any money on the house that way."

"And what do you say?"

"It depends on the situation, but mostly I tell them that my livelihood depends on their purchase regardless of who I am officially representing. Therefore, I'll try to do the best I can to make sure they're happy. Plus, you're selling them on who you are, the kind of person they're dealing with. Back in my office I have all of these plaques on the wall, you've seen them, so from the very start of our relationship they know I know what I'm talking about."

"So what's the point here?"

"Point is that by state law I have to get them to sign a paper saying they know I'm representing the seller, and this is my personal way of getting them to do that without raising their suspicions."

"Then what?"

"Then I prequalify them. Because I'm a broker I can do that, and also because I've worked hard to have relationships with various mortgage institutions, so, for example, when discount points are high I can usually shave them a bit."

"Then what?"

"Okay. So after I prequalify them for a particular priced home, we usually go to lunch. During lunch I learn as much as I can about who they are, who they have been, and what their dreams are."

"How do you do that?"

"Bud, you're new in town and your company has moved you here and you didn't know this place existed until you looked for it on the map. You need a friend, an advisor, someone who will see to it that you don't live where you don't want to and you don't spend more than you have to. So I have to know a lot about how you see the world and your place in it."

"You want perspective, right?"

"I want perspective, but I also want reach."

"What's reach?"

"Reach is where they can go, where they want to go, but haven't been able to get to. It's in their heads, and usually they will tell a stranger a whole lot more about it over lunch than they have ever told a family member."

"Give me an example."

"Okay. Last week there was a woman from Atlanta whose home there was just leased by the State Department. She owns a company here and decided to buy a home in Huntsville, but it has to be just the right sort of place to maintain her image. Plus, she didn't know diddley about Huntsville. So I sent her a book on the history of the town, I sent her the names of people she would want to know about, and I spent a day taking pictures of homes that aren't for sale but that are in her price range. I called her every day, learned a little more about her from each phone call, and provided all of this as a service to her at no charge."

"What happened?"

"Nothing yet. She's still looking. But we have established a relationship, a business relationship, and I expect she'll close on one of three properties by the end of next month."

"How did you determine her, uh, reach?"

"By asking her. Most people will tell you what you want to know if you just ask them. So I asked her what a dream home would look like, and she gave me square footage and a basic description of the sort of neighbors she wants to have."

"What did that tell you?"

"It told me she wanted a small mansion in the Twickenham section that would have some history to it, for the stories she could tell her Atlanta buddies."

"Yeah, but there aren't that many homes for sale in Twickenham."

"That's right. That's where it gets interesting. And that's why I took the pictures I did and sent them to her."

"You mean if she likes one of them, you'll approach the owner and ask if it's for sale?"

"Not exactly. I'll approach the owner and tell them I have a customer who will buy their home for a certain price, and then, if they agree to it, I work out an arrangement with them about my commission."

"More money."

"A lot more money for Drew, and the woman gets the home she always wanted, and the seller gets a price well beyond what he thought it was worth."

"Okay, so you sell a house for more than it's worth. How does that work on an appraisal?"

"In this case there doesn't have to be one because it's a cash deal. But even if it wasn't, appraisers generally appraise a home for right around the selling price. They know the price going in, and unless there's something really wrong with the place, something structural, for instance, there isn't a problem. And if there is a problem, and it isn't structural, then I make a few calls and get another appraiser."

"This all sounds fairly easy and straightforward."

"So does playing the guitar, pal, so does playing the guitar. But there's a world of difference between a guitar player and a guitarist." He smiles. He is referring to a past conversation of ours, and I know exactly what he means.

I turn around and see the assembled realtors nodding. They have learned something, something they can use. Basically it's a line, a good line, that will fit into their own sales narratives, their own relationships with consumers, maybe even their own lives.

We get back into the blue Volvo.

"Man, did you see old Lubie Poole back there taking *notes?*" This from Dave, who seems fired up.

"He's been trying to figure out a way to do that disclosure statement without pissing people off for six months now, and you just gave it to him." This from Mary Frances, who is getting a kick out of it.

"Yeah," says Drew, "but can you see ol' Lubie trying to do it the way I do it?"

Everyone laughs. In the laughter you are swirling back to Dave's imitation of Drew earlier, playing air guitar, and to my own role as guitar player to his role as the guitarist in WHITEDOG. I am thinking that you can know how without even being able to, and that sort of knowledge is really an absence of power, an imitation of a performance that will always come off as an absence of power and an imitation of performance.

"That was a pretty good little lecture you gave back there," I say. "I didn't know Mr. Thompson could teach real estate."

Drew laughs louder. "You can't teach real estate. You can teach the rules, the laws, the procedures. You can tell a few stories that have some value. But you can't teach real estate, you have to feel it."

What I hear in that last sentence, because of the way he draws a breath when he pronounces it, is "You can't teach real-at-stake," which I read as "You can't teach (when what's) real (is) at stake." It reminds me of something I have been saying lately: "You can teach people to speak, but not to communicate." Here again there is something that can't be seen that is more real than what can be, something felt perhaps only in the presence of metaphors when metaphors work on you from the inside out and leave in their wake a lingering for their own long echoes, when to try to repeat them out of context is to destroy·them entirely, which is like trying to repeat the past, which isn't like anything because it just doesn't work.

1 8

The next series of Dreams were all suburban digs, each home like its catty-corner neighbor, alike in their invitations to comment on how a garage turned this way or that makes the whole thing special, the crisscross logic of patio dwellings, of planned urban communities where X on the map marks the same kind of spot regardless of street address.

There must have been ten of them, from looking at my notes, the hand-drawn scrawl becoming with each number smaller and less significant. This was the part of the caravan where we switched from tapes to FM radio, where the conversation began to get stale, focus on the weather, sports, lunch. What were we thinking about while our mouths were working on these rituals? I can remember nothing, but nothing as a space that I inhabited rather than as a void, as a place to go to when the dreams of life and the life of dreams collapse. This is the place, or space, that I go to when I need to recover that nil feeling, that blankness that increasingly defines parts of my life. Viewed from the outside this is empty space between conversational episodes, and the tendency is to focus on the episodes; viewed from the experience of it, the episodes of talk merely bypass the center of it, this essential blankness in the womb of no feeling, while I travel along fast lanes at speeds increasingly random, being driven by somebody else, wearing, really *wearing* as if for the very first time, my shades.

I come out of it and check my watch, squint into the hazy yellow sunlight, feel once again the heat that eats at you in the South in the summer, name the month, and remember my name. Maybe I've been asleep, or maybe I've just been working.

Doors open. I open my door. Everyone steps outside and looks around. I step outside and look around. My eyes recognize Madison, recognize the gas station and fast-food stop, recognize the realtors. I see a picnic table with two men eating big burgers and drinking cold quart beers. The men are in T-shirts and faded jeans and are both missing the same front tooth. I turn away from them and see a sign that reads: "McDick's: Famous for Almost a Month, Over Twelve Burgers Sold."

I enter, hoping only for lunch.

19

We are inside a full-service convenience store cooled down to just above frigid by a couple of old two-ton window units whose working whine and complaint inspire a decibel level, that, if pitched a bit higher, could easily shatter glass.

Three heavyset goodtimin' mid-life women from Madison in white chef's aprons bebop to Elvis's last number one hit, circa 1969, called "Suspicious Minds," while they steam-heat the burgers, slice up the Better Boys and cut up the iceberg, and toss Wonderbread buns through the air. They enact his vocal performance visually, lip-syncing the words:

Caught in a trap, can't walk out
Because I love you too much babyyyy

Oh why can't you see, what you're doin' to me
When you don't believe a word I'm sayinnnn . . .

We can't go on together with suspicious minds,
We can't build our dreams with suspicious minds.

The woman with the butcher knife, iceberg, and tomatoes, whose name tag announces her as DeeDee, is singing to Drew, swaying her hips and pouting her lips, and for a moment he joins in this impromptu performance with air guitar and attitude.

I order a burger-no-mayo from a name tag labeled Cindy, who invites the order with her eyebrows only, and who does not miss a single word in the song while all of this transacting goes on.

Behind me file in the other realtors checking out the luncheon options, which range from Betty's handmade sandwiches to factory-packaged Oreos. Amid the roar of the air-conditioning and the rush of the crowd there is talk about what is cheap, what would be easy, what tastes good. There is laughter, movement; we are in the America of rapid consumption, where green dollars and nourishment exchange hands and are, in the moment of exchange, exactly the same thing, having exactly the same meanings even though they are never exactly the same.

This is the America of money, food, music we know the words to, the playfulness of sexual innuendos with waitresses, and the forces of air-conditioning and sudden hunger brought on by the onslaught of familiar symbols, luncheon rituals, and a known sense of place. This is the America of regress and renewal, of a consumption that gives imagination to all that we consume.

Ethnographer always, I ask Cindy about McDick.

She giggles, blushes, and takes comfort in the giggles and blushes of the other two women, who have apparently overheard my question. "There is no McDick?" she says in that overly sweet elongated ultimate vowelness that for me always sounds like it ends in a question mark and that defines, at least for me, the root cause of the odd innocent decadence in the Southern female accent. "We are all three of us divorced? And off the alimony we started this business?"

"And all of our ex-husbands were assholes?" This from Betty.

"And so we called this place McDick's?" This from DeeDee.

Glad I asked.

"We hate men?" says Cindy, grinning at me as she finishes my burger and hands it over the counter.

"Honey, did you put the *rat* poison on his like I did this one?" This from DeeDee, who has handed her work to Drew.

"No, I think I forgot to?" replies Cindy.

Elvis ends this episode:

We can't go on together with suspicious minds,
And we can't build our dreams on suspicious minds.

There it is. I hand over green money to a woman who has just told me how she feels about me by talking about men in general. I will not like what I eat for lunch today, I can just feel it.

"With women like this around it just shows you why there are a lot of gay men these days," says Dave to Betty, with semireal disgust.

She smiles, and then deliberately points the knife at his throat. "Have a nice day?"

20

In the war between women and men, a tactical guerrilla war fought in the jungles of hearts and minds, a war in which the body is fodder for skirmishes, skirmishes that escalate when the weapons of choice move from outward gestures inward along the tender corridors of desire and hope and fulfillment, mining each harbor in turn, destroying those resources, making damn sure there is no way out, there ends up being no way out.

None.

This is how I carry my histories with me, like old songs that remind me of a past that lives, that distorts, that complicates, on and on and on. What keeps me going is all the pounding of energy and nerves; I hear it, figure it's the beat of my life music, and just go with it.

This is everyday life where everyday life is a struggle just to get by despite all the laughter and promises I make, all the false hope I wear on my many faces, all the confidences I share with others who are, themselves, also engaged in the war, caught up in the struggle, also managing faces.

This is about women and men, real estate and what's real-at-stake, the music of business and the music business, the everyday and its attendant emotions, who you are when you do what you do and who you think I am when you do it, all the pretexts and contexts and posttextual traumas, small and unearned as they are. For to earn the right to a reading is as important as what you find there; when the often desperate, inarticulate collapse of places and persons and meanings at first dislocates and then threatens to replace you, it is what you have lived through rather than read into that sustains whatever life particle is left.

All now is entropy and wonder, jazz music for a Fender guitar.

This is what it feels like, don't try to make sense of it, let it induce rather than inform you, go with this sentence into whatever lies beyond before you find yourself gone.

2 1

The last dream on this particular tour is west of Madison, a country property. This is the West Madison of the upwardly mobile, the kind of country property that has nothing to do with country living, and where the only farm animals decorate the china.

The realtors are anxious to get through this, to conclude this part of their day, to return to the office or their families, to meet their lovers for real or imagined affairs, to go shopping or whatever it is they will do. I seem to be the only one interested in reading the text that is this country house, a text whose spine includes a den with shelves full of unread books surrounding a mail-order diploma from a mail-order law school just above the certificate from the Dale Carnegie Institute.

How stable is this binding?

Everything else in this house is perfect.

But will it sell, and sell quickly?

Is it true that when we purchase a property we inherit its ghosts? Is it true that when we move in there are memories and emotions and maybe even whole scenarios that refuse to move out with the previous owners? I remember worrying about that in Ardmore, even writing about it in my last book. I recall the moment when my well-meaning neighbor told me that both men who had lived there drove silver Corvettes and ended up divorced; I remember him telling me this when he came down to see my new silver Corvette. I recall also how it felt to sell my silver Corvette not long after, and still I ended up divorced. Is this the eery part of what is implied by the phrase "unique sense of place?" or is it merely a coincidence, something like displaying a mail-order degree prominently on the wall of an otherwise perfect American country home?

Is the right question:

A. What's wrong with this picture?

Or:

C. Is there anything wrong with this picture?

Or is the right question lost in the absence of a *B,* somewhere between what we can say about what we sense and know and what lies elsewhere, or the always evident possibility of a *D* that we cannot even begin to know?

If there are no true texts, how can there be right questions? And if this is true, do all the right answers exist only in the shadows?

I am, of course, playing with metaphors here.

Aren't I?

2 2

I fell in love with Sandra, the woman from upstairs, my ex-wife's now ex–best friend.

I ask myself, again, how do you show how an attraction grows? How do you explain, in linear words that move across margined paper, that which is not linear, that which does not work within margins?

There are some who would tell you that this had been in the stars for a long time. But what do the stars know? And can you trust the judgment of people who believe in movements of stars, who calculate their effects in a language that is ineffable?

There are some who would tell you that this was a large mistake, that I was moving too fast, as if speed was the force that determined the important outcomes, or that speeding into love was like some traffic violation, a cause for a warning, or a ticket for a dressed-up appearance for a dark-robed court. But my dad always told me, "He who hesitates in love and war often loses it," the "it" in this case being the love that is life.

So who would you believe: your dad, who survived the last world war to die in a marriage to your mother, or those who fear for you because they fear most deeply for themselves? And besides, does the passage of so many days really mean anything other than the passage of days? You can live for a long time with someone, wake up one morning and realize you don't know them at all. This is the truth, as I have lived it, so I can't believe merely in the passage of time.

And there are those who told me to do whatever made me happy, those eternal ontologists of the grin. But happiness is experienced as ebb and as flow, in thought and in action, and cannot be held still even when named and known. And besides, what has marriage to do with happiness? If that was all there was to it, the marriage license should come with some nice chemical dependence that would intoxicate away all the miseries of love.

In the end we decided to tell virtually no one. We eloped from friends and family, from readers of stars and hearts, from believers in happiness and time.

We flew to Jamaica and did the big vow scene on the beach. Our minister was a very serious black Episcopalian who, the day before, had told us the true history of women and men in marriage, an unexpected talk on a mysterious island that mesmerized us with its insights and truths. Our witnesses were dark handsome strangers who, an hour before the ceremony, made a big colorful heart out of the flowers they would later ask us to stand inside of, and that then they would gather up and place at our feet. This, all of this, against the mid-afternoon movements of gentle tides and breezes, making even truer to the eye the pastel attitudes of the watercolor sky and the Caribbean sea.

And then it was evening, pink hibiscus blooming and scented air and the gradual appearance of hushed stars amid the wine and chocolates and laughter, the ocean's beautiful rhythmical lapping; and then came to us the warm surround of night.

24

I am back at the office, the white building with the sign out front that says only TMT.

The realtors are back inside, most of them, and most of them are on the phone. Drew asks me if I want to talk to Mr. TMT before I leave. I nod.

"Mr. TMT, this is my friend, Buddy Goodall."

I reach out and shake a hand that does not shake back. I look at an old white man who is obviously dying of cancer, a tall stick figure still wearing the executive uniform, his gray eyes already halfway to somewhere else.

"How many homes did you see today, Drew?"

"Thirteen dreams, Mr. TMT," Drew replies.

"How many you gonna sell before you go home tonight?"

"As many as I can, Mr. TMT."

"That's not good enough." Mr. TMT appraises me as he says this, as if he has already had enough of Drew's bullshit and wants to see what kind of bullshit I am made of.

"They worked hard today, Mr. TMT," I say, for no particular reason.

"Hell, they was hardly working." There is not the hint of a grin on his lips as he mouths this. "Got to keep after the family all the time, isn't that right Drew?"

Drew looks down. "If you say so, Mr. TMT." Read: "Yes, Father," spoken by one of the delinquent sons who that night will most certainly be out in the nether reaches of America searching rural everywhere for hell and beer and poontang.

It may be instructive to note here that Drew Thompson was reared strict Southern Baptist, carried a Bible to school every day until he was a sophomore in college, and was minister of music to a small country church before he gave his soul to rock n roll and broke with his father over the hypocrisy of deacon religion.

"Damn *right* I say so. *Damn* right." His hand moves to my elbow and gently, but firmly, pushes me out of his way.

No wonder babies cry in here. In my heart, for a brief but certain moment, I wish he would simply die. This is the report, you understand, from the friend who just saw his pal put down, the same friend who has been hearing consistently negative stories concerning the "father" of this particular business family.

"Sorry about that," Drew offers. "But that's Mr. TMT."

"It's okay," I say. "I just got even."

2 5

I'm on my way home, feeling uneasy, restless. I can't name why.

I glance repeatedly into the rearview mirrors. I am thinking through the experiences of this field day, connecting points of departure with previous lines of argument, feeling my way along the tracks of the narrative, hoping for help from known metaphors. When I reveal my methods to students (via Gareth Morgan's work), I tell them to think of each metaphor as a prism and the organization being studied as light. Pass the light through the prism, turning it each time to reflect the lean and language of the particular metaphor. Like light through a real prism, each turn reveals new colors, conceals ones you've just seen. Then put as many of the prism tracks together as you can, work with their artistry, and the result is a narrative. The goal should always be to chart the path that got you there, as well as to create meaning.

At a stoplight I see a realtor from a rival company taking a SOLD sign out of the trunk of his Aries. He carries it, along with his hammer, to the middle of a front lawn, looks at the sign, and then laughs out loud. He walks quickly back to his car, reopens his trunk, and removes a FOR SALE sign instead.

I wonder what he makes and how much it costs him. I wonder about his laughter, his clothing, the way he loosens his tie. I wonder why he drives an Aries. Have I learned anything today that would help me explain any of what I have just seen?

There is a lady in blue jeans by the side of the highway selling roses for a dollar. Are they still the color of blood?

There is a bumper sticker on a bottle-blonde's white IROC-Z in front of me that screams IF IT SWELLS, RIDE IT! Her vanity plate says BYEBYE, and her tag date whispers *expired*. What does all this mean, given the tactics of the existing struggle?

Slowly I rev my engine, check my mirrors.

The radio voice says missiles were fired in Beirut today, and the stock prices soared. Is there any connection? Local legislators are worried about gridlock but are hesitant to make changes in the highway system. The price of an average new house in Madison county rose to $97,500 last month, the consumer price index rose by some garbled margin, and wages and unemployment remained the same. Right now it is 3:35, 94 degrees in Huntsville, 80 percent relative humidity. Tonight look for thunderstorms and severe lightning, lows in the mid-70s. Tomorrow, continued humid, hot, and hazy. . . .

I feel the heat through the windshield, rev my engine a little more, this time to boost the power of the air-conditioning. The guy with the right and wrong real estate signs pulls in behind me, tilts up his Ray-Bans, and tosses back a long mouthful of Coke. When I examine him in the rearview mirror I see Willy Loman at this end of the twentieth century. I do not see his individuality, I do not see his uniqueness, nor, if he bothered to look, would he see mine. Ours is a culture of caricature that finds it convenient, maybe necessary, to read genre fiction into empirical fact. I learned today how easy it is to read the surface of me based on similar limited data, my life as loosely constructed daytime drama, my life summed up in a nutshell, my future imminently cliched. So who are you, Mr. Willy Loman of real estate and rearview mirrors?

He yawns, largely.

There is a commercial for *Indiana Jones,* then one for new-car financing, then one for mobile homes.

There is a song on the radio, but I miss it thinking about America, imagining the Kansas of it that Sandra and I will soon experience, she with concerns about Southern fiction with visions of Western truth.

The song that comes on the radio is indistinguishable from the last song on the radio, and even the one before that. This is the new station in town, specializing in music with words that don't stick with you and a beat whose thumping constancy drives me mad. If I were poor and angry and already bothered by this early summer heat, this adolescent bleating and banging would encourage me only to want to kill somebody.

I could change the station, but I don't.

Instead I begin a mad dance in the interior of the car that obviously scares hell out of the elderly couple in the old green Plymouth next to me. But I move into the music, get with it, shuck and jive, shuck and jive. The real estate dude behind me drops his glasses, crushes his Coke can, wipes his mouth, places both hands on the wheel. The chick in the IROC plays circles with her hair. The elderly couple look taut and Baptist and mean.

Shuck and jive . . .

The light changes to green and I fire up the tires, go into the redline, pass beyond 100, disappear under the bright yellow caution light on the edge of the Madison county line

I am not writing all of this.

All of us are writing this.

Some of us race toward the horizon and figure in a moon; others of us see the moon and forget about the sky.

37

Months later I will look back on this day and read it differently. Maybe there was a blue moon on that horizon and there really was no sky.

Maybe it was all Kansas.

Guns'n'Roses, not roses the color of blood.

Not real estate.

Not even real-at-stake.

This way: I went outside one day, left early to go with Drew Thompson, etc., on caravan for TMT.

Read that sentence again, please; focus on "left early," words that your first reading may have left out.

I went on caravan, saw thirteen houses, which the realtors joke about as "dreams." I listened to their music, asked them to tell me what it was like to be in the business, to work for TMT, and to do caravan. I watched them live and work, briefly. I ate lunch after an interesting encounter with three divorcees who ran the place. I went back to the office, met Mr. TMT, drove home. I got home a little after four o'clock.

This was Drew's account.

Self, Other.

From Charlene real estate queen, the experience gets talked about this way: I didn't feel good all last night, and then I find out in the business meeting that some college professor is going to ride with us today. I think I sold him a house once, or maybe just listed one. He stayed out of the way, though. I saw a house I think I can sell this week, and another one that's a good prospect. Old T [TMT] didn't look good at all today, and when I went in to talk to him he said if he had to get to heaven before me he'd damn sure lock the gate . . .

Now try this one, which, maybe, is just a dream:

She pulls off the road near a pay phone outside of Huntsville. She makes a long-distance phone call, nervous, obviously distraught. The phone call warns of unspecified danger, but a danger that is intentionally directed, involves a third party, and includes the words "Something terrible is going to happen to him."

Around 9:00 A.M. a young man with a gun pulls to the side of a quiet suburban neighborhood. He has been told that I am the enemy, he has been lied too, he has been pumped up. He has also been told that I leave for work every morning around nine-fifteen. This intelligence apparently is the result of some investigative work done beforehand. The gun is loaded, the safety is off.

Nothing happens.

I left early, remember?

Eventually, he just gets tired and goes home. On his answering machine is a message from the woman in California explaining to him that he has been misled, lied to, and there is no reason for violence. And there is another message, this one from another woman, telling him she is sorry, but there is no need to deliver that special wedding present after all.

The war, and fortunately the music, go on.

AFTERWORD: THE TEXT INTERVIEWS ITS
AUTHOR

TEXT: The mysteries of self, Other, and context. That is what writing ethnography is all about. This is its license as well as its challenge . . .

AUTHOR: To understand self, Other, and context requires more than description and interpretation. It requires, I think, going beneath the often cosmetic surfaces of cultural traffic to where symbols mingle with the driven stuff of life.

T: This is the territory of the emotions, the realm of mystery, fate, God, and feelings. For it is down here, and really only down here, that our otherwise politely stated, socially constructed realities take shape and have meaning. It is a curious thing that humans have theories to explain everything under the sun except the feelings inside of themselves and the God some of them say created them. It is curious also that experiences we feel most deeply do not in fact have adequate names or ready-made forms of expression.

A: Everyone's experience of life is her or his own, so in some way our accounts are shot through with autobiography and fiction. Everyone's experience of life is also mostly enacted for or in the presence of others, so in some sense a full explanation must include biography and guess. And everyone's experience of life is lived out in contexts that include antecedent and consequent conditions, so there ought to be a kind of historical evolution evident in the work. Because I believe all of these things to be true and because I see them worked out best in ethnographies, I see no other way to proceed, to advance the art, other than by example, experiment, disclosure, and speculation.

T: Some of your colleagues will disagree.

A: That is to be expected and, if I'm lucky, to be learned from.

T: Some will say this is mere self-indulgence, as if what they practice isn't, whether their laboratories are found in texts that inhabit libraries or their experiments are conducted in controlled settings with sophomores.

A: I'm glad you said that and I didn't. And some may find this kind of work merely entertaining. Well, then, be entertained! There is much to be learned from entertainment, I think.

T: The only certainty there is about any of this is that years hence none of it will seem like it really matters, and yet, in its passing, all of it will.

A: You are beginning to sound more and more like me. And in that voice you might ask: Will I ever truly understand Willy Loman, or Drew Thompson? Probably not. Probably can't.

T: Will you ever be able to claim that your experience of TMT as an organizational culture is anything more than your own experience of those aspects of the culture that you were able to name and share?

A: No, I think not. But I think you're really asking if I think I might have missed something important, something that may have changed my interpretation of these events. Perhaps, but how could I know that which I didn't experience, that which wasn't told to me, or that which was shared only among others with whom I never came into contact? What do you intend with this sort of question, the need for a survey or questionnaire, some fancy new math? Whose text are you, anyway?

T: Yours, of course, and the readers'. But let me go on. Do you think you have arrived at some important truth because you have had, as Scott Fitzgerald puts it, "these privileged glimpses into the human heart"?

A: Yes. And no. And maybe.

T: That's a good postmodern response. But was it, for example, really necessary to add the bit at the end about the potential—even if it was only a dream—for murder in this story? Did that really help understand the organization, or its participants?

A: Given the wording of this question, I suppose the best answer (although not necessarily the right one) is no. But wording it differently, putting it within the context of what I am trying to do with you, would also seriously alter the answer.

T: Would you elaborate, please?

A: In my view, when we conduct a study there is a lot going on around us that we simply do not see. How can this be represented? Why, for instance, does the narrator look nervously into the rearview mirror, and how come he doesn't know why he feels uneasy? Didn't you ever have a day when you felt uneasy and didn't know why until later?

T: Yes, usually when you're working . . .

A: Did it affect your mood, your work, what you thought about, how you acted?

T: That's a strange question to ask of the object of your own creation. I think it's better left to your readers.

A: Very well then. Also, there are a lot of clues given because of the way the story is told, its inclusion of women and men as topics that move beyond the margins of real estate, the way song lyrics are read and responded to, and so forth. But how these clues fit together isn't revealed until the end because, in fact, they weren't known by the narrator until the end. I could have titled the piece "Dreaming the Anatomy of a Murder" and placed the sniper in the plot from the very beginning, but that's the television version, and it allows the reader to see (foresee?) everything, privileges the end of the story from the very beginning, and encourages a misreading of what was going on while it was happening. Life doesn't make a good screenplay without serious cuts and rearranging, but it can make palatable ethnography.

T: But doesn't "palatable ethnography" require serious cuts and rearranging? Aren't you just straining to be poetic here?

A: I don't think so. I think the issue comes down to one of perspective. Ethnography is either done in first- or second-person singular. It is written from the point of view of the ethnographer—

T: But isn't that part of the problem? Isn't that both a privileged reading and a source of latent jingoism?

A: Somebody's got to be the voice, somebody's got to do the talking, and somebody is surely having the experience. I agree with the need for caution, and I do try to give voice to those others who are within the realm of the experience, but there are no perfectly true texts, right?

T: How would I know?

A: Please don't start that again. How do we know what we know, how do we do what we do, how do we know what we do, how do we do what we know? Talk like that may get you a reputation at cocktail parties, but it won't help you write.

T: I don't get to attend cocktail parties; I'm the text, remember?

A: Sorry. Well, do you have any more questions?

T: Just one. In the end, what do I mean?

A: You mean you don't know?

T: Well, from where I'm positioned I have an interpretation, of course. But since you are the author, I thought I'd ask you. What does "Free Fallin Through the Streets of Thirteen Dreams" mean?

A: It means exactly that. From where you are positioned you will have an interpretation. *Of course.* And it also means that no matter where you are positioned in relation to this text, *everything counts.* Or, put a little differently, you are what you read, and you read what you are.

T: Can I ask one more question?

A: Go ahead, but this has to be the last one.

T: What happens to me now? I mean, after this presence as a chapter in a book, where will I go?

A: The afterlife of a text is a matter of great mystery and much speculation. Some say that either you will go into an already crowded and smelly wastebasket that will eventually be emptied into an incinerator or you will end up as a xeroxed ghost in a clean manila folder inside a nice filing cabinet in some important professor's office. But there are others who believe you will return in some altered form, maybe as an object of critique in a book or journal, or maybe just as a reference in somebody else's work.

T: Sounds to me like this is pretty much it.

A: That's my view. But it's only one person's interpretation. And by the way, I want to say how much I've enjoyed working with you and the readers on this project. Without everyone's help this whole idea wouldn't have gone anywhere.

PART FOUR Touring Culture: Participating in the Mystery While Observing the Other

Observing Otherness

Fundamentally, empirical science is an enterprise that seeks to
develop images and conceptions that can successfully handle and
accommodate the resistance offered by the empirical world under
study.

—Herbert Blumer

Carnival is a pageant without footlights and without a division into
performers and spectators. In carnival everyone is an active
participant, everyone communes in the carnival act. Carnival is not
contemplated and, strictly speaking, not even performed; its
participants live in it, they live by its laws as long as those laws are
in effect; that is, they live a carnivalistic life. Because carnivalistic
life is drawn out of its usual rut, it is to some extent "life turned
inside out," "the reverse side of the world."

—Mikhail Bakhtin

Perspective by Incongruity

—Kenneth Burke

GOING OUT, COMING IN

Can you hear in the approach the sounds of distant music? Can you
feel it? Listen:

The critical site of the Other in fieldwork is problematic. As a site of
cultural inscription, the Other has been defined historically as an exotic
or alien species (McGrane 1989), someone to be engaged, observed,
probed, and ultimately "understood" as a cultural product as well as the
coproducer of cultural texts.

The act of defining the Other as culturally distinct, exotic, alien, is an
interesting rhetorical move that carries with it intriguing strategies for
writing ethnography. To maintain that distance requires a delicate balance
in the narrative between observer self-doubt and self-discovery that folds
into what can be perhaps best described as the "contingent certainty"
about what you have observed. The result, for a reader, is a gradual dialogic
constructing of varying degrees of textual authority, of the author's *ethos,*

that depends on reporting stories that display rich textual description and detail (a grammar of knowing, capable of establishing familiarity and commonplaces) set within a broader narrative context of general ontological uncertainty and difference (a rhetoric of mystery, capable of inducing belief).

Coinciding with the conventional purpose of observing the "otherness" of others in travels to foreign lands and exotic peoples, ethnographers have always coordinated a deeper journey into the exotic reaches of ourselves, to chart along with the outward manifestations of the Other the equally strange and occasionally dangerous realms of the great unknown within. Reading these tales I have always been struck by their resonances with the first line of Dante's *Inferno*, which, when translated, begins, "Midway along the journey of my life," and goes on to chronicle a trip simultaneously inward and outward in which the quest is both a search for the truth and consequences of others' lives (in this case focusing on the theme of evil) and an attempt to satisfy the astonishing sacrifices of the human soul, or, if you will, given our twentieth-century lingo, the human *self*.

I am struck in these narratives not only by what seems to be a centering strategy that always returns to the self the yield of the trip, but also by the striking mid-life qualities associated with the need to locate metaphysical purpose and importance in routines, rituals, and choices that we have participated in as well as to explore the symbolic dimensions of the actions and words of others.

Surely the ethnographic songs in celebration of otherness would be self-indulgent and often self-congratulatory tunes if it were not for the fact that the knowledge gained from the journey into the exotic lands of otherness can be gotten at only by a simultaneous passage into selfhood. I am speaking here not just of the acquired knowledge written in travelogues, guidebooks, analyses, and histories of foreign peoples and places, but of the broader issue of what it means to be human among other humans with whom one shares neither the commonality of experience nor the understandings that such commonality assumes. Perhaps this is one reason why in our postmodern recognition of fragmented experiences, of a lack of common understandings or shared meanings even among so-called "Others of our kind"—relatives, neighbors, colleagues—we now find the inarticulate oddity and native strangeness once associated only with those who did not share our color, race, religion, economics, or education.

If the everyone and everywhere of human experience is now potentially exotic, we are living in the expressive world of rock n roll. For it is in rock n roll that the experience of otherness begins in untethered, often inarticulate emotion, offering a codependent code within the music, lyrics, style, and attitude of shared activities that reveal the deeper possibility of hidden meanings and the hope of shared messages. As the Beatles put it on *Revolver,* this sense of freedom is another way of saying the word "love." For the practice of interpretive ethnography—the research and writing equivalent to rock n roll—this is a way of acting on the Bakhtinian advice to recognize and accept the polyphonic voices of carnival as well as to engage the Other as a source of interdependent mystery whose very interdependence asks difficult questions of the self.

This is the mystery of rock n roll, the mystery of love, and this is the problematic assumed by the practice of interpretive ethnography. To make these connections clear, or at least clearer, I devote this chapter to philosophical and methodological issues involved in private investigations of the public lives of the Other. I hope to provide a framework for such investigations that recognizes and accepts differences between self and Other rather than attempts to repress, speak for, or subsume them. To accomplish this purpose I will, first, develop an argument about the nature of interpretive ethnographic reality as existing within what I term "the plural present as the communicative dimensions of experience." I will use this foundation, then, to explore how the writing of the interdependent, interpenetrating experiences of self and Other may be done and to explore some of the problems evident in that passage.

Can you hear the music now?

THE PLURAL PRESENT AND THE COMMUNICATIVE DIMENSIONS OF EXPERIENCE

Conducting fieldwork and constructing narratives involve interdependent dialogic and rhetorical processes. Both the fieldwork and its narrative begin in mystery, and move, using the vehicles of empirical observation, experience, and encounter, through a field of representational possibilities for "meaningful orders of persons and things" (Sahlins 1976) to some sense of completion or resolution, however contingent or partial.

By applications of intelligence to the ever-expanding, ever-evolving texts, the observer/writer creates dialogic foundations for understandings induced rhetorically by the language of the experiences then said to "be-long" to the scene (Burke 1965, 1969). The ongoing narrative—the tale the teller shapes and tells about the experience as she or he moves through it—strives in words and writing strategies that are *not* equivalent to the experience to capture the "story" in and of the critical site or *context* (Geertz 1988; Langellier 1989).

I am interested here in the nature of the critical site, or context, from the perspective of the observer/writer *and* the perspective(s) of the Other. Let us agree, at the outset of this exploration, that a large part of the territory claimed by the terms "critical site" and "context" is the contested space known in everyday talk as "reality." Furthermore, let us also agree that the word "reality"—as it is normally used in everyday speech to refer to the "empirical"—refers in fact to *trifurcated sites of meanings bounded by the communicative dimensions of experience.* I apologize for both the structuralist implications and the awkward poetic of this phrase, but it is, as we will see, descriptive. It isn't pretty, but it will have to do.

I use this awkward phrase for the following reasons:

1. The word "reality" simultaneously points to or assumes the existence of a physical, "natural" world of facts, and yet privileges our own phenome-nological constructions and interpretations—all selectively perceived and processed—of those facts (see Berger 1970). These privileged readings may be based on observations and beliefs about how people and things work, how people and things are, or what people and things ought to be. All readings thus constructed are privileged, and all privileged readings have some basis for justification, verification, negation, playfulness, or some artistic combination thereof.

2. Our constructions and interpretations of "reality" are created and constituted in symbolic codes that invite participation in their meanings at both digital and analogic levels (Goodall 1983; Haley 1976). These meanings at once make all symbolic codes into metaphors, as well as metaphors about metaphors, and at either level (and often both at the same time) invite participation in a reading of "reality" that is necessarily partial and not necessarily true. Language is our attempt to order chaos (however you want to read this juxtaposition, wherever you want to place the emphasis), to make something out of everything and nothing, and to render all things at once immediate and personal as well as distant and abstract (see Olney 1972).

3. The site that we call "reality" is a discursive space in the communica-tion dimensions of experience (van Peursen 1972). The communicative

dimensions of experience are the dialogic, linguistic, contested spaces in which we make discourse, converse, offer arguments, bargain, and negotiate with some Other to support the metaphors we believe best represent and account for what we have lived through or thought about (see Gunn 1982). It is within the communicative dimensions of experience that we bring the word "reality" into the realm of both legalistic argument (Toulmin 1958) and narrative rationality (Fisher 1984), choice domains of discourse that suggest rules, rituals, and boundaries that, in the act of their speaking, appropriate, aggregate, and/or negate various alternative constructions of "reality" according to some intention or purpose.

I am in accord here with the view that "reality," at least in an objective sense, exists and that its existence constrains what can be said about it (Railsback 1983), but that it cannot in any complete sense actually be communicated or yield "objective truth" (Goldzwig and Dionisopoulous 1989). Our words aren't large enough to hold the all of "reality," but even if they were the space for their enactments as well as any claims made about them would still be contested. "Reality" exists, then, both as an objective presence outside of the metaphorical filters of human language and within the imaginative and linguistic realms of the communicative dimensions of experience. It is, however, only within the communicative dimensions of experience that narratives about "reality" exist and do the business of inducing us to listen and to participate in their constructions.

The communicative dimensions of experience are socially construct*ing* as well as socially construct*ed*. This means more than is usually implied by the invocation of the familiar Peter Berger and Thomas Luckmann (1967) phrase, because the trifurcated simultaneous plurality of "reality" put forth here asks us to conceive not of one dominant, consensus site for negotiations of our co-constructions of meaning, but rather invites us to participate in an ongoing multivocal process of various counterconstructions, various sources of metaphorical approach and political resistance to the shifting sites of meanings (see Morgan 1986; Mumby 1987; Norton 1989). There is, strictly speaking, no one "reality" available to the mutually constructed and constructing communicative dimensions of experience; there are, instead, multiple *copresent* realities.

I do not claim any of this as novel insight on my part. For generations similar claims have been made by philosophers, poets, psychoanalysts, literary theorists, scientists, novelists, and mystics who, however they gained access to the consciousness which embodied this observation, located the site of the problem in the translation of experience to the experience of the translation. What this entails for the interpretive ethnographer is important because it places—much like the balance of weights in the hands of Lady Justice—equal emphasis on self *and* Other, research *and* writing, truth *and* beauty.

The trifurcated view of "reality" has serious implications for the constructing rhetorics we develop to represent the always dialogic nature of fieldwork. John Van Maanen (1988), for example, describes realist, confessional, and impressionist tales as ways of writing narratives that display, in their different stylistic embodiments, different ways of reading and representing "reality." But more important, he recognizes that "ethnographies are documents that pose questions at the margins between two cultures," and, with Roland Barthes (1972), he sees this act of creation and representation as one of "necessarily decod[ing] one culture while recoding it for another" (4). Hence, there is no "transparent" text any more than there can be a "neutral" language code or a truly "consensus" reality.

For these reasons I am at home with the idea of a "plural present." I use this term to stand for "multiple copresent realities" because it is shorter and more poetic and suggests the always diverse, contested, and contingent nature of context, self, and Other as interdependent, interpenetrating features of any interpretive ethnography. The "plural present" is a way of capturing the spirit of diversity, of recognizing differences, and of placing self and Other on equal dialogic and rhetorical footing while releasing from that sense of capture the freedom to explore an imaginative field of representational possibilities for the experiences of living and writing culture(s).

To get at the implications of the "plural present" requires more than a philosophical appreciation for the ways in which reality is constructed. It also requires, I think, an appreciation for how the experiences of fieldwork and the experiences of textual construction are themselves shaped and formed. By "shaped and formed" I mean to convey something I hope is implied already by my use of the "plural present" because it is so difficult to say. It goes like this: Every journey outward into a culture, even your own culture, embraces a sense of what it means to be the Other within the experience of discovering the self; at the same time, every journey inward toward the centers of self embraces a sense of what it means to be confronted as the Other by the self. The result should be both distance and sympathy, mystery and curiosity, a desire to alter combined with the feeling that what is experienced must be left somehow alone. It is to these interpenetrations of self and Other that the term "plural present" is directed.

Reading Back to the Future II *as Ethnography*

Consider, if you will, the film *Back to the Future II.* This is a film (otherwise probably forgetable) that inspires me to read it (at least on one level) as a narrative about the practical problems of doing and writing about fieldwork. You will recall that "reality" is, in this film, trifurcated, but in the analogic sense that means taking place at three different, simultaneous times (1955, 1985, 2015) while remaining in the same critical site or context of a small town. More important for our purposes, there are dual senses of self and Other as active, real actors within these simultaneously existing realities: the "Doc" (1985) is not the same as the "Doc" (2015) or as the "Doc" (1955), or, for that matter, as the "Doc" (1885) who will be a character in the sequel. The same is true for the hero, for his parents, for his girlfriend/wife, and for Biff.

Read one way, this is a film about the changes that occur as a result of our choices of action in moments in time. Very well, that is one interpretation, and a useful one. But read another way, this is also a film about what happens when mystery and curiosity converge on critical sites of self and Other, and on the self *as* Other, and the Other *as* self. For me this is akin to investigating a culture that you participate in on a daily basis, but going into that experience with an eye toward a closer, more exotic reading of what happens there. Sure, signs can be read differently, and often this reading occurs because the signs have been changed and the change—as well as the message of the signs—is what says something about the culture. This also happens in the film. But the reading of things should never be isolated from the reading of persons, as I have tried to show in chapter 5.

There are moments in this film when the hero, the villain, and the wizard intermediary "Doc" all confront who they have been and will be from the perspective of who they are. The message of each one of these encounters is essentially the same: don't look—or better yet—don't be seen by that other self, at least not closely or for very long. This is what happens when you confront the self *as* Other, which should tell us something about our basic attitude and approach to studying the Other at all. It is an attitude, and an approach, of both mystery and curiosity, but it is also one of *fear*. In the film this fear is expressed as the potential cause of a cosmic interruption, a warp of space and time, that may lead to the destruction of the universe. Strong terms, even when spoken in the quasi-comic voice of the "Doc."

Let us go into the body of that metaphor and see what keeps it alive. I believe that at its heart, which is the heart of the pervasive sense of fear that is expressed as a warning, is the issue of the nature of reality and the relationship of the observer to it. What the film shows us is the plural present; but it works very hard in its narrative structure to deny reality to it. The journey into the future, into the past, is one that must be undertaken only because it will get us back to the safety of the known present with some security that the future and the past are in harmony, that time and space exist as a continuum.

In many ways this message can stand as an important critique of cultural ethnography. As observers we try to link the past, present, and future in sentences that underscore their perceived (desired?) linearity and our ability to act upon and interpret that linearity. In the act of writing we create the world, call it into existence, order and arrange it, give voice to self and Other within a context we alone have constructed. In our curiosity about the Other we construct stories about the experiencing of him or her or them, place the stories and the experiences within the frameworks of our understandings, locate their meanings within our extant texts. We observe, but often fail to *see*. We ask questions, but we do not admit that the questions are often asked because we are curious about who we find ourselves to be among them, not because we are curious about who they are to themselves.

One of the subtexts of the film is the need we feel to marginalize the experiences of the Other when their questions, behaviors, and understandings conflict with our own. Jennifer—the girlfriend/wife of the hero in the film—is put to sleep when she asks about the overall purposes of their journey, rendered senseless and voiceless. The hero's mother is similarly marginalized throughout the film as a constructed presence whose body and mind are modified to meet the demands of the men in her life. Although she is viewed with sympathy, she is also viewed as a victim of space and time, a person who cannot speak unless spoken to, a woman who is comfortable when watching men perform and happy only when preparing and serving them food and drinks.

Feminist critique here is obviously useful. But I am after a different kind of problematic, one that complements gender-related issues but that also concerns itself with the depiction of the plural present, the ways in which a film about time travel can be read as a textbook about writing ethnographic experiences of context, self, Other. Read this way, the eye of the camera is really the "I" or self telling the story, and it is a story of the plural present in which depictions of all of the characters are secondary to the progress and plot of the film. Interpreted one way as narrative theory, this is good, even inventive storytelling; interpreted as ethnography, it reveals how limited any story, any depiction of the plural present, must necessarily be when access to self and Other is controlled by the demands of making the tale always relevant and relatively coherent. Viewed this way, how "good" or "useful" would it have been for the camera to have focused on the plight of the mother? Good or useful for *whom?*

Experiencing the Other for Whom?

Writing ethnography in the spirit of the plural present is a way of recognizing the always contested nature of context, self, and Other. It is a step in the direction of narrative progress, I think, to try to get at the dignity of the Other in the same ways that we try to get at the dignity of self. But the process—both of research and writing—is interdependent and interpenetrating. It is done within the communicative dimensions of experience, which means that all of it can never be depicted and what is selected for depiction has a reason for being there. Interpretive ethnography is about opening up the texts of plural present realities by opening up the ways in which such construction can be experienced and the ways the construction can be carried out, but it makes no promises about gaining neutrality as a result.

The experiencing of the Other must always be accompanied by an awareness of self: this much is clear and I think always true. Similarly, the experiencing of self in the quest for the Other must necessarily be accompanied by an awareness that the desire for the experience is often motivated by concerns that have little to do with the Other: we want to have the experience, acquire the understanding, write the article or book. This is not always as clear or true, and it depends, always, on the observer. It is also true that the motivations may change as a result of the fieldwork, as in Dwight Conquergood's work with the Hmong refugees in Cambodia and Chicago (see Conquergood 1985; 1987).

The point here is that even the plural present comes with motives that are, as Kenneth Burke has taught us, "shorthand terms for situations" (Burke 1965). Our quest for the Other, for the experiences and experiencing of them, is limited by who we are and what we want to do even when we make every known effort to display their dignity, the diversity of their lives, and their differences from us. That said, the issue here returns to a series of methodological questions and problems, issues that have to do with the constant, if awkward, weave of interdependence and interpenetrations in plural present texts and metaphors of the Other that are also, simultaneously, texts and metaphors of self. Let us begin with the methodological issue of preparation.

PREPARATIONS FOR THE PLURAL PRESENT

We live on a blue planet upon which exist texts of the Other. It has not always been so.

Imagine a mid-sixteenth-century ethnographer about to embark on a three- to five-year-long trek into the nether reaches of a land about which he (or she) knows little more than a name. It will take, probably, ten or eleven months of long walking and close suffering to get there. Ditto for the return trip, if disease or exotic rituals don't do him (or her) in first. When he (or she) finally gets there, there are no guarantees. We are not talking reservations at the local Holiday Inn here.

Now imagine how one would prepare for such a journey. Remember, we are still in the imagined world of the mid-sixteenth century, a time when it was literally possible to have read—as did Milton a century later—every book that had ever been written (at least books as they were known to exist in the Western world). But let's say there are no books about the place where you plan to live and work, nor is having read a book any particular currency in conversations with those who do not share your language or sense of perspective; let's say, in fact, that you are going to write "the" book and that is the reason for your journey, another fact of your mission that will be utterly incomprehensible to those with whom you stay and learn.

How would you prepare?

This is, of course, a convenient fiction. We do not live in the world of the sixteenth century and there are no places on the blue planet that have not had at least something written about them. If things get too tough in the field we can check into a Holiday Inn and watch MTV, get a decent meal, go to see *Back to the Future II*, get back in touch with whatever it is that we feel we are missing or that we have simply left behind. Even if the purpose of our trip is to "get away" in the hope of getting in touch with something even more primal than our own lives in the city, chances are pretty good that we won't be able to, or at least not for very long.

I am reminded here of Paco Iyer's (1988) quest for the East, in which he found evidences everywhere only of the West, or Bill Bryson's (1989) return to America after fifteen years in England, a trip on which he hoped to find at least one quintessential, metaphor-inspiring American small town, and went back to England not only without metaphors but also newly estranged and overwhelmingly disappointed. The point here is that if you set out these days to find the Other, whether that Other is an idea (like a "foreigner," or the quintessential small town) or a myth (like the quintessential small town or whatever exotica you sense lives in the East), you will inevitably confront an increasingly global and mediated community where geography no longer easily separates the civilized from the spartan.

To go out in quest of the unknown, where the unknown is defined as some distant place and its citizens whose immediate and long-range differences from you mark them (not you) as exotic, is to begin your trip with a flawed logic. Ethnography is no longer about "you" in the quest or conquest of "them"; it is about the voice that emerges from the context(s) you share, it is about the choices you both make in the relational territory you jointly develop. It is about the plural present.

No guidebook can adequately prepare you for this experience. For it is experience, when all the fancier language about purposes, themes, and outcomes is done, and precisely the experience of being alive and finding out what that means to you—that is the only tangible guide. Joseph Campbell (1988) put it best in a conversation with Bill Moyers: "People say that what we're all seeking is a meaning for life. I don't think that's what we're really seeking. I think that what we're seeking is an experience of being alive, so that our life experiences on the purely physical plane will have resonances within our innermost being and reality, so that we actually feel the rapture of being alive. That's what it's all finally about, and that's what these clues help us to find within ourselves" (5).

We don't go out in search of the Other, but of the experience of being with the Other and of the learning that can occur there and only there. Context, self, and Other are interdependent and inextricably intertwined, not only into and with each other, but into and with the experience of the moments we share. To go into those moments—into the here and now of the there and then rather than into some mythic, exotic elsewhere—that is our quest and our singular good fortune.

RECOVERING THE CONVENIENCE OF FICTION FOR DEPICTIONS OF THE PLURAL PRESENT

There is another sense in which I want to explore the notion of convenient fictions, this time by recovering the map for the territory of the plural present it purports to cover.

I have thus far in this chapter been concerned with the philosophical and methodological issues involved in plural present investigations of the Other and with the "convenient fiction" of being able to prepare for a journey into the land of the Other, insisting that such preparation is neither possible nor desirable. This time I want to look at the pronounce-ment of convenience in fiction as a way into the *expression* of what is encountered when Otherness is finally confronted and must be produc-tively dealt with within the communicative dimensions of experience. I am, of course, using the term "fiction" to refer to research and writing styles that seek to represent truth and beauty (Goodall 1989a) and *not* to perpetrate further the annoying habit modernist theorists have of separat-ing fiction from nonfiction as true from false. Fiction, for me, is not about make-believe any more than rock n roll is about youth.

Fiction is convenience. For the ethnographer, fiction is a way of experi-encing yourself and Others as both subjects and characters within narra-tives and a way of seeing the contexts you share as a weave of vocabulary and motive. It suggests possibilities for writing that recover the evocative territory of the plural present of human actions, emotions, conversations, and fantasies by allowing for accurate maps of how those territories come into existence in the here and now of the moment, and for what happens when that happens. Fiction, like the lives it recovers, is about choices made between self and Other and about how those choices are displayed as textual clues. It is about the mystery that surrounds us when we enter, as a character enters an ongoing scene, that time and place where something happens that changes forever the shape and dimensions of what we know, who we are, what we do. *Back to the Future II,* revisited. This time read it as a metaphor for narrative, as a film (read: convenient fiction) about the depiction of the plural present.

Fiction is not just a way of writing the plural present; it is a way also of experiencing the ethnographic quest for the plural present, a way of immersing oneself in the rock n roll, a way, finally, of recovering expressive forms of knowing through expansive forms of showing. Fiction, in the doing of research and writing, requires presence, voice, and positioning, a way of accessing those aspects of the plural present of every context that make it part of the scene, a way of accessing those aspects of self that make you a player in the unfolding drama, and a way of accessing the Otherness of Others that shows, that bodies forth, that reveals. For fiction works best when individual human complexity blurs into the universal human condition, and at the site of the blurring is a story that induces interest in the read you can give it as well as in matters of character, plot, conflict, and outcomes.

Notice here that I am including in what counts as fiction the experience of the read as well as the experience of researching and writing what is ultimately read. Here too is rock n roll, not just as a style or styles of music but as a read given to a situation, a way of accessing through experience the evocative materials of interpretation and meaning.

Which brings us back to interpretive ethnography, which, at this end of the book, brings us back again to the issue of accessing Others. One way into this issue, and a very important one, is through the metaphor of the tourist.

NEUMANN'S TOURIST

Mark Neumann's work centers around the concept of the "tourist." He positions the tourist at a crossroads of culture and cultural studies and sees in the experiences of tourists "the ways culture travels through our lives" (1988b, 15).

For Neumann, accessing the tourist is a matter far more intricate and complex than, say, just hanging out at the Grand Canyon (Neumann 1990), playing blackjack and craps at Vegas, Reno, or Wendover (Neumann and Eason 1988), or watching the choreographic movements of crowds who construct knowledge and experience in the museum that is the world (Neumann 1988b). At the core of his research is the concept of "Otherness" and the ways in which "Otherness" can be accessed through experiences and written about at the discursive intersection of fiction and autobiography. Mark Neumann is definitely a rock n roller, an ethnographer, and I'm proud to say I've drunk, gambled, and jammed with him.

Neumann's world of the tourist begins with an existential premise, a line taken directly from a novel by Albert Camus: "We are all special cases." From here he reads into the photography of published artists, such as Richard Avedon (1988a), more than crafty snapshots of poses, faces, and costumes, seeing through them into a tourist's world of middle-class values and voyeurism that verifies the demand to be special cases appreciated for the complexity of our own individual trip. Photographs are one of the ways we access "Otherness," one of the ways in which the experience of being human in a famous site can be captured and about which stories can then be told. So it is that through the serious photographs of an Avedon or the holiday art that we all have at home that "Otherness" is joined to self and context. The photograph comments, in fact, on the positioning of self within context whether we are the person behind the camera or the subject in front of it. Whoever takes the picture has an angle on the story, but what is the story when *you* are the one compelled to take a picture of it?

It is in the joining of the photographer to those photographed as well as the conspicuous presence and consumptive value of these contextual phenomena in our culture that suggest a much larger issue: Part of the experience of "Otherness" is what we ask them ("Could you tell me how . . ."), ask of them ("What do you think makes geysers happen?"), or ask them to do ("Would you pose next to this wooden Indian for me, please?"), or, in our fear of the asking, simply steal from them when their backs are turned and their attention is elsewhere directed. How many photographs do you own of someone you've never met, some interesting body, some alluring view?

Neumann's tourist is an intersection of culture and cultural studies and a reminder that regardless of the direction taken at that intersection all roads eventually lead back to the activity of driving, walking, or just roadliness in which the metaphors of self serve as both drivers and passengers. So the question then quickly becomes one not of direction—for all roads do in fact lead somewhere—but of the attitude we take when we travel. Are we competent tourists, content to make an experience out of our explanations of that which we see ("All the dirt from the Grand Canyon, honey, is what made California"), however wrong or skewed we may be? Or are we naive observers, gaining the experience ("I've never been here before, but I didn't think it would be like this!") and comparing it to what we think we knew about it before we acquired it? Or are we to locate ourselves somewhere in the gray in-between, partly naive and partly competent, always observers, sometimes explainers, involved in finding in the experience a story of our lives?

Neumann's answer is also mine. It is the rock n roll answer, the interpretive ethnographic answer, the answer that loves the experience of otherness because it does come back to this: *mystery*. Although Neumann, like me, finds it in the philosophical work of Gabriel Marcel (1949a, 1949b), he also finds in the fiction fragments of Dave Eason (1987, 1988, 1989), which include fine lines such as this: "A phantom, I floated unfreely through the summer of my departure, longing to be made real in an immediate and acute feeling, any feeling." Mystery is the attitude, the right feeling with which to begin the ethnographic, rock n roll quest for Otherness that inevitably wraps itself into contexts that bring you out a different, sometimes a very different, sort of person.

TAYLOR'S LOS ALAMOS

Bryan Taylor's voice is not as raw as mine, or for that matter Mark Neumann's. It is a voice somehow more tender, jazzier, more serene. His attitude toward otherness is also one of mystery; however, it is the voice of mystery that surrounds Los Alamos as a site of nuclear meaning.

His angles of approach differ in qualities that make them intriguing. His first study (1988) was of texts written about the Los Alamos experience, and in them he locates scientific and bureaucratic sentences that balance, for their narrators, the more dramatic *sentence* that Los Alamos threatens to pronounce for the rest of us. His second study (1989) was of photographs, this time photographs not of tourists to the place that is Los Alamos, but of family members, persons in whose connections can be located the various sites of nuclear meanings. These are the workers in nuclear plants, most of whom are dying from unnatural causes, if one considers chemical invasions and resultant psychological disarray unnatural causes of death for those who voluntarily expose themselves on a daily basis to the elements of serious nuclear chemistry.

Taylor's work is not yet ethnography, and in many important ways cannot ever be. Twice he has been denied access to Los Alamos, both as a visitor and as a researcher. His immersion in nuclear culture cannot be completed with the requisite on-site visit, much less a prolonged stay. So the question becomes, how can you access Otherness if They won't let you in?

Taylor's solution is to use all the means currently available to him and to keep trying to gain access to that place where he really wants to go. Along the way he makes contributions that help educate him as well as the reading public so that when he finally gets there he will have ground to explore that he has not already covered. His other alternative is to go undercover in the nuclear family, find a way in as a worker, penetrate the secret code. This is far riskier business, but it is possible, and, in the case of Bryan Taylor, it may even be likely. For he too likes the experience of mystery, and the mystery of rock n roll.

ONCE YOU HAVE FOUND THE OTHER, WHAT THEN?

Otherness is not about what happens when the ethnographic you gets out of the office and just walks around. That is just getting out of the office and walking around. Call it exercise, call it good for you.

Otherness is not about going somewhere, even somewhere as exotic as Montego Bay in Jamaica or Tiananmen Square in Beijing, and testing your particular read of what it will be like. That is just testing your particular read of what it will be like, albeit exotic. Be sure to take your passport, and perhaps your American Express.

Neither is Otherness about what I am doing now, on this page, sitting as I am behind my clone thinking about the grander experiences that lie ahead of me, such as lunch or my evening walk through the Avenues with Sandra, or tomorrow's departmental retreat. These are just thoughts, and sitting behind my clone thinking them doesn't get me any closer to Otherness.

Neither does all of what I have been arguing so far add up to Otherness. Otherness is not an argument, after all. It is not a subject, it is not a chapter, it is not a place, a site, or a stare.

It is an *experience*.

It is an experience that involves me and somebody else and the plural present of our shared context.

It is an experience that involves me, somebody else, the plural present of our shared context, and while we share the moment of it, something happens.

I don't know what it is.

Maybe, probably, neither do you.

In fact, while it is happening it is little more than a feeling, an emotional undercurrent that moves time against the soul. Like mystery, like mystery blended with curiosity.

It does not do any figuring. It does not, at the moment, require any figuring out. I am there with somebody else, that's all, and this *thing* happens. Maybe it happens to me, maybe it happens to the somebody else, maybe it happens to both of us, or maybe it happens somewhere in-between or around us or up there somewhere in Thought Heaven, from whence all Great Notions spring.

I don't know. And I certainly don't know for sure.

What I do know is that this thing happens. It's like the experience of jamming that Eric Eisenberg (1990) writes about when he says that what matters is the jam, the coordinated action of two (or more) people, nothing necessarily cerebral about it, certainly nothing about shared understandings anywhere in it.

What gets shared is the plural present.

Eric Eisenberg, by the way, is a consummate rock n roller. I've jammed with him and learned from the experience.

So anyway, this thing called "Otherness" happens. It is an experience that makes me, in this case, quiver a little. It is an itch, an oddity, something awkward and neat, but it passes. Too often, too quickly. In its wake I catch up with part of what went down inside of it, and what that is makes me feel like I know what the word *estrangement* means, for the first time, maybe for the only time.

Estrangement becomes the mystery.

And that is what Otherness is, and is all about.

ONCE YOU HAVE FOUND IT, NEVER LET IT GO

The problem is, if you have experienced Otherness, and if you are an ethnographer, then you have to write about it.

This is where *love*—the freedom to love—comes in.

You have to love the Other as you love your self. And you have to realize that your love is contextualized, that it exists between persons and with things, and that its existence is created in sentences, sentences that always add up to less than what has passed in that feeling of the plural present. It is, at the same instant, to realize that the word *love* is not love, that its four-lettered map is never the full-bodied flesh and blood territory of the experience.

But you still have to write. At least I think you do.

This is where you and I, reader, return to fiction. This is where this chapter, with its insistent voice, its argument, its clowning, winds down, where the you and I that we have created in this particular here and now part ways.

I will go into the next chapter, but I'm not so sure about you. That too, is part of the experience of us and of our essential, existential Otherness. But I wanted to let you know where I was headed, and to ask you along.

This is the return ticket to rock n roll. When you turn the page, if you turn it, you will be there, looking over my shoulder at Otherness.

This time the mystery is in the audience.

Do you hear them?

Listen:

10

Knowing Your Audience, Knowing Yourself:
What Is This Thing Called Rock n Roll, Huh?

What is needed is a working relation between concepts and the facts of experience wherein the former can be checked by the latter and the latter ordered anew by the former.

—Herbert Blumer

The human sciences are sciences about man and his specific nature, and not about a voiceless thing or natural phenomenon. Man in his specific human nature always expresses himself (speaks), that is, he creates a text (if only potential). When man is studied outside a text and independent of it, the science is no longer one of the human sciences.

—Mikhail Bakhtin

The conclusion we should draw from our thesis is a belief that the ultimate metaphor for discussing the universe and man's relation to it must be the poetic or dramatic metaphor.

—Kenneth Burke

STORMY WEATHER

Willie Moffatt's is a Cajun fern bar and restaurant on University Drive, just down the hill from the BMW-and-Buick dealer and across from the chain Italian place that serves soft garlic loafs free at lunchtime and has the audacity to call them breadsticks.

That's okay, nobody complains but me. Everybody else just walks in there with their thirty-dollar haircuts and suited for success, stuff their mouths with *faux* breadsticks, and don't notice that the food that comes after is genuine chain pre-pak, and served lukewarm at that. The parking lot glows with money. It's the shine of the times.

Over at Moffatt's, where I am, there are fewer cars in the parking lot, less overall shine, but the food and the company is much better. This is the noon hour, and in here the only guy with a thirty-dollar coif is the chef, Black Maxie, which ought to tell you something. Besides, there is

a brand-new set of neon on the marquee outside that tells another part of
the story:

APPEARING TONITE!

LIVE!

HUNTSVILLE'S HOTTEST ROCK N ROLL BAND!

WHITEDOG

On the way here—just after the weather forecast predicting heavy
thunderstorms and lightning to begin later this afternoon—I heard the
radio spot on WTAK. It began with a few scorching bars of one of our
Led Zeppelin covers, then the announcer's voice cut in: "You've heard
about them all over town, now come and hear them, live tonight at
Willie Moffatt's, WHITEDOG!" Then the background music changed to
something cooler and the announcer cut back in: "Willie Moffatt's is
proud to feature WHITEDOG tonight, and if you come early you can
hear them perform the new WHITEDOG hit 'I'm Gonna Run to You.'"
Mike Fairbanks's sweet vocal track lifted out of Drew Thompson's lead
ride with the song's beginning words: "Do you remember, the times we
shared . . ." Then the announcer came back in with the tag, "Be there
for live WHITEDOG tonight at Willie Moffatt's."

Not bad, not bad at all. I'd go. I'd pay to go.

Then it hit me. This has been happening a lot lately and I'm not sure I
like it. I'm driving along and hear something about WHITEDOG on the
radio and I start tapping my hand, maybe singing, liking very much what
I hear, and then BAM! it slams into me, just like that, that what I am
liking is me.

I'm in WHITEDOG. That's my rhythm guitar on the radio.

The odd part is that I have to remind myself of it.

It's like some kind of queer amnesia. It's like looking at an old photograph and suddenly realizing that the guy in the middle with the chicken
and the grin is you. No, actually it's more dramatic than that. It's experiencing yourself as the other, an estranged version of seeing yourself as
others see you, and then, just when you are feeling it, the whole social
construction collapses, and when the dust clears that one magical window
on the self disappears.

I am back inside myself, in the singular I of multiple me's, turning off
of University Drive, pulling into the parking lot at Willie Moffatt's,
preparing myself to prepare for tonight, something I could not have ever
prepared myself for, as it turns out.

Once out of the car I am feeling like just a regular guy in ordinary blue jeans standing next to his car, in this case a white Mustang GT, feeling the hint of fun and madness that is everywhere at this moment in the air. Maybe it's the weather, the news of the impending storm against which is the here and now of this breezy but otherwise perfect day.

I don't know what it is. I just know something is.

Something. There is something in the air, something heavy on the way here. Something I'll have to deal with out there near the horizon, sweeping up from the south and west, moving this way fast.

Maybe a tornado.

I take a deep breath, inhale the close surround of life. In the middle of it I smell the garlic from the chain place across the street. Garlic is an alluring scent, its pungent sweetness belying the ugly undercurrent of its nature, almost human when looked at this way, the bulb of it like a world unto itself and its clove looking all too much like an exploded heart.

ENTER THE SWEET MYSTERY OF MY LIFE, MISS CINDY

Once inside I smell not garlic but the four peppers that make Cajun spicing what it is, a zydeco shuffle along the summer of the tongue, a mouthful of bubbles that hot and squeak.

Cindy is the manager. I see her leaning sweetly over the bar, exchanging smiles and lies with a salesman who has definitely loosened his tie and plans to make a long afternoon of it. But not in the way you might think. Cindy is friendly, but that's always as far as it goes, although, like this salesman, you can always dream. She is a tall, handsome woman after thirty with cascading ruins of brunette hair and that classic twinkle in her dark green eyes that promises a story you would like to hear. She is married to a mostly unemployed musician, a big, long-haired ex-biker with a surprisingly gentle nature whose name I never catch but who seems to answer to Hal.

Anyway, I walk in along the brass rail and she sees me and says, "Hi!" like I'm the best news she's had all day. I smile and wave and keep moving because to stop and try to make something out of it would bruise what we have and I wouldn't like that. Besides, I'm a little late and Roadie Dave is fiddling with the board, which means most of the hard work of the setup—the lifting and unloading and stretching and taping—has already been accomplished, and part of my job, which is to keep Dave away from the board until Drew gets here, needs attending to.

"Dr. Bud!" says Roadie Dave. He looks guiltily at me, like a child caught with his pants down and his hands full. He tries to smile.

"Dave, how're you doing?" This from an old part of me, the part of my upbringing that always encouraged making a polite introduction before turning mean.

We shake hands. "I got here early with the truck and set up everything."

"Thanks, Dave. I appreciate that." I really do appreciate it. This is grunt work and I am increasingly feeling a bit too long in the tooth for it. Anybody who has played rock n roll knows what I mean. There is far more work involved than the glitter and glamour you see on MTV.

"I plugged in the mikes and heard this little squeal coming from somewhere, so I thought I'd check it out." Big smile, because he knows this is against the rules.

This is a Big Mistake.

Dave is our roadie, not our soundman. But ever since Mr. Puckett, our soundman, got transferred to Atlanta, Dave has taken it as a sign from the rock n roll God that he is about to move up in the WHITEDOG organization.

But it is not meant to be.

Simply put, he has no talent for it. Twice we have tried to teach him, and twice we have ended up doing a first set that, from the audience's vantage, was all cymbals and bass guitar, which makes it tough to recognize even something as familiar as "Louie, Louie." Both times Mr. Fairbanks has lost patience with Dave, because Dave has shown a remarkable propensity for zeroing his energies in on the lead vocals: the louder Mr. Fairbanks sings, the less volume he gets. So Mr. Fairbanks has sworn to choke Dave to death the next time it happens.

This is the weave of the context on this story.

"Dave." I put my hand on his shoulder. I sigh. "Dave, I'm going to have to beat the shit out of you. You know that, don't you?"

"But Dr. Bud, I was just . . ."

"No buts, Dave. What's the rule?" I am looking down at the floor now, shaking my head and putting on my very best *disgusted*.

"I know what the rule is, but Dr. Bud . . ."

"Dave. The rule." Now I am looking directly at him with an earnest expression that lies uncomfortably at the intersection of caring and pain.

If Dave was a dog at this intersection, he would be one of those big, fat, happy, and not terribly bright dogs, an Irish setter gone too early to table food who bounds out in front of the truck anyway.

"Okay, Dr. Bud. The rule says I'm not supposed to touch the board until Drew or Mike gets here."

"Very good, Dave. And why do we have that rule?"

"We have that rule because Mike will choke me if I fuck up the board."

"Right. And what happens after that?"

"After Mike chokes me, I die and he goes to jail."

"And then what?"

"The WHITEDOG band will have to find a new lead singer."

"Exactly. And what's the problem with that?"

"There is no better lead singer in the world than Mike."

"Precisely." I remove my hand from his shoulder. "Now show me what you did before Drew or Mike gets here and I will try to save your life."

"Thanks again, Dr. Bud." Dave looks relieved. Within the text we have created this scenario has become familiar. I don't understand it, but there it is. I mean, here is this grown man, all 250-plus pounds and nearly thirty years of him, a guy who had until recently major hardware responsibilities for a Fortune 500 computer firm, and a genuinely nice guy at that, and he somehow can't help getting himself into trouble. He's got an ex-wife who is still suing him after all these years, four kids that he is devoted to, a mother he moved back in with after his divorce, and somehow, somehow in the interior universe of discourse that lives inside his head, he can't quite get anything completely right.

But we love him, this poor country-Southern son-of-a-bitch WHITE-DOG roadie. He quit his job mostly to spend more time helping us out. And now his ex-wife is suing him because the money stopped coming in. But he doesn't care. He is having an experience, as he phrases it, the time of his life. "That's what life is all about, Dr. Bud," he once told me, eternal Silver Bullet in his fat hand. "That's what God put us here for. To experience it, the all of it." He grinned his big toothy grin. "Ain't that right, Dr. Bud?"

Who am I to argue?

I think about this while I repair the damage he has done to the setup of the board.

Cindy, audience to all of this, brings me a beer. "Nice job," she says, dark green eyes twinkling.

"What?"

"Handling Dave. That was fine." She puts her hand on mine. It is warm, and that is all it is. "You have a very nice touch."

Then Cindy, and the mystery of her, walks away. I bet she's kind to all the animals.

ENTER NOW, MR. DREW THOMPSON

Drew Thompson, aka the astonishing Drew Thompson, saunters in just after one in the afternoon.

Today he is costumed in one of his business suits, so he curls his beige jacket around the arms of a waiting chair before stepping up to the stage to check things out. This is part of his transition ritual, a ritual we have all learned to go through on the days that catch us moving out of the world of commerce and into the world of commercial rock n roll. Watch this because next Mr. Thompson of TMT Real Estate, on the way to becoming the astonishing Drew Thompson of the WHITEDOG band, will fire up a Camel Light.

He fires up a Camel Light. See what I mean?

"Hey man," I say from the rear of the room, back where the board is and from where Dave has just retreated to go hide in the men's room for awhile.

"Hey man," comes the ritual reply. Part of the male-bonding thing is what just transpired. Did you catch it? Don't worry, you'll see it again. Then we'll talk about what it means.

Drew checks his mike connections, then does his own personalized job of hooking up four sets of footswitches to his Rocktron Multiplex effects unit, the only unit he allows to rest on top of his Peavey power amp. He does this part of his ritual slowly, carefully, engulfed in bluish smoke. Within the ritual he at first loosens, then removes the tie, rolls up his sleeves, coughs. He looks up when the cigarette is spent, calls out for a drink, and at that moment has become, although not yet fully in his costume or voice, once again a WHITEDOG.

Cindy brings him a drink. He drinks only Johnny Walker Red, Johnny Walker Red on ice. From the shadows at the rear of the room I watch their cheerful exchange, different from my experience, and smile to myself. How is it that we ever believe we can know another person, somehow convince ourselves that we can get inside of someone else, when all the evidence suggests quite the opposite?

Dave bounces out of the men's room a new man. If I didn't know better I'd swear he does drugs. But drugs are off-limits for Dave as for the rest of the WHITEDOG band. Or, I should say, we limit our intake of drugs to caffeine, alcohol, tobacco, the noxious polluted oxygen of life, and maybe, just maybe, the occasional controlled substance.

This is the rock n roll life, as I have known it.

Drew completes his check of the gear and then joins me at the board. In truth I know almost nothing about the board, so my fooling with it is limited to reversing whatever damage Dave might have done. Then I turn everything over to Drew, who creates the WHITEDOG sound. He actually studied commercial music in college and worked for awhile for a band down in Mobile as a mixer, so whatever he says, goes.

While he works we talk. We talk about the weather, the cloudiness and humidity of it, guess what it will mean for the crowd tonight. We talk about his day as a salesman, and during this conversation the salesman at the bar, dreaming of an afternoon with Cindy, pays his tab and walks out. We talk about room acoustics, but during this talk I just listen, knowing almost nothing about the language of acoustics. Then we talk about women and beer, and laugh together because this is part of what men do. Somewhere in the midst of these preparations I restring both of my guitars, polish the necks and bodies, retune.

Four hours pass. The sky outside is darkening and bitter and eerily green, its wind sudden and harsh; the air it brings with it is hot and damp, heavy with ozone. We can feel the closeness, the intensity in the narrowing eye of the coming storm.

ENTER MIKE FAIRBANKS, STAR AND GUY

We are awaiting the arrival of the rest of the WHITEDOG band. Everyone is always late, this is part of it, this thing called rock n roll in which time matters only if you think it does.

And when you are the star it hardly ever matters.

Have you noticed lately how time, in all of its pretensions, such as age, deadlines, history, and so on, doesn't matter as much as it did? Maybe it's just me, but I don't think so. I think it is part of the rock n roll of social life, in which all of us are increasingly encouraged to witness ourselves as stars and in the witnessing to do away with time, at least temporarily. I am reminded here of how old we are getting to be, those of us who were part of that mythical Woodstock that everybody seems to have attended, and how young we still seem to be. Look at the photographs of your parents when they were your age. Go ahead, do it. What do you see?

You see the movement of time against the soul. You see otherness. You see time that mattered.

This is where Mike Fairbanks, star and guy, walks in. Actually, Mike Fairbanks *never* just walks in. He walks in like he owns the place, which, in a very real rock n roll way, he does. For Mike Fairbanks, Mr. Fairbanks—his name when wearing his sharp Italian business suits; " 'Banks" to the other guys and "Oh *Michael*" in a very soft voice to all the women who always seem to want him in ways that are clear and really quite impressive—for 'Banks is the star.

He is the leader, and the lead singer, of WHITEDOG.

Let me tell you about him.

'Banks is a guy's kind of guy in the old world, certainly prefeminist way. He is a true friend, a beer drinker, an exceptionally talented athlete, and he is smart and very hardworking. In 1984 he was the last man cut from the United States Olympic hockey team, an event that changed forever the direction of his life. As he puts it now, he realized he was never going to be good enough in that sport to get where he wanted to go, so he altered his course. He still went on to star on and eventually captain the hockey team for the University of Alabama in Huntsville, but we are talking scholarship, a way to get through college without draining the old man.

That's where I met him. He became my advisee in the Communication Arts department, the kind of wise-guy student who wins your favor because behind all the hype and quickness is something special, something raw and honest and maybe even true. He graduated on time with a solid grade-point average and was elected, at the beginning of his senior year, president of the student body. Rare among athletes, wouldn't you agree?

He went on to work for Intergraph, then moved over to B-BCSC as a Quality Leader.

What a title. It's perfect.

But Mr. Fairbanks, for all his talent, has a bad case of women.

Women, it seems, fall for him instantly and then, after their time with him, either end up his lifelong friend or hate him with an intensity that is pure and unyielding. In the four years I knew him while he was in college he always had the same story. He'd meet a girl, he'd tell her he was just out for a good time, she'd hear these words but would interpret them to mean that somehow she was different and therefore she would be the one to change him, and then there would be the inevitable scene with the old girlfriend confronting the new girlfriend with him confused and in the middle, which he would interpret as a clear sign of his interest in good times guaranteed for all but which the old girlfriend would see as an end and the new girlfriend would see as a beginning. It was like that, it was like that, it was like that.

Radical feminists take note: it always takes two to party. You may believe that men are all liars and cheats, which mostly we are—I've always said that given half a chance a man will become a dog—but what is it in women that makes you believe you can change us, that makes you not only open the door but give us an invitation to outright dogness?

We are all pitiful hopefuls. Men, women, and dogs.

But, as I have said, Mr. Fairbanks is a guy's guy from the old world, and with killer Italian handsomeness and a big heart he is the kind of rare young man who exists, it seems, solely to be the star. The problem is where, after all the high school and college athletics, after the schoolbody presidency, after all the lesser glories—after all this has been done, has been conquered, where can he find the right place, the appropriate context, from which to launch his imminent stardom?

His world is one of insistent energy and interesting contradictions.

He is like physics after Einstein.

Call him 'Banks, shake his hand, see him as a star and guy.

Anyway, he walks in. When you picture this, picture a young Frank Sinatra, still a little unsure of himself but covering up extremely well by playing the King. Picture him moving up to Cindy, arms outstretched, picture her falling into them, picture all of this in the soft lights of playful make-believe that is, at the same time, somehow real. "Baby," he says, and that is all he says, and that is all he ever needs to say because in the moment that is that word, she is his.

You gotta love this guy. You've got to.

"Hey man," I say.

"Hey man," he replies.

"Hey man," Drew says.

"Hey man," he replies.

There is an easiness to rituals like this. There is much comfort living in them.

"Dr. Bud, did Dave follow all the rules?" This from 'Banks, right on cue.

In my best Monty Python fake-peasant British accent I say, "All but one, sir. All but one."

'Banks rears his eyebrows, joins in on the accent. "And which one might that be, sir?"

I pretend not to want to say. "It was a very *small* rule, actually, sir."

"Quick, man, let's have it."

I cover my face with my arms in a tragic gesture, say only, in a small accented voice, "The one about touching the board, sir. That one. But only that one."

"I must choke him, you know."

"Oh, but I wish you wouldn't, sir. Not this time. He's been, well, pitiful, sir, ever since I caught him. I chastised the bastard meself. I shouldn't think he requires choking, not today sir."

"I don't know. I still feel the need to choke him. It is a rule, you know."

Drew walks over, joins in the merriment. "I think it was such a small rule that you should overlook it this time." Drew puts his hand on 'Banks shoulder. "Do it for us, sir, for the good of the band."

"Oh, very well then. For the good of the band."

'Banks points a finger at Dave, who, during this scene, has been perched sulkily on a barstool, Silver Bullet in hand. "You've been very bad," says 'Banks. "Do you repent?"

"Oh hell yeah," says Roadie Dave. "I fuckin' *repent.* I mean it. I really do."

We break up in laughter.

Dave looks at us, "What's so funny, guys? Huh? Huh?"

This only brings more laughter, Cindy and the barman this time joining in.

Dave shakes his head and does his very best Sad Dave look. "I'm just an asshole, I guess."

He looks pitiful, then hopeful, but is a WHITEDOG nevertheless.

"Well, he may be an asshole, but at least he's *our* asshole. Isn't that right?" This from British Drew.

"That's right," says 'Banks.

And that's the end of it.

'Banks walks over to the stage, fully the young Frank again, and tests his mike. Outside there is the bump and roar of distant thunder.

ENTER THE BASSMAN, AND THE BASSMAN'S GIRLFRIEND

I. B. Alexander, the man who fingers expertly the Yamaha five-string bass, walks in with his silent girlfriend on his arm. He is dressed in black and black leather, and looks like a Detroit hood; she is dressed in creamy pinks and whites, and looks like the Detroit hood's girlfriend, which is what she is.

I. B. Alexander (the initials don't stand for anything; at birth he was christened that way) is not a hood, although he is from just outside of Detroit and does look the part. He is a quiet guy with a degree in finance who works in a bank, but when he is onstage with WHITEDOG he becomes someone else. He becomes I. B., resident wild man, the guy who dances around a lot while he plays, the guy who at some point in the performance will lie on his back on the stage and continue to play his bass, the guy who will release from that somewhere within some indefinable something that gets the crowd in a particular sort of mood.

It is a frenzy, this mood. There is an odd mix of anger and comedy in it, the sort of anger and comedy that I. B. himself exudes in conversation—that is, when he talks, which isn't often, which is why when he is what he is onstage with WHITEDOG there is something crazy in it, something that matches the unresolved craziness in the everyman aspect of any crowd. And it is something that, when performed, *works.*

I. B. Alexander walks in, removes his bass from its velvet case, tunes it, checks it, returns it to its case, turns around and is suddenly I. B. Gone is the part of him that is Alexander, that reads like a banker, that includes a degree in finance and all the experiences those words somehow suggest. What we have in its place is I. B.

"Hey man," I say.

"Hey man," he replies.

"Hey man," from 'Banks, and then Drew, and then Roadie Dave.

I. B. just grins. It is a big, sudden grin that takes over his face, and then just as suddenly as it came is gone. He doesn't say anything else.

He walks over to his silent girlfriend, they look at each other, and then leave to get some food before the show.

Normally we would do a full sound check, but our drummer isn't here and the dinner crowd is beginning to come in and Cindy doesn't like us to do a sound check with the dinner crowd around. 'Banks is unhappy about this, but it will pass. It is time to go to the Kettle.

We walk outside just as a thundercloud breaks above us and rain pelts into the ground around us. Overwhelming ozone, penetrating heat. A jagged smear of bright yellow lightning happens. Then it happens again.

I am still thinking tornado.

The traffic on University Drive is already trouble.

THE KETTLE

This is the part of the ritual where we go home, shower and change clothes, and then meet over at the Kettle for the $4.99 Sirloin Special. It is an interlude in the drama of the band, a good place for reflection.

So here it is.

This is a chapter about the experience of Otherness, in this case Otherness that is defined as an audience for a rock n roll band. I have introduced all of the band members except the drummer, whom I will get to when he shows up, which will be just before the show. In those descriptive rhetorics of introduction I have chosen words to body forth who they are, as well as who they appear to be. I have done this because it is important, I think, to realize that regardless of where our performances take place we contextualize the eloquence of it by taking from the whole cloth of self those threads of life that we believe fit both the demands of place and the demand curve of the audience in it. Partly this is planned performance, but partly it's not. It is this thing we do, or that is done to us or for us or that comes out of us from the vague somewhere of our continuous conscious/unconscious territorial struggle, our soul jamming with and against the police of our being, the emerging surface display of our innermost outermost knowing and doing.

This is depth rock n roll, the force of pure, inarticulate feeling that shows itself, finally, in expression. What is important here, though, is the recognition that this is precisely what is happening in the audience, in the Other, in the very seat of Otherness, wherever that is and whatever phenomenology informs it. What moves us also moves the Other.

The result, if you take Kenneth Burke's tack, is identification. But identification is a large word with decidedly modernist implications. It speaks to structural considerations and bags the force of emotion, the essential drive and panic of "suspended agitation" (this is Dave Eason's phrase) that marks postmodern living. Increasingly I think Burke was right, probably exactly and precisely right, about his main historical period, but not for the rock n roll of ours. I can read his critical work, say, "Wow, that's neat," multiple times, but still never fully believe that his words speak directly to my experiences.

There are differences, differences that matter.

I want to leave that thought right there and go back into the narrative. I want to return to the band, go inside the Kettle, remember the feeling that is in part due to the terrible storm that is still out there brewing. God, those skies are dark. Lights are on everywhere a good hour before they should be.

Something is about to happen. I just know it.

THE KETTLE, THIS TIME REALLY

The waitress who serves us is older than dirt. She wears a uniform whose name tag identifies her as Barbara.

She has been seeing us come in here before shows for many months now and knows the order by heart. But she always asks us anyway. It is part of it, part of the experience of it, part of the rock n roll that includes Barbara.

We like her and always leave a big tip.

Outside the rain is heavy and the sky is bruised by its own blacks and blues. Maybe this is the end of the world.

We order, we joke around, we eat. Somewhere a Nero fiddles.

I find out, through 'Banks, that my ex-wife and her boyfriend are going to show up tonight, a fact that makes a certain turn toward uneasiness occur around the table. I try to dispel it, but they know I'm just faking it.

"So." Drew pauses, puts on his long face and very best British accent. "Do you think you should try to strangle her?"

"No, I think not." This from me, also in British.

"I think we should *all* strangle her." This from 'Banks, who is obviously just kidding. "Then we should strangle him, just in case."

"Just in case of what?" Me, this time.

"In case of . . . Oh I don't know, good measure or some rot like that."

Back in my own voice, I end this conversation. "I'm not going to do anything. She's coming to see the band. And besides, I've invited Sandra."

Looks are exchanged everywhere around the table. I have just entered the strange world of Otherness for both Mike and Drew, turned a corner onto a mean street down which lies danger, only nobody knows where it will be or what it is. They are watching me go down it, they want to warn me, but on their faces I read all of this and they see that too.

"Perhaps we should strangle her too," says 'Banks. We all break up.

If Kenneth Burke is still right about one thing (although I must add that I think he is still right about a lot of things), it is that comedy is the only thing that can save us.

This is where we are when Barbara brings our food. "What's so funny?" she asks.

"Nothing," I say. "Nothing's funny." Then I begin laughing uncontrollably. There are tears in my eyes.

"Something's wrong with this one," Barbara says. "He don't even know why he's laughing." She looks oddly pleased to see me having a fit. Imagine how happy she would be if I was choking.

She has her reasons.

This is a woman I tried unsuccessfully to interview. She said, "What for?"

"For a book I want to write."

She laughed. "You want to write a book?"

I nodded.

I might just as well have told her I was planning a leisurely walk to the moon. She left the table quickly in a way that let me know she either didn't believe me or didn't want to be interviewed or both. The next week I tried again. This time she said, "No, I wouldn't know what to say."

"Just tell me what you think when I ask the questions."

"I don't think," she said. "All I do is work."

I place that statement here as evidence. Of what I am less certain.

Tonight when I finally manage to calm down and stop laughing she is still staring at me. "You write books, huh?" She shakes her head. "No wonder the world is crazy."

I place this in evidence also, because I think she would want me to.

BACK AT MOFFATT'S, WHERE MR. FRENCH IS

The trip back to Moffatt's is slow because University Drive is littered with accidents. The storm is a little Vietnam, a war being fought heroically all around us while we are studying our fame. Red-clay mud has

swept over the roadways, making the surface as slippery as the movement
of troops at night, or metaphors to college sophomores.

Is that an ambulance I hear in the distance?

Moffatt's neon lights welcome us as us, as WHITEDOG, as in appearing live tonite! See Mom, I always knew my name would end up in lights!

Inside now we see Michael French, aka The Kid, our drummer. "Hey
man," he says when he sees us.

"Hey man," says Drew.

"Hey man," says me.

'Banks just walks to the bar.

"What's with him?" This from The Kid.

"You weren't here, so we couldn't do a sound check."

"So?" Michael grins, all cigarette and lips. What you have just heard
and seen is his essential attitude, best summed up in an album title by
Joe Walsh: *Nothing Matters, and What If It Did?* Then the grin, the
cigarette, the lips.

Michael French is nineteen. He dropped out of ninth grade to devote
his life to full-time rock n roll.

He lives at home with his parents, who are supportive. His father is a
long-distance truck driver and his mother, I don't know, I guess she just
stays at home managing Michael, his brother and sister.

They want him to be happy. They hope he'll be rich.

They live in the woods outside of Decatur, Alabama, next door to
Michael's small rehearsal building and sound studio. This is the kind of
rural area that is difficult to enter except through the imagination. You
turn off a two-lane blacktop that has no shoulders, drop off the other side
onto a pot-holed dirt path, and are at once greeted by the haunting bark
of several large inbred guard dogs. The sign on the fence says BEWARE!
and you do.

It is always dark here, due mostly to the overgrowth of trees, but also
due to that hidden territory of the human heart that darkens life when
fear seizes it, sends all the light to the eyes and all the blood to the ears
and waits, *waits*. But, like the rural real estate we have already been into
and come out of, there is nothing, really, to fear here. Nothing that is,
except the Other, the Otherness of the imagined Other, the life you
have imagined for the Other, your own sense of guilt and tragedy and
strangeness that may have nothing at all to do with what this is about.

I was always happy to see Michael there.

Things lightened up considerably after that.

Michael used to be a metal-head. Still is, but knows the steady money
around here is in classic rock n roll. He sings and plays a fine metal guitar,

but his instrument is the drums. He began playing when he was four and was starring in a country band at nine. He practices four hours a day every day of the week, approaches his practice seriously because it is his calling as well as the localized site of his career, plays the drums with a highly professional attitude. He is nineteen, but only sometimes.

He is the one the young girls go for, with his perfect, chest-length, pin-curled hair and his tall, angular good looks. Very European, actually, which is very unusual for a rural Alabamian. He is the one who wears the loose, torn T-shirts and either flashy pajama bottoms or skintight black shorts, always the lime-green tennis shoes, always the Marlboro cigarette. He is quick in a way that suggests his lack of formal education has not really hurt him, a testimony to what American high schools don't do anymore as well as to what his parent's did.

He once said to me, "Dr. Bud, I respect the hell out of you for what you're doing. I mean you're a doctor, a teacher, and you can still rock n roll." He was sincere, and I appreciated it. From the Otherness of him those words told me not only who I was, but also why I was standing there from his perspective.

This is The Kid, genuine as the weather, young, raw, a new pistol loaded with great expectations.

Repeatedly I have heard him say that rock n roll is his life, by which he does not mean just music but the whole experience of what he is and what he is doing. He can't imagine it any other way. He knows that the difference between the low bucks he is making and the high bucks he is working toward is just a bit of luck and a lot of hard work away. He visualizes it like an athlete visualizes victory. Every night is his night; there is just no point to yesterday, and tomorrow we might evaporate.

So here is Michael French, drummer and Kid, living the rock n roll life in the burning here and now of a cool eternal always.

Applaud him, America. He is your new native son.

FIRST SET

About a hundred people are crowded into this little fern bar when we mount the stage for our first set. I see among them my ex-wife, Donna, her boyfriend, and over on the other side of the room Sandra and her friends. This is going to get interesting. There is a big nasty storm all over town tonight.

Ethnographer always, I am driven to want to watch.

But to watch is also to play, and after tuning up and warming up with a few of the flashier chords I know, I find myself suddenly in the middle of my first dual lead ride with Drew doing "The Boys Are Back in Town," a classic Thin Lizzie number that always gets the crowd moving.

Onstage, if you are in the audience, we are five. From left to right there is me and my '57 Strat, I. B. and his Yamaha bass, The Kid and his Tamas, 'Banks and his cordless mike, and the astonishing Drew Thompson over there on the right wearing his Gibson and a smile. During the first set we seduce the audience to movement, get them up dancin', get them dry enough to order more beers from the waitresses who know that when WHITEDOG plays they make the big bucks.

"Boys Are Back" ends and "Two Tickets to Paradise" begins, immediately. 'Banks is already having fits over his inability to hear himself on stage and is gesturing to Roadie Dave back at the board to turn his monitors up. Dave, as usual, turns them down. This doesn't affect the crowd because what they hear comes from the Internationals that face them, but there can be a big difference between what you hear onstage and what the audience hears out on the dance floor.

It is like giving a speech and feeling that your nervousness is showing and everybody sees it, which they mostly don't, which is oddly disconcerting. It calls into question the whole notion of what it is that they do see, even when you aren't nervous, even when you aren't giving a speech.

While this little drama takes place I am thinking that we drew a larger crowd last week than Eddie Money did, and here we are playing one of his songs. That was our Space and Rocket Center gig, playing for the Intergraph International Users' Conference, where about three thousand people got so far into what we were doing that they wouldn't let us stop. When the woman in charge of entertainment threatened to unplug us, I leaned down to the audience and said, "She wants us to stop playing, do you?" and witnessed, firsthand, what effect the right rhetoric can have in a crowded room. They picked her up and carried her outside, deposited her on the lawn, and locked the door. We kept on playing until somebody had a heart attack and the ambulance folks had to come to the rescue, allowing the woman in charge back in, this time with her guards.

That was fun; that was rock n roll. That was what happens when the audience becomes part of the show, something WHITEDOG has a bad habit of inspiring, something we love to do. When it was over at the Space and Rocket gig there were suit jackets, many ties, and even a pair of lacy underwear left on the floor. One leftover guy who had obviously had too much to drink wanted to get into a serious conversation with us about his road trip with the Stones. We left him on the floor, passed out over the power cords. Another guy, fully sober, an executive with money and access to the company's Learjet, wanted to fly us with him to his beach place in Florida.

But we have daytime jobs and can't do it.

He promises to get us down there sometime and we promise to do it.

This is bullshit but it's a part of it and this is also part of rock n roll.

We are playing our sixties stuff when I come out of this memory, my fingers doing "Good Lovin' " and seeing a full dance floor. 'Banks is out there with them, getting everyone hot and making every one of them feel like a star. Already, this is getting to be Large. Outside the rain keeps thundering down.

Forty minutes later we end the first set with The Kid's heavy-metal version of "Wipeout." Over in the corner by Drew a young girl is getting seriously drunk, her legs crossed and moving to a quickening pace of mimic fornication, her cheeks flushed, her mouth a pink pout. In front of me a guy is watching me play, trying to commit to memory what I am doing so that when he goes home, maybe with that girl, he can play it too. Between these two individual audience members lies the whole continuum of rock n roll as social life, as experience, and as music.

So tell me, reader, how are these ends different from the ends of your life? Are you going to tell me you don't walk around full of unreleased emotion? Are you going to tell me you don't dream of satisfaction, of self-display? Are you going to tell me your own fragmented life doesn't have music to go with it, to help you when you need more than anything else to feel again, and to feel again like this?

Get out of the way.

BREAK ONE

"Hi, Bud," she says.

This is Donna, the woman I once loved and was married to. What would you say?

"Hi," I manage. I am fiddling with my gear, retuning my guitar, trying to seem occupied and wanting to seem distant. Lightning breaks across the room, filling it suddenly with a great and awful light. In the split instant of its sinister glow I recognize her face and see its sadness and its resistance to sadness, its stern resolve to be okay in this new life she has chosen.

She stands there, waiting. For what, I no longer know.

I only know I don't feel connected to her at all. She is now as different and strange to me as anybody I don't know.

"Excuse me," I say. "I have to go meet some people."

I brush by her. Even her perfume is foreign.

She stands there for a long time, they tell me later.

I walk over to Sandra and her friends. She smiles at me, but I can tell this is difficult for her. She and Donna were big friends for a long time, which was for the years that led up to last week, which was when Sandra told Donna that we were dating.

Lord, why does life make us difficult?

There's enough hurt and pain to watch without having to contribute to it.

I put away a couple of bourbons, which have the combined effect on me of spring water.

Sandra looks stunning tonight.

I don't know what's right any more.

"Dr. Bud, come on man, it's time to play." This from 'Banks. He has had his inevitable scene with Dave over the monitor sound and is anxious to get back onstage.

I stand up, and Sandra touches my sleeve. "If this is too uncomfortable I'll leave," she says. She is serious and I appreciate it but I don't want her to go.

"No," is all I say. And then I say it again, louder.

SECOND SET

I look out over the audience and see a large party, a crowded museum of faces, costumes, and attitudes.

Who are these people? Why do they come here?

Playing rhythm to our Hendrix and Led Zeppelin set does not involve very much thought. Hendrix and Page were great lead artists, so this is all about the astonishing Drew Thompson, and over here on the corner of the stage good ol' three-chord me is just along for the ride. 'Banks is fully in his element now, out with the crowd, and I. B. is warming up to his full stage presence. He leans over to me and reminds me of a chord change I usually miss and we laugh about it. The Kid is all punch and run on the drums, really playing them, not just keeping the beat.

So it is within this weave of context I consider, seriously, the audience.

It's been my experience that the people who come to hear us play on Friday and Saturday nights are willing partners to the dance of life. They work hard to make a life space that includes the full range of themselves and collectively claim that the one thing they fear is neither death nor nuclear war but emptiness. They don't want to wake up one morning at the edge of their own endings and wish they had done, had experienced, had lived.

So they go out there. And when they get out there they go for all of it. "It" is never defined, but with Joseph Campbell I tend to believe "it" is the experience, the rapture of living, and not some esoteric meaning for life.

They don't believe the news. They talk about it like any other television show, call it "Just Media."

They believe instead in the lyrics of rock n roll.

They don't read much outside of thrillers, newspapers, the occasional sports magazine.

They hear the cool infrastructure in the heat of the music and want to recognize it in the known causality of their lives.

They all went to college or want to or are in college now. They want the profits of college. They want to have had the experience of it with the radio on.

They believe in wrapping themselves in the slick among Japanese cars, but still want to be seen wearing the German eventually.

In the meantime they settle for megawatt stereos.

They know exactly what's on TV.

They can sing the theme songs.

They can talk about love, they can talk about marriage, but they can't talk about love and marriage in the same breath and keep it together.

They can sing about the words, though, all night long.

They can talk about each other a lot.

When they do, they do the lyrics of life.

They do believe, I repeat, do believe, in the power of money. Nothing comes close to it in their prayers. Nothing.

No surprises here. Rock n roll is a commerical enterprise.

So much for the generalities.

When you speak with them you find individual voices that are desperately happy in the struggle to define and know and live in their own mysteries, mostly unhappy in the everyday routines of jobs and lives. So they live half the time or more outside of themselves, avoiding the boredom that is the real enemy inside.

This is the outside that is the inside of rock n roll, the part with a strong beat that empowers, energizes, feeds the ego and makes you a star, if only in your own car, if only when you see yourself singing in the silver screen of your own rearview mirror.

Once we experience ourselves living on the outside of who we are through the inside of rock n roll we never look back. For it is here, maybe only here, that dreams come true. It is here, maybe only here, that words *and* music go together, make something of themselves, and in the making make us something as well.

This is better than church, better than school.

Make life, forsake war.

This makes us want to make love rather than just get laid.

This is a big sex metaphor, isn't it? It seems like I have always lived by this particular river.

Maybe the whole thing is a big sex metaphor, rock n roll as fucking.

But not *just* fucking. Never that. Not anymore.

Maybe fucking is the metaphor. The word that charges headfirst into first mysteries and feels good at the same time. Is this the first principle of rock n roll?

Oh, sure, there are a few in every crowd who are not even aware of mystery, who do want to *just* get laid, preferably with *just* someone new and *just* on a regular basis, but press them as I have pressed them on this and you hear within all that boredom something they prefer to hide deep inside themselves, some presence, some awareness, but they are not sure of what.

They have no metaphors.

Fucking, for them, is *just* fucking.

Rock n roll is *just* music.

I have witnessed their boredom and found it only dull.

This is where their Otherness, for me, breaks down, and something else opens up just a little bit, but neither you nor I can quite squeeze inside it. Our words won't work, they don't speak to their experiences.

And that is what is wrong with them, and that is what makes what they do feel wrong, and that is why when they do *just* get laid, with someone new and on a regular basis, which is easy enough, it is never enough.

You have to go inside the mystery of self to find the mysteries of life. You have to get inside the mysteries of life to know what enough is, and then you have to recognize in the drama of the mystery where enough is in the mystery that is the Other. Just opening up a little bit won't do it; you must be willing to risk it all, you must be willing to venture, no, to find the *ad*venture inside.

You must own this experience, not just buy into it.

Bakhtin, by the way, came to this one from an entirely different vantage a long time ago. In his time and country there was no rock n roll; instead, there was carnival. This is what he found there: "not a spectacle seen by people; they live in it, and everyone participates because its very idea embraces all people" (1984b). For Bakhtin, this form of social life was evidence of the presence of an absence in people's lives, something he termed the "second order," something to resist the "first order"—the bureacracy, the boredom, the rule-bound authoritative voice of every-body's ordinary life.

I have never met an audience, by the way, that wasn't also the show. This is rock n roll, their Bakhtinian carnival. They know that even if they don't use those words, that's why they come in their best cars, wearing costumes, acting out all those mirrors they have played in while the radio, the stereo, or MTV supplied the metaphorical rush. The few bucks they pay to get in is not to hear the band, but to jam with us, to filter their own unutterable feelings through our perishable breath, to dance inside the music of self and Other and context even if they never leave their tables.

Let's examine them closely. Enter their Otherness.

See that woman at the table over there, the one alone with her make-up whose make-up is a cover-up of something she experiences as skin but knows, way down deep in her heart, is something that's just plain missing? See how she flirts with the guy posing at the bar as the friendly cowboy, the one with two tequilas in his multiringed hand? Can you feel her hesitation? Can you sense his next move?

We are doing "Love Stinks" now, by the way.

He doesn't really want her, and she knows it. Probably she doesn't want him either. But they are here in the downtown now of tonight, and they aren't getting any younger. He walks over slowly, letting her see him as he wants to have her see him, still muscular, not an ounce of fat, good meat that through his precious smile he hopes turns into something better than that in her eyes, a good heart maybe, maybe just good for a laugh. He asks her if he can join her; I see him mouth those familiar words, she says something flip but smiles, so he joins her and it goes on like that, it goes on like that, and it goes on.

They are living in the show tonight. Let's hear it for them.

If this read is true, rock n roll is for them a metaphor for the open road, that wide and spacious head territory that allows for, maybe encourages, the chance meeting of strangers and opens up certain possibilities for life. Here the radio plays only their favorite songs. Their lives, as they have know them, live only in a narrative, and that narrative, for whatever reason, has not yet been enough.

They are ready for danger, they hope for love.

Watch how gently he takes her hand now, how his smile has become laughter, and how she laughs with him and returns his touch. Now let us look away, leave them alone.

There are Others here enough to watch. Consider with me, if you will, the young among us.

I don't have as much empathy for the young any more, now that I'm no longer pregnant in that way. By young I mean demographically somewhere between seventeen and twenty-one, old enough to drink illegally in Alabama but usually get away with it, old enough to vote and marry and pay taxes and acquire things, but we all know there are issues involved here that those numbers and statements can't catch.

These days the young among us seem to be impenetrable in their awkward Otherness, and I, for one, wonder if I was ever really young in that same way. But that is like asking to examine the photographs we spoke of earlier, the ones of our parents when they were our age, so here again we come up with this strangeness of time and its absence, and the turn life in general has taken with the advent of rock n roll as something much greater than music, much longer than youth. The young nowadays look infinitely younger than I remember looking, but they dress much better and seem less inclined to be driven by wild ideas.

Mostly, they resist the rock n roll life. They come here because they have nowhere else to go, and this is only a place to come to, a place to get dressed up for, to be seen in, a place in which they can purchase experience, buy a drink. They don't know the music.

They want to live rich as engineers.

This is a metaphor, I think.

I made a point of spending time with Michael French, for just this reason. I guess I was trying to get in touch with nineteen again, some foolish middle-aged nonsense notwithstanding. He was nineteen, not between seventeen and twenty-one, but it was as close as I was likely to get. I wanted some vestige of youth, anyway.

But Michael French was only nineteen part of the time, like when he would call women pussies and claim he didn't care how they got him off so long as they did.

Talk about your basic engineering attitude.

Even 'Banks, who was never appalled by anything that had to do with the word or fact of pussy, was appalled by that one.

But as I was saying, that was a rare display of nineteen for Mr. French.

I remember one night after the bar closed and he and I sang "Every Rose Has Its Thorn" all the way through by ourselves in nearly perfect harmony. I remember how in his eyes I thought he was seeing something in the language of that song that was just beyond his reach but at the same time was close enough to be part of his life experience. I thought that at that moment of sharing I had discovered something about him; but maybe not. Our experience together was just jamming, just coordinated activities we both knew the words to, and given the wide differences between us that may have been the all of it, and in a very important way that was enough. I thought I had discovered something about his nineteen as well, but I hadn't. Nobody has been nineteen like Michael French.

At least nobody I know.

I'm thinking about all of this while we're ending our second set, ending it with "Whole Lotta Love." This is the set, by the way, in which love is the theme and love is the football; the messages we play run the full course but always come back to the essential yearning that sticks love with an identity somewhere between great pain and great pleasure, love as a word in a series of songs that collectively suggest a lot more and a lot less than love itself ever remembers being. It all ends up in a climax gush and scream, but the gush washes out in a sea of movement and beer and the scream fades even among the best lungs.

Then it was God's turn to speak.

Thunder shakes the building and the lights dim, but our instruments—thank you sweet rock n roll Jesus—never fail us. Maybe God is speaking to me directly, warning me about my tendency to generalize, to move from the individual to the group, the here and now of rock n roll to the always that never is and never will be. And maybe Jesus, who was, after all, God's rock n roll son and who did, after all, die once already for our sins, is up there jamming with the WHITEDOG band and doesn't want the song to end.

I don't know.

I left the church years ago, preferring the energy of faith to the boredom of religion.

What I do know is that when the lights come up I see the cowboy and his new sweetheart closer to each other, holding hands and oblivious to God, Jesus, or the weather, and I swear I know that cowboy is telling that lady the story of his life.

The girl in the corner with the previously fornicating legs is now on her feet in front of Drew, dancing for the pleasure of it, sweat dripping off her blonde bangs onto the parquet dance floor.

'Banks is making sweet hard love to the microphone, holding on to that last high note, that one great rock n roll climax, holding on to it until his throat is raw as freshly butchered red meat, holding on to the high note of it because it's one of the best messages in the whole of rock n roll.

I. B. is on his back, the banker no more.

The Kid is out there in drum hyperspace, doing physics and biology and the higher math that gets you there.

Sandra is dancing, dancing into her own space, her own future.

And Donna, Donna is out the door.

This would be the last time I would ever see Donna, because sometimes, just sometimes, we get exactly what we ask for.

Ohhhhhh . . . yeahhhhhhhhhhhhhhhhhhhhhhhhhhhhh.

BREAK TWO

There is a scene in every mystery where the narrator tries hard to figure out what this all adds up to.

There are just such scenes in life.

Sandra and I are doing just that, over at that table by the Miller Genuine Draft sign in the corner. We are talking it out, this thing that has happened between us, and all around the words of this conversation is the fact of how someone we once thought we knew could become someone else entirely.

This is another way of experiencing Otherness.

For Others do change. Through the scenes of life that they enact, or that they enact with us, they *become*. Constantly they become. So it is never enough to define them, to come up with some word, some language, for who and what "they" are. For what they truly are is changing, often right before our very eyes.

I have been guilty all night of this.

But rock n roll is not perfect and some of us do wear glasses. Our vision may be corrected to 20/20, but how we interpret what we see hardly ever is.

Maybe it can't be.

This is where the physics becomes poetry.

This is where new metaphors begin.

Sandra, we are surrounded by music and fools, but we have some good friends too. We are packed with our own memories and filled with the fluffy stuff of shared dreams. I just know it.

Sandra, my heart engine has been shut down for a long time, and there is a big hole in it. I've been all out of fuel. But when I look at you I see a restart and maybe in time a full recovery.

I don't care about God, Jesus, or the weather any more.

I know that somewhere there is always a storm.

I know that prayers go somewhere, if only into outer space.

And I know that this thing called rock n roll is deep inside of me and even when I quit the band to move to Utah I will just be moving it somewhere else.

This is who I am. Can you stand it?

What I am saying here, San, is can I interest you in me?

She doesn't want to answer this now, not in here, not in the context of this night either. But there is a certain quality in her expression, the soft blue movement of her eyes, that gives me strength.

How is it, reader, that two that were once Others can become you and me?

What is this next song?

I know I don't know it, but can I learn how to play it?

THIRD SET

The third set is rowdy, *always*.

We are nearing the midnight hour and there have been many beers, leers, fears, and gestures expressed and consumed. Styles of speech are loose and often slurring. All this and a whole lot of weather too.

We do the Doors justice with a long WHITEDOG version of "Road-house Blues" that slides into an even longer "Red House," through which the audience becomes one with the mood of the music, which is a mood made up entirely of sweet, dirty blues.

Rock n roll almost always comes to this.

It is *hot* in here. Every sense of the term.

We have upped the ante on hot as a metaphor, moved into a whole new way of making emotional poetry out of the here and now.

From where I am standing this scene looks like a Baptist version of hell. Everyone has the look of pure drunken fornicating ruin and nowhere is repentance in sight. The Angel of the Lord has joined hands with the Holy Ghost and is headed for the soft backseat of an old Chevrolet parked in the lot outside. And that angel is *ready,* honey, and I wouldn't be surprised if the Holy Ghost was carrying a gram or so of coke, either.

And we all know, don't we, exactly what that means?

All the so-called good people have gone on home, and only the best of the rest are left. Madness and alcohol and loud electric music that have slurred the collective speech now blur the individual distinctions between self and Other, bodies and souls rub and bump and grind, there is slut dancin' going on right down in front of me, and all those previous good intentions about making love instead of getting laid have somehow turned around, lost the sanctity of their borders, their logics trashed in the overall lost-and-found frenzy.

Some of this anticipated sex will actually happen, but mostly it's just a big attitude and the swell of an expansive feeling. Mostly this is just nineteen looking at seventeen like I was looking at nineteen earlier myself. Mostly this is just rock n roll after midnight, when, as Eric Clapton and the WHITEDOG band put it, "You just let it all hang out."

I am out there in the emotional poetry myself.

This is one hell of a loud poem we've got here.

One hell of a *fuckin'* poem.

Fuckin' A! Fuckin' *allll right!*

This is the part of the night in the social life of rock n roll where who are you is no longer the right question. Who are you has become will you or won't you, do you or don't you. We are talking coordinated actions here. There is nothing cerebral about it.

We have moved out of head physics and into emotional poetry, out of the medium-cool questions and into white-hot answers.

There are only two possible answers. One continues the hot, the other does not.

And, from a rock n roll point of view, only one of them is correct.

It's when you get home, later, in the much later that is tomorrow, when you cool off. That's when the questions start coming at you again.

Talk about your basic patterns.

What is this thing called rock n roll, huh?

THE END OF THE NIGHT

Twice the lights have been purposefully dimmed and "Last call!" has been called out.

Finally we have to stop. We ride Hendrix out on "Hey Joe," which talks about women and guns from the point of view of the hands that hold them.

Now it's past 2:00 A.M. and the last rowdies have been teased out, tossed out, or just guided to the door where their wandering can continue elsewhere.

Inside the lights are up and the air is cloudy and gray. Outside the storm has passed into Tennessee, leaving wet streets littered with downed trees and roofing, the aftermath of ozone and havoc. There is a lingering presence, too, of something ineffable and mysterious, something that a dark storm always leaves behind, maybe just a readiness to see life a little differently, maybe a knowing brought out of the fury of the sky that nothing will ever be quite this way, or the same, again.

At the door I fire up a Camel and think of Popeye. He liked all kinds of music, he loved to dance.

Sandra's gone home and promised me some time tomorrow.

Tomorrow night we will play here again. The Saturday crowd has always been different, their difference a sum that adds up to a certain sense of mystery that becomes what we will play to. The order of the songs will change, and with it the physics of all this and the poetry.

All the dramas will evolve, all the actors will appear in new clothing, and there will have been an entire day on the blue planet between this and then, an entire day with its time and its weather.

Nothing much will change. But it will go on.

This is still rock n roll.

'Banks joins me at the door, gives me a look that is somewhere between I'm tired and I wish you'd quit smoking. I love this guy. I am going to quit smoking, but only when I leave the band and this town and drive across America to Utah.

There I can be clean again.

There are the higher altitudes.

"Good work, man," I tell him. He shakes my hand and we are men together.

"Super job," he replies. "We really packed the house tonight."

"Yeah, we did."

"I'm going home, get some sleep. Sound check tomorrow at four?" It is not really a question; 'Banks is the leader and this is his decision.

"Fine. I'll be here."

'Banks slips his jacket over his shoulder, finishes his drink, turns back around. He lifts his right hand and raises his voice, announces his farewell. Everyone stops, replies. Sinatra again and perfect, aware of the essential attitude of closure, of the need for endings that he will always claim he is no good at, but is.

See him now, reader. See him walking outside to meet the ozone and the night on his own terms, one strong man against the odds and the women and the weather, one performance ended and one night closer to his dreams. He gets inside his big machine, a burgundy T-Bird Turbo Coupe, and the first thing he does is turn on the stereo and slide in a tape.

He's still working.

This is still rock n roll.

I. B. and his silent girlfriend move by me; he says good night for both of them. He is carrying his bass in its case and his woman on his arm. He is stylin'.

He is gone.

This is still rock n roll.

The Kid has already been outside with his girlfriends, choosing among them, I guess, for the honors still available. He is a smile, a cigarette, and lips. He gets his jacket and tells me he's got "places to go and people to see." I am barely hearing, having spent the past six hours standing next to my Fender Pro 185 amp at sonic volume, so it comes to me as "places to go and people to be," which seems more than right.

I wish him well.

This is still rock n roll.

Drew and I will drive home slowly with the radar on. When we get there it will be 3:00 A.M. in this time zone and we will still be wired. We will drink sour mash bourbon and trade talk about women and music and money for a while, laugh and smoke Camel Lights, a couple of guys on the quiet other side of a fine rock n roll night.

Then we will run into the end of the night. It will stop us suddenly, cut us off from wherever we were and leave us sleeping. In our sleep will be nothing.

In the distance and mist a slow black train will pass.

Somewhere in Tennessee a tornado will finally touch down. It will kill two children and tear up the land. An old man, snatched up from his sleep by the swirling whirl and curve of the storm, will come to in another county, still under the covers in his bed, bolt upright against a lone tree that stands at the corner of a cotton field.

A new song, by a new band, will soon be released.

All the answers will become questions again.

But there is still you, and me, and this thing, this thing called rock n roll, between us.

PART FIVE Coda

11

Putting It All Together: Mystery Is the Detective's Metaphor

The road to empirical validation does not lie in the manipulation of the method of inquiry; it lies in the examination of the empirical social world.

—Herbert Blumer

Two voices is the minimum for life, the minimum for existence.

—Mikhail Bakhtin

It is a craft of the faintly damned and the inveterate outcast who take up the calling in the first place. May their souls be saved elsewhere.

—Douglas Birkhead

DISCOVERY/MYSTERY

This has been a book about the discovery of mystery. It has also been about the mystery of discovery.

This book has also been a series of stories about the mysteries of rock n roll as a form of life and interpretive ethnography as rock n roll. Read together as I have read them together, they provide the metaphor of discovery as a way of experiencing the writing of social life. Chapter by chapter, these intertwining tales have investigated various ways in which context, self, and Other are interdependent and interpenetrating sources of discovery, and at their common heart is always a discovery of mystery.

This is the last chapter in this particular volume, but the discoveries and mysteries continue. There can be no completed self any more than there can be a completed understanding of the Other, no more than rock n roll or experience or the contexts that give voice to them can be fully captured and expressed. We all move along, defining the borders, negotiating the boundaries, living our lives.

This book has been a reflective space, a pause in that movement. In that pause discoveries were made. They were made in the language of

259

metaphors—of context, self, and Other—and persons and things were exposed to those metaphors. In their contingent terms and through the readings of performances they inspired, I discovered interpretations of cultures, the significance of certain signs, of certain clues, of certain symbols, and what got written about was a certain yet contingent moment in the meanings of persons and things.

Mine is the voice—the metaphor—of an organizational detective. It is a voice acquired from a part of a secret history of the twentieth century, a history that whispers about accidents of genetics, timing, conversations, and purposes that conspired to create me in the image of real and imagined ancestors. It is also a metaphor derived from my experiences as a compulsive reader of contextual clues, a seer of mysteries in the vague in-betweenness of persons and things, an agent of interpenetrations. It is a metaphor made out of the languages in which I was trained—rhetoric, social science, literature—languages that bring out latent critical tendencies, that conspire to evoke drama in the everyday, that encourage an essential suspicion that is itself a source of desire and satisfaction.

But this detective, his voice(s), his metaphor, is not content to remain aloof in the pause of the reflective moment. I am too much the participant ever to remain indoors for very long. The detective that is me needs now to move out of these pages and back into the flow, to go outside and do the walking around that opens up new cases, that provides for new mysteries, that induces me to play in and with the ever-present rock n roll of social and professional life.

Before that happens there are some obligations that need to be met. This is the place for summing up and tying in, for commenting on what has happened in these pages and for predicting the future, at least as far as research and writing interpretive ethnography about American cultural experiences are concerned. To do this I will divide the discussion where in the world it cannot be divided, into manageable units of thought that will appear as manageable units of thought instead of as quick glimpses of a calm spectral light in the toss and swirl of purposes that suddenly cross paths, which is how this sort of thing often happens out there where you are, away from the pages of this book.

The fictive divisions are drawn from three desires, three sources of intrigue really, that have been discovered as a result of writing these texts. It is as if the detective's reading of clues on one case suddenly coalesced to produce a reading of what was essentially another case, a different and more speculative case, one that recurred with a nagging consistency throughout these investigations.

To make matters more complex, this happened not once, not twice, but thrice. By then the clues could not be ignored.

These clues were also elusive, gaming little devils. They were the kind of clues that kept me up late at night tracking them down, trying to chase and corner them, reading into them, finding connections between their presence in the context of self and Other that comprised the text I was then living in and the meanings suggested by that presence—and that text—in my life.

I believe I have caught up with them. They aren't devils, though. They are symbols, and not even symbols of devils. But they are LARGE symbols, bigger than You and Me. They must be approached carefully and given more than one reading. I recommend we do it together, like this:

COMMUNICATION

Because I am a detective trained in the arts of rhetoric, you might suppose that my interest in communication would be natural, if not all-encompassing. To tell the truth, it was for a number of years.

But sometime during the winter in 1986, for reasons that now seem in memory cold and vague, I stopped being attracted to this symbol. I moved away from it and into the broader symbolic domains of culture and cultural studies. I did this because something was wrong with my own conception of communication that could not be repaired without relocating all of it— both the conception and its repair—in the incongruities and displacement that come from immersion in a foreign language, a language that makes you think about your native tongue, and think about it *differently*. My occupation, to use Kenneth Burke's (1965) language, had become a preoccupation, and thus preoccupied I had a trained incapacity to see. I needed a change.

For years I had more or less accepted that communication relies on shared understandings, that it is a process that creates consensual relationships. This assumes, I think, that to "have communicated" means to "have had" shared understandings, which in turn assumes a metaphysical alignment of cognitive space as well as a congruence of the complex systems of biological and electronic materials of cognition.

Furthermore, I assumed that shared understandings became permanent fixtures in the enacting of relational processes. This means, essentially, that you and I can create what the ancient Greek and Roman rhetoricians called "commonplaces"—literally places to go to find things to talk about that we can both understand. Maybe the elite Greeks and Romans did that, but ours is a very different world. Assumptions of simple symbolic similarities must coexist with assumptions of profound differences in how those symbols get produced, enacted, read.

Here again, in the intellectural baggage we have inherited from the wisdom of the ancients, it is *shared understanding* that drives both the motives and outcomes of communication and that sums up whether or not communication has been "successful" or "effective." Think about that for a minute, please.

At first it seems a little bit like liberal economics, doesn't it? We are speaking here of shared understandings as a code for commonly available resources, a code that suggests a neighborly, helpful community of user-friendly symbols. "Shared understandings" is a feel-good term, and in the flow of that feeling there is a steady undercurrent of cerebral and behavioral niceness. There is a politeness about this metaphor of inquiry and response that leads suggestively to imminent consensus, to relationships that can be constructed in a highly principled manner on agreements, and those agreements become a sort of firm, unyielding, unchanging foundation upon which is then built a rational life of harmony, sympathy, and ease.

We could even go a little further, as have some theorists, and suggest that communication based on shared rules for constructing "legitimate" understandings—such as Jürgen Habermas's (1979) theory of communicative action—would lead to a better world, a world in which everybody knows what is going on because the only things going on have meanings that everybody has negotiated and understood. God, that is comforting, isn't it?

But it doesn't work in practice. And, as comforting as it sounds at first, the longer I think about it the more disgruntled I become. In a world of universal rules and rational argument, what gets marginalized is diversity, complexity, emotion, voice, resistance, and change. This begins to be a sinister plot, not a good idea. This begins to sounds like the Thought Police to me.

Even the World Court, where rules for argument are strictly enforced and everybody is supposed to abide by the outcomes, has seldom achieved its utopian vision of justice. Bigger nations still ignore the legitimate claims of littler nations, and because (thank God!) there is no World Army to enforce the decisions the losers often just yawn and walk away. Let's have some more fun in the air tomorrow, they say. Here again, however, it is not the absence of a World Army that is entirely to blame; it is the faulty conception of communication that assumes shared understandings are at the core of "proper" or "appropriate" or even "productive" human relationships.

Are you uneasy yet? Ready to retreat to a kinder, gentler metaphor, even if it is flawed?

I know how that felt—at least I know how it felt inside of me (who am I, after all, to assume I know how you feel?)—because it was the feeling I lived in for a couple of years while suffering from communication apprehension of a different kind. It is the sort of head problem that won't go away because you've wrapped up so much of yourself in its solution. It is also the sort of head problem whose existence in your head is part of the problem: you can't very well go to a physician and say, "Look, Doc, I don't believe in communication any more. And I don't think much of shared understandings, either."

Walker Percy (1989) has a marvelous analogy that fits here, one that he applies to a similar problem in literary studies. He says that when you get this sort of bad feeling about the wrong directions your discipline is adopting, it is like standing in a crowd at a party and finding that you need to advise a friend that he had best attend to his fly. Something is open that shouldn't be, something might show that might not ought to, and yet most of the party crowd is walking around as if that is okay. Now, the problem here is no mystery. There is clearly something amiss; the difficult question is what are you going to do about it?

In my previous collection of Huntsville tales, I attributed this feeling of malaise to the way in which communication scholarship was being written. That was a first step toward the larger issue of what communication is *about,* a way of working the detective method on cases that revealed—through practices of reading and writing, and in those practices confronting context, self, and Other—clues to this larger mystery of communication. We are speaking here of "communication" as an empirical fact existing in the everyday practices of American culture at the end of the twentieth century, not "communication" as a contested term in the literature of various disciplines.

That was one way to begin to answer the question.

In this collection I have gone deeper into those clues of everyday practices of "communication," bringing to the reading a more complete investigation of context, self, and Other. These investigations have, in turn, taught me that the cases presented here have been *about* their individual topics and subjects as well as *about* the mysteries of communication that were found within them. This was to be a book, if you turn back to the Preface, that addressed the everyday practices of rock n roll as social life and as an analogue to the writing of interpretive ethnography; it was also a book that wanted to add to the scholarly conversation about "communication" ideas about presence, voice, and positioning.

Well, that is what I intended to do, but it turned out to be only a part of what needed to be done to tell the story, to answer the more difficult question. When I realized that, the story got bigger and the answer more elusive. And it was in the telling that it got bigger and more elusive.

As I mentioned earlier, writing this book has been a process of discovery. Principally, it has been about the discovery of an answer to that difficult question about "communication" where "communication" refers both to the empirical world of social practices and to the literary world of contested terrain. To get at the "it" that refers to both of these territories, I have displayed *mystery* as an alternative approach to the problem-solution, technorational methods that have traditionally informed the literature on the complex phenomenon we call "communication." It is important to note here that mystery, either conceptually or practically, does not buy into shared understandings. It engenders an attitude of suspicion, of inquiry, of private investigations of "the meaningful orders of persons and things."

Here again I refer to the groundwork set in place by Kenneth Burke, Herbert Blumer, and Gabriel Marcel. Each in his own way approached the idea of communication in social relations—and of social life—as a mystery; each in his own way worked out the terms of his own sense of context, self, and Other in the dramas of everyday life read into and sometimes against the literature each was reading and committing.

From Kenneth Burke (1969) I have learned to see mystery as the basis for reading differences as important to the attributions of significance to the acts and conditions of communicating. I have also learned how to read mystery as the heart of desire, and desire for communication as the transcending of social estrangement.

From Herbert Blumer (1970) I have learned to see mystery as embedded in the symbols we exchange when we communicate and to find in their ambiguities and strategies sources of self and Other. Symbols are exchanged. They are also performed and interpreted, and when this happens it happens *not* according to some commonly seen internal genetic image on which are written the commonly understood rules for behavior that assume shared meanings. Instead, they are read against a larger screen of the experiences of living and of discovering who we are in the truth(s) of those experiences.

It is in and through the experiences of living, in and through the acts and conditions of participating in relationships, groups, and cultures, that we discover who we are, what we are about, and decide what we must do. Like the flickering light of phenomenal knowledge that characterizes the dancing images on the back wall of Plato's metaphorical cave, our knowing is never perfect, never certain. But our doing is. And it is from doing—from making and sharing activities that involve the sharing of symbols—that we come into being, and from that being learn what we know.

We are not rational animals, but we do have the capacity to act rationally.

We are not animals that share understandings as a result of communicating, but we are animals who can share acts of understanding and exchange symbols in acts that we can name as communication.

We live in the phenomenal Big Cave, and the shadows that dance against the back wall are not dancing for us, but because of us. While the shadows dance we go about the business of living.

From Gabriel Marcel (1950) I have learned to appreciate anew a version of existential phenomenology that values human agency and at the same time admits to caves, to shadows, and to mystery. I have also learned to read mystery as an invitation to participate in the rock n roll carnival of social life, and to locate within that participation the idea that shared practices—not shared meanings—form the "how" of communication. I have also read into his work that the further reflective mysteries that haunt the difficult questions of "why?" and "what for?" may be used to comment upon the "how" of communicating, may give to our space for understanding "communication" various ceilings and floors, but that those comments should not be confused with direct, active participation. Ontology is not epistemology, although their boundaries often blur.

So I come to this alternative construction: *Mystery is intrinsic to our attempts at understanding communication.* Mystery suggests that communication is not a problem to be solved, but a life force to be experienced. Ontology, in this case, precedes and informs epistemology. What we know about communication depends on what we do as participants in its interdependent processes, its shared activities. The quality of our knowing depends upon the quality of our participation and the quality of language we bring to the shaping of what we do and know. Communication is not about shared understandings, even though they can and do occur. For me, communication is about *shared activities* that make possible negotiations about the meanings of contexts, self, and Other. It is indeed a process that creates relationships, but within that statement lies buried a much more profound message, and that message has to do with the negotiation of boundaries.

Communication as the Negotiation of Boundaries

What happens when we share activities? The answer to this question depends on how we do what we do when we share those activities. The "how" question here refers to the issue of negotiating boundaries, by which I mean the boundaries of context, self, and Other as well as the ways in which our talk and actions will be interpreted. I am referring here to walking around in everyday cultural life and to the lives that we lead in and through our scholarly conversations that occur when we act as participants in the literature.

As I pointed out in the first essay in this volume, the border metaphor is pervasive in ethnographies that address issues of communication and culture. As human beings we live on the borders of territories we have ourselves negotiated, marking our spaces, our values, our heritage, our sources of expertise, our individual sensitivities, habits, desires, and passions, with speech and with silence. We move together, we remain where we are, we drift or split apart because the activities we share in that space become meaningful (or not) as shared activities, and in the act of sharing (or not sharing) them we are always conscious of the borders, the boundaries.

In some communication activities, as Douglas Birkhead (1989) puts it, the whole point is to blur those boundaries, to test them, to move them closer or to push them back. In other activities, as Eric Eisenberg (1990) puts it, the effect is one of mutual blurring, so that we lose sight of the established markers and have to negotiate the meaning of this new thing that we have created, this new space we have manufactured out of words and actions, through the activities we continue to pursue. This is what he means, I think, when he tells us that "jamming" is communication as organizing, and organizing is, this way turned, a way of using the experience of communication as transcendence.

Viewed in these ways, then, communication is about the ways and means of negotiating boundaries. It is also about the experiences we have and interpret when we are doing this. Too often in our professional discourses about communication we have neglected the role of experience and interpretation, not as facts we can pack into sentences like this one, but as sources of information about where the boundaries are and how they get negotiated. Experience is where we collect the data of life, and whether those experiences are gathered from reading, writing, observing, feeling, sensing, moving, being, listening, or speaking, they always involve boundaries that must be negotiated because they involve boundaries we call self, Other, and context.

So it is that the journey chronicled in this book took me inside out, literally. What is presented here are the processes through which I moved and shared activities with Others, immersed myself in experiences, and discovered that the mystery that led me into these private investigations— a mystery I thought was about self, Other, and context—was really another, more pervasive mystery about communication as the negotiation of boundaries. But there is one additional aspect of boundary making, blurring, and breaking that I need to articulate.

Presence, Voice, and Positioning as Boundaries

In the Preface I mentioned that one of the contributions I hoped to make to the ongoing scholarly dialogue concerns the writing of interpretive ethnography. Specifically, I wanted to address the issues of presence, voice, and positioning by showing, through the activities described on these pages, how these practices can inform an expanded notion of what constitutes studies of communication and culture. Here again I am negotiating boundaries, this time professional and written ones.

Presence is rapidly becoming an outdated issue, at least as far as book-length manuscripts are concerned. Since I began this project several presses have launched new scholarly series in communication and cultural studies, and all of them seem open to interpretive ethnographic work. Journal space is still limited, but the limitations seem less a matter of head space than page space and quality submissions. Perhaps this will change. But if it does change, it will do so not because of shared understandings or some essential consensus we have reached about scholarship; rather, it will change because in the acts of writing and reading we will have negotiated new boundaries that include what has previously been marginalized or negated.

Voice is still very much a concern. What I have tried to do here is to display the interpenetrations of voice, the polyphonic qualities of the contexts of social life, and to suggest, following Mikhail Bakhtin (1984, 1986), that as researchers and subjects of research we speak through and in several voices. For me, the issue of autobiography is essential to the practice of interpretive ethnography. Knowing where I came from, what my vocal heritage is and has been—both the "real" and the "fictive"—plays an important role in monitoring what I think I am reading into situations and the motives and behaviors of the Other. I find in my voice traces of persons past and present, real and imagined, and in that discovery I find legitimacy in the opening up of my texts to the multivocal qualities of those whom I study and with whom I share activities.

In a way, this sense of multivocality is reminiscent of R. D. Laing's (1971) notion of "mapping." Laing uses "mapping" to refer to the ways in which families reserve for children the voices, behaviors, and patterns of experience they have read from the texts of other family members' real and imagined lives. It is a metaphor that suggests that life is a territory and a journey, and the mapping process allows families to re-create known territories and thereby reveal a preferred path for their offspring. This is another way of negotiating the boundaries, of inscribing on the body in question other bodies from the text. The journey of my territory has certainly been shaped by the textual patterns established by my friends and relatives, and I can't now pick up a copy of *The Great Gatsby* without seeing my father's face, without feeling a Carraway to his grander visions, without reading his escape from a past and a family he wanted to forget into the territories I have myself been through.

Positioning the author in the text is a practice that follows logically from the acceptance of multiple voices and of communication as the negotiation of boundaries. To negotiate boundaries requires knowing where you and the Other are standing, which in turn requires placing yourself, as well as the Other, in a specific context. To speak through multiple voices, to display the multivocality of all contexts, requires attaching the voices to the bodies and—again—placing those bodies somewhere in the unfolding story. Notice, please, the word "in" toward the end of the previous sentence. The idea of positioning requires the narrator to be placed "in" the story, not to stand outside of it. Sometimes this means, as I tried to show in the narrative about group decision making, acquiring the voice of a voyeur. But even then this is a voyeur whose body is present on the scene of the action and whose voice moves through a variety of possible influences in the working out of the story.

So I hope, at this end of the project, that I have kept my promise to make good on the writing experiments for presence, voice, and positioning. What I have tried to do is show (rather than tell) what I mean, to place in print the experiences I want to share with you, and to display in that showing why prose dedicated to democratic propositions inherent in this rock n roll worldview can provide a different angle on research and writing about communication and cultural studies.

ROCK N ROLL AS INTERPRETIVE ETHNOGRAPHY; ROCK N ROLL AS A FORM OF SOCIAL LIFE

Len Hawes offers an educationally inspirational and practically therapeutic course in conversational analysis at the University of Utah. It requires the instructor and students to live in the theories it teaches. He too believes in communication as the negotiation of boundaries, but he takes the topic of boundaries into mutually constructed conversational space. When he does that, one of the voices he uses is that of the eighty-four year-old-save-the-trees activist in the play *My Dinner with André* (Shawn 1984), who, upon meeting the protagonist, inquires where he is from. "New York," replies Andre.

> And he said, "Ah, New York, yes, that's a very interesting place. Do you know a lot of New Yorkers who keep talking about the fact they want to leave, but never do?" And I said, "Oh, yes." And he said, "Why do you think they don't leave?" And I gave him different banal theories. And he said, "Oh, I don't think it's that way at all." He said, "I think New York is the new model for the new concentration camp, where the camp has been built by the inmates themselves, and the inmates are the guards, and they have this pride in this thing that they've built—they've built their own prison—and so they exist in a state of schizophrenia where they are both guards and prisoners. And as a result they no longer have—having been lobotomized—the capacity to leave the prison they've made or even to see it as a prison." And then he went into his pocket, and he took out a seed for a tree, and he said, "This is a pine tree." And he put it into my hand. And he said, "Escape before it's too late." (92–93)

Len uses this dialogue to illustrate a variety of lessons, but I want to appropriate here only one lesson, and that is the lesson of research boundaries and how they are constructed. Communication is, according to the late Richard McKeon (1970), "the architectonic art capable of informing all disciplines and subjects." Despite the freedoms inherent in this claim, ours has often been a prison-house of research and writing practices, constructed in much the same way as the activist's understanding of New York.

We are talking boundaries here.

We are talking escape.

We are, therefore, talking about rock n roll.

Rock n roll is a form of social life and is used here as a metaphor for the research and writing practices of interpretive ethnography. If rock n roll is an experience of communication that creates new boundaries—as music, as fashion, as history, as art, as a way of knowing, as a way of being, as a way of doing—then it seems reasonable that to capture that experience (so far as capture is ever possible for that which is by nature resistant and changing) requires a form of research and writing that is also capable of negotiating new boundaries.

But rock n roll is never just about the negotiating; it is more properly about the experience of reading self into the texts of the Other, and it is about an interpretation of context that prizes shared activity over shared understanding. Rock n roll, finally, is not a solo concert to an audience of one, but—to borrow from Bakhtin again—a carnival event. It is a place for resistance to the established order, for the reign of laughter and madness, for the overt and nuanced displays of multiple copresent voices, and for the blurring of boundaries between artist and audience, music and dance, life and lives.

In the carnival presence that is the everyday experience of rock n roll, dreams come true, but only for a little while. It is an experience that induces you into its emotional centers, holds you on its seductive lap, and when you wake up or come to you find that what you went through was better than where you are now, so you go out again in search of that ageless feeling of being alive, that sensuous rush of immediate, close experience, of rapturous carnival, of daring pleasure, of sharing activities that lift you up and out of the everyday wash of identities, roles, jobs, work, age, and fear into a negotiated, playful, intoxicating space that transcends all of that for all of *this*.

Rock n roll is like a tornado. It comes down like a hammer and within its moment changes forever everything it touches. Sometimes it destroys, sometimes it rearranges, and sometimes it just moves things and persons around for a little while. While it is happening it happens intensely for all those who are caught up in it, yet where it is not happening life goes on as if nothing has happened. This is a strange phenomenon, but as a metaphor it awakens another part of the reading I want to give to communication and culture.

Several times in the previous chapters I have dropped into the middles of sentences a phrase that reads something like this: "the side-by-side existence of the modern and the postmodern." What can this mean? From the angle of everyday cultural experiences, this phrase means precisely what it says: you can't walk through a city without observing that architecture, art, literature, politics, and film representing modern and postmodern ideas coexist. There has never been, nor will there ever be, a total replacement of the modern by the postmodern. More important for our discussions here, individuals who walk around with us in the cities also represent those side-by-side territories, and many of them currently seem to enjoy the inevitable blurring of the genres they suggest. Persons and things, reader, persons and things . . . . When I read these together, I, at least, cannot escape the fact of the simultaneous plurality of the postmodern and the modern and the endless variety of its blurrings.

So it is that the practices of communication in everyday life testify to the plural present. We use all the available channels of discourse and deportment in our cultural displays; there is dominance and resistance, and resistances even to the resistance. Ours is a culture pattern that, however grudgingly at times, is fashioned out of the spirit of representative democracy *and* bureaucractic incorporation; ours are cultural experiences made out of the interpenetrations of work and leisure, cultures and subcultures, permanence and change, arts and artifacts, memories that differ about the meanings of the past and visions that differ about the shape of the future. It is toward that sense of commonality, alternity, and plurality that I locate the "side-by-sideness" of the modern and the postmodern.

We can live in a variety of places.

We can listen only to what we think is right.

Rock n roll music can be modern (Elvis, the Beatles, Roy Orbison, Linda Ronstadt), postmodern (Rolling Stones, Sex Pistols, Laurie Anderson, Talking Heads), or a blur (Fine Young Cannibals, Bobbie Brown). Rock n roll experiences can be shaped or informed or negated by the music, by its rhythms, its lyrics, its inducements to be. Turn the channel and you alter the reading; what happens there alters the meanings you give to life.

This has all been one large metaphor, maybe.

The point I am trying to make is that if you use terms like "modern" and "postmodern" or "rock n roll" to refer to the experiencing of social life, you are engaged in the negotiation of boundaries. If you want those boundaries to be drawn with clear definitional spaces, that says as much about you as it does about the realities you are reading and trying to represent. Similarly, if you want those boundaries to be read within the mysteries of given cases, as I do, that also invites a critical blurring of autobiographical interpretation with the reading you provide. There is no rock n roll without a performance, and that performance involves an invitation to read self into audience and context, and context and audience back into self.

The boundaries are always being negotiated. The lines we draw, the definitions we compose, are artificial forms of intelligence. The empirical spaces represented by the boundaries we draw do not exist separately from each other until we make them do so. That is why our experience of being at the margins, living on the borders, is so meaningful and so intense. There we realize that we are moving within the territorial space that is the prison-house of our mind. This is the prison-house of the languages that disciplines, corporations, and nations induce us to speak. And for a moment, just a necessary, fleeting, contingent moment, we realize also—with André—that we exist as victims of these languages, simultaneously the inmates and the guards.

These are the margins as they appear to me at the end of this reading of the twentieth century. They are margins that ask us to push against what we have taken for granted, what we claim, what we claim to know. They are margins that work with the beauty and truth of metaphors—not just beauty, not just truth, but both together. And they are margins that, like the experiencing of rock n roll as social life, like the interpenetrations of researching and writing interpretive ethnography, like the feeling that begins in a mystery of context and pulls you into deeper mysteries of self and Other, like prisons with inmates who are also the guards, require self-implication if change is to be sought.

These are the margins where the futures of scholarship—and social and political changes—are being negotiated. It is a negotiation that begins with shared activities—reading and writing, speaking and listening, jamming together, tearing down the Wall—that renegotiates the boundaries of who we are and what we are doing simply by participating in the doing of *that*. It is not a scholarship—or a life—about Us watching Them, but about I communicating with Thou. This story is not about dominance but participation, and its theme is not solving problems, but instead discovering mysteries of the plural present and participating in their wonder.

ENDINGS

This is where this tale ends.

In my last book it ended with the detective turning out the lights, thinking about going home, thinking about stopping for a sandwich and a beer along the way. He didn't know what was waiting for him.

Sometimes it's hard to know where the boundaries are.

This book has been about the discovery of those boundaries, about the what and how that was waiting for him. It is about what he encountered when he thought he was heading home, what it was when he got there that brought him back out again, this time playing a sea-foam green '57 Fender Stratocaster. Read this way, where this book begins is where the band begins, and the discovery here has been about rock n roll as social life. In it the detective moves through a year of close observation and music, gets out of a bad marriage and walks into a new life. Yeah, this is one way to tie in the ending with the beginning of the story. It's true enough, but seems driven too hard by form and not enough from the heart.

There are other ways of telling it. Consider this one: On the way home the detective—driving a candy-apple red 1967 Mustang GTA—stops at a traffic light on University Drive, the one by the municipal golf course, and sees a friend lifting a golf bag from his trunk. It is a beautiful spring evening. The air has been rain-washed and there is promise in the seductive scent of lilacs that bloom in the dooryards everywhere. He gets out of his car, walks over to his friend and is seized, once again, with an irresistible feeling, that subtle pull, that wild call, and there is in that moment of true feeling the spirit of mystery . . .

That's another way of telling beginnings and endings, of wrapping up the story before entering the next tale. It is also accurate, which means here true to the facts. Chronologically precise. But narratives about mysteries that inevitably lead to discoveries often find that their geneses are elsewhere, out of chronological time, away from the real space in which facts roam, in an ineffable somewhere asynchronous and megafactual in which that irresistible feeling captures immediately and takes permanently hostage the detective's perishable breath. Sometimes that sudden and irresistible feeling is a prelude to something else, something that maybe the detective had perhaps forgotten he had along with him or perhaps had just mentally misplaced.

What is it? It is this:

There is a clearly recognizable voice whispering out of the permanent past, making space for a new and different sense of the plural present. It is a distant whisper and until now an almost invisible past, a voice within you that had lain quiet in memory for a long time, and then for a long time afterwards was simply forgotten. This whisper, this voice, has chosen for some unknown reason this spring moment to awaken, to beckon, to speak to its bearer a Siren's language, to make intoxicating promises on lilac breath.

This is not a case of possession, but of discovery.

Self, Other, context. Negotiated boundaries, these. Temporal illusions, optical fallacies. Ours is a shared planet and a common life force: what connects us is mysterious and vital; what separates us is negotiable.

Shared activities, not necessarily shared understandings. Let us talk together, play music the way we feel it, make something positive out of emptiness, loneliness, and nothing.

And this:

Past, present . . . future. Negotiated boundaries, these. Words that make history make wars. We are a genetic unity, our bodies and ourselves, carrying inside us a story of biological wisdom for keeping the party going that transcends all the narratives of space and time. Yet we deny it. Instead we walk around with the consensus three seconds that we seem to believe constitutes the present as if naming it makes it so. Reduce the complexity and you live a narrow life.

Smell the lilacs, I say. Feel the presence not just of boundaries, but of transcendence. Organize life for bliss, which is not hedonism but the following of your heart, writing poetry into the madness, finding music in the silences of night, listening to the inner voices that connect you to the past, to the future, to yourself, to the Other, to contexts, to consciousness.

Everywhere is always . . . .

This is what the detective in me was thinking about when this story neared its close and I found myself already reading clues for another case. If these sentiments seem private, the sort of free association of words and the mysteries of life that we have all experienced but rarely disclose, then ask not whether this is the place to disclose them but why sentiments about mysteries are suspect in the first place. This, too, after all, is only a negotiated boundary.

I think I need to end this now. This is where, and how:

My father's voice is the one I hear when I return again to his difficult questions. I feel it inside of me especially when I am close to the sea. There, usually at night, I see in the boats moored against the docks a narrative unity, see in their rocking the roll of a deeper mysterious sea, feel in my heart their rhythms and their beat, a beat that takes me ceaselessly back into the past where these boats on this sea stand for much more than that, and what gets implicated in their stories is the discovery of me.

References

References

Aaron, D. 1978. *Studies in biography*. Cambridge: Harvard University Press.

Anderson, C. 1987. *Style as argument: Contemporary American nonfiction*. Carbondale: Southern Illinois University Press.

Ardrey, R. 1967. *The territorial imperative*. Garden City, N.Y.: Doubleday, Anchor.

————. 1970. *The social contract*. New York: Atheneum.

Aristotle. 1954. *The rhetoric and poetics*. Trans. W. R. Roberts. New York: Modern Library.

Bakhtin, M. M. 1981. *The dialogic imagination*. Trans. Caryl Emerson and Michael Holquist. Austin: University of Texas Press.

————. 1984a. *Problems of Doestoevsky's poetics*. Ed. and trans. C. Emerson. Minneapolis: University of Minnesota Press.

————. 1984b. *Rabelais and his world*. Trans. Helene Iswoldsky. Bloomington: Indiana University Press.

————. 1986. *Speech genres and other late essays*. Trans. V. W. McGree. Austin: University of Texas Press.

Bangs, L. 1988. *Psychotic reactions and carburetor dung*. Ed. Greil Marcus. New York: Vintage.

Barthes, R. 1972. *Mythologies*. London: Paladin.

Bastien, D. T., and Hostager, T. J. 1988. Jazz as a process of organizational innovation. *Communication Research* 15:582–602.

Bateson, G. 1936. *Naven*. Stanford, Calif.: Stanford University Press.

Baudrillard, J. 1988. *America*. Trans. Chris Turner. London: Verso.

Becker, E. 1962. *The birth and death of meaning*. New York: Free Press.

Bennett, H. S. 1980. *On becoming a rock musician*. Amherst: University of Massachusetts Press.

Benson, T. W. 1981. Another shootout in cowtown. *The Quarterly Journal of Speech* 67:347–406.

Benveniste, E. 1971. *Problems in general linguistics*. Trans. M. E. Meek. Coral Gables, Fla.: Miami University Press.

Berger, P. L. 1970. The problem of multiple realities: Alfred Shutz and Robert Musil. In M. Natanson, ed., *Phenomenology and social reality: Essays in memory of Alfred Shutz*. The Hague: Martinus Nijhoff.

Berger, P. L., and Luckmann, T. 1967. *The social construction of reality*. Harmondsworth, Eng.: Penguin.

Bersheid, E., and Walster, E. 1978. *Equity theory and research*. Boston: Allyn & Bacon.

Beyer, J. M., and Trice, H. M. 1987. How an organization's rites reveal its culture. *Organizational Dynamics* 15:4–25.

Birkhead, D. 1989. An ethics of journalism. *Critical Studies in Mass Communication* 6:283–94.

Bitzer, L. F., and Black, E., eds., 1970. *The prospect of rhetoric*. Englewood Cliffs, N. J.: Prentice-Hall.

Blumer, H. 1969. *Symbolic interactionism: Perspective and method*. Englewood Cliffs, N.J.: Prentice-Hall.

Bochner, A. P. 1977. Whither communication theory and research? *The Quarterly Journal of Speech* 63:324–32.

Booth, M. 1976. The art of words in songs. *The Quarterly Journal of Speech* 62:242–49.

Brockriede, W. 1982. Arguing about human understanding. *Communication Monographs* 49:137–47.

Bruss, E. W. 1976. *Autobiographical acts: The changing situation of a literary genre*. Baltimore, Md.: Johns Hopkins University Press.

Bryson, B. 1989. *Lost continent*. New York: Harper & Row.

Burke, K. 1965. *Permanence and change*. Indianapolis: Bobbs-Merrill.

———. 1969. *A rhetoric of motives*. Berkeley: University of California Press.

———. 1989. *On symbols and society*. Ed. Joseph R. Gusfield. Chicago: University of Chicago Press.

Calas, M. B., and Smircich, L. 1987. Reading leadership as a form of cultural analysis. In J. L. Hunt, R. Baliga, C. Schriesheim, and P. Dachler, eds., *Emerging leadership vistas*. Lexington, Mass.: Lexington Books.

Campbell, J., with Moyers, B. 1988. *The power of myth*. New York: Doubleday.

Camus, A. 1964. *Carnets*. Paris: Gallimard.

Carbaugh, D. 1988. Cultural terms and tensions in the speech at a television station. *Western Journal of Speech Communication* 52:216–37.

Cheney, G. 1983. On the various and changing meanings of organizational membership. *Communication Monographs* 50:342–62.

Chesebro, J., Foulger, D., Nachman, J., and Yanelli, A. 1985. Popular music as a mode of communication, 1955–1982. *Critical Studies in Mass Communication* 2:115–35.

Clifford, J. 1978. "Hanging up looking glasses at odd corners": Ethnobiographical prospects. In Daniel Aaron, ed., *Studies in biography*. Cambridge: Harvard University Press.

———. 1988. *The predicament of culture: Twentieth century ethnography, literature, and art*. Cambridge: Harvard University Press.

Clifford, J., and Marcus, G. E., eds. 1986. *Writing culture: The poetics and politics of ethnography*. Berkeley: University of California Press.

Coetzee, J. M. 1984. *Truth in autobiography*. University of Cape Town New Series Inaugural Lecture 94. Cape Town, S.A.: University of Cape Town.

Connor, S. 1989. *Postmodernist culture: An introduction to theories of the contemporary*. New York: Basil Blackwell.

Conquergood, D. 1985. Performing as a moral act: Ethical dimensions of the ethnography of performance. *Literature in Performance* 5:1–13.

———. 1988. Health theatre in a Hmong refugee camp: Performance, communication, and culture. *The Drama Review* 32:174–208.

———. 1989. Poetics, play, process, and power: The performative turn in anthropology. *Text and Performance Quarterly* 1:82–95.

Conrad, C. 1988. Work songs, hegemony, and illusions of self. *Critical Studies in Mass Communication* 5:179–201.

Dance, F. E. X. 1970. The concept of "communication." *Journal of Communication* 20:201–10.

———. 1980. Swift, slow, sweet, sour, adazzle, dim: What makes human communication human? *Western Journal of Speech Communication* 44:60–3.

Davis, W. 1986. *The serpent and the rainbow*. New York: Simon & Schuster.

De Certeau, M. 1984. *The practice of everyday life*. Berkeley: University of California Press.

De Man, P. 1971. *Blindness and insight: Essays in the rhetoric of contemporary criticism*. New York: Oxford University Press.

———. 1979. Autobiography as de-facement. *Modern Language Notes* 94:920–30.

Denney, R. 1964. *The astonished muse: Popular culture in America*. New York: Grossett & Dunlap, Universal Library.

Denzin, N. K. 1989. *Interpretive interactionism*. Newbury Park, Calif.: Sage.

Derrida, J. 1976. *Of grammatology*. Trans. G. Chakravorty. Baltimore, Md.: Johns Hopkins University Press.

Di Prima, D. 1988. *Memoirs of a beatnik*. San Francisco, Calif.: Last Gasp.

Eakin, P. J. 1985. *Fictions in autobiography: Studies in the art of self-invention*. Princeton, N.J.: Princeton University Press.

Eason, D. L. 1987. Editor's note. *Critical Studies in Mass Communication* 4:i–ii.

———. 1988. Editor's note. *Critical Studies in Mass Communication* 5:i–iii.

———. 1989. Editor's note. *Critical Studies in Mass Communication* 6: i–ii.

Egan, S. 1984. *Patterns of experience in autobiography*. Chapel Hill: University of North Carolina Press.

Eisenberg, E. M. 1984. Ambiguity as strategy in organizational communication. *Communication Monographs* 51:227–42.

———. 1988. Jamming: Organization and ectasy. Paper presented at the Summer Conference on Interpretive Approaches to Organizational Study, Alta, Utah.

———. 1990. Jamming: Transcendence through organizing. *Communication Research* 17:139–64.

Elbaz, R. 1987. *The changing nature of the self: A critical study of the autobiographic discourse*. Iowa City: University of Iowa Press.

Ellis, D. G. 1980. Ethnographic considerations in initial interaction. *Western Journal of Speech Communication* 44:104–7.

Fetterman, D. M. 1989. *Ethnography: Step-by-step*. Newbury Park, Calif.: Sage.

Fish, S. 1980. *Is there a text in this class? The authority of interpretive communities*. Cambridge: Harvard University Press.

Fisher, W. R. 1984. Narration as a human communication paradigm: The case of public moral argument. *Communication Monographs* 51:1–22.

Fiske, J. 1989a. *Understanding popular culture*. Winchester, Mass.: Unwin Hyman.

———. 1989b. *Reading the popular*. Winchester, Mass.: Unwin Hyman.

Francesconi, R. 1986. Free jazz and Black nationalism. *Critical Studies in Mass Communication* 3:36–49.

Gallagher, K. 1975. *The philosophy of Gabriel Marcel*. New York: Fordham University Press.

Garfinkel, H. 1967. *Studies in ethnomethodology*. Englewood Cliffs, N.J.: Prentice-Hall.

Geertz, C. 1973. *The interpretation of culture*. New York: Basic Books.

———. 1980. Blurred genres: The refiguration of social thought. *The American Scholar* 29:2.

———. 1983. *Local knowledge*. New York: Basic Books.

———. 1988. *Works and lives: The anthropologist as author*. Stanford, Calif.: Stanford University Press.

Goffman, E. 1959. *The presentation of self in everyday life*. Garden City, N.Y.: Doubleday, Anchor.

Goldzwig, S. R., and Dionisopoulos, G. N. 1989. John F. Kennedy's civil rights discourse: The evolution from "principled bystander" to public advocate. *Communication Monographs* 56:179–98.

Gonzalez, A., and Mackay, J. 1983. Rhetorical ascription and the gospel according to Dylan. *The Quarterly Journal of Speech* 69:1–14.

Goodall, H. L. (1983). The nature of analogic discourse. *The Quarterly Journal of Speech* 69:71–79.

———. 1989a. *Casing a promised land: The autobiography of an organizational detective as cultural ethnographer.* Carbondale: Southern Illinois University Press.

———. 1989b. A cultural inquiry concerning the ontological and epistemic dimensions of self, other, and context in communication scholarship. In G. M. Phillips and J. T. Wood, eds., *Studies to commemorate the seventy-fifth anniversary of the Speech Communication Association.* Carbondale: Southern Illinois University Press.

———. 1989c. On becoming an organizational detective: The role of intuitive logics and context sensitivity for communication consultants. *Southern Communication Journal* 55:42–54.

———. 1990. Interpretive contexts for decision making. In G. M. Phillips, ed., *Teaching how to work in groups.* Norwood, N.J.: Ablex.

Goodall, H. L., Wilson, G. L., and Waagen, C. L. 1986. The performance appraisal interview: An interpretive reassessment. *The Quarterly Journal of Speech* 72:74–87.

Greene, Bob. 1988. Louie, Louie. *Esquire,* September.

Gregg, R. B. 1971. The ego-function of the rhetoric of protest. *Philosophy and Rhetoric* 4:71–91.

———. 1984. *Symbolic inducement and knowing.* Columbia: University of South Carolina Press.

Grossberg, L. 1984. Another boring day in paradise: Rock and roll and the empowerment of everyday life. *Popular Music* 4:225–28.

———. 1986. Is there rock after punk? *Critical Studies in Mass Communication* 3:50–73.

Gunn, J. V. 1982. *Autobiography: Toward a poetics of experience.* Philadelphia: University of Pennsylvania Press.

Gusdorf, G. 1986. Scripture of the self: "Prologue in Heaven." Trans. Betsy Wing. *The Southern Review* 22: 280–95.

Habermas, J. 1979. *Communication and the evolution of society.* Boston: Beacon Press.

Haley, J. 1976. *Problem-solving therapy.* New York: Harper & Row.

Hannah, B. 1989. *Boomerang.* New York: Samuel Lawrence.

Hawes, L. C. 1977. Toward a hermeneutic phenomenology of communication. *Communication Quarterly* 25:30–41.

Herr, M. 1977. *Dispatches.* New York: Knopf.

Hickson, M., III. 1983. Ethnomethodology: The promise of applied communication research? *The Southern Speech Communication Journal* 48:182–95.

Hymes, D. 1962. The ethnography of speaking. In T. Gladwin and W. Sturtevant, eds., *Anthropology and human behavior.* Washington, D.C.: Anthropological Society of Washington.

Irvine, J., and Kirkpatrick, W. 1972. The musical form in rhetorical exchange. *The Quarterly Journal of Speech* 58:272–89.

Iyer, P. 1988. *Video night in Kathmandu and other reports from the not-so-far East.* New York: Knopf.

Jackson, M. 1989. *Paths toward a clearing: Radical empiricism and ethnographic inquiry.* Bloomington: Indiana University Press.

Janis, I. L. 1982. *Groupthink.* 2d rev. ed. Boston: Houghton Mifflin.

Jay, P. 1984. *Being in the text: Self-representation from Wordsworth to Roland Barthes*. Ithaca, N.Y.: Cornell University Press.

Kantner, R. M. 1977. *Men and women of the corporation*. New York: Basic Books.

Katriel, T., and Philipsen, G. 1981. "What we need is communication": "Communication" as a cultural category in some American speech. *Communication Monographs* 48:301–17.

Keller, E. F. 1985. *Reflections on gender and science*. New Haven, Conn.: Yale University Press.

Kerr, M., and Bowen, M. 1988. *Family evaluation: An approach based on Bowen therapy*. New York: Norton.

Klein, J. G. 1982. *The office book: Ideas and designs for contemporary work spaces*. New York: Facts on File.

Knupp, R. 1981. A time for every purpose under Heaven. *The Southern Speech Communication Journal* 46:377–89.

Korzybski, A. 1933. *Science and sanity*. Lakeville, Conn.: International Non-Aristotelian Library.

Kosokoff, S., and Carmichael, C. 1970. The rhetoric of protest. *The Southern Speech Communication Journal* 35:295–302.

Kroker, A., Kroker, M., and Cook, D. 1989. *Panic encyclopedia: The definitive guide to the postmodern scene*. New York: St. Martin's Press.

Krueger, D. L. 1982. Marital decision-making: A language-action analysis. *The Quarterly Journal of Speech* 68:273–87.

Lacan, J. 1966. *Écrits*. Paris: Editions de Seuil.

———. 1968. *The language of the self: The function of language in psychoanalysis*. Baltimore, Md.: Johns Hopkins University Press.

Laing, R. D. 1965. *The divided self*. Harmondsworth, Eng.: Penguin.

———. 1971. *Politics of the family and other essays*. New York: Pantheon.

Langellier, K. M. 1989. Personal narratives: Perspectives on theory and research. *Text and Performance Quarterly* 9:243–76.

LeCoat, G. 1976. Music and the three appeals of classical rhetoric. *The Quarterly Journal of Speech* 62:157–66.

Lefebvre, H. 1971. *Everyday life in the modern world*. Trans. S. Rabinovitch. London: Penguin.

Leirus, M. [1946] 1984. *Manhood: A journey from childhood into the fierce order of virility*. Trans. R. Howard. San Francisco: North Point Press.

Lejeune, P. 1974. *Exercises d'ambiguité: Lectures de "Si le grain ne meurt" d'André Gide*. Paris: Lettres Modernes.

———. 1989. *On autobiography*. Trans. Katherine Leary. Minneapolis: University of Minnesota Press.

Lévi-Strauss, C. 1955. *Tristes tropiques*. New York: Antheneum.

Louis, M. L. 1980. Surprise and sense-making: What newcomers experience in entering unfamiliar organizational settings. *Administrative Science Quarterly* 23:225–51.

Lurie, A. 1981. *The language of clothes*. New York: Random House.

McGrane, B. 1989. *Beyond anthropology*. New York: Columbia University Press.

McHale, B. 1987. *Postmodernist fiction*. New York: Methuen.

McKeon, R. 1970. Communication as an architectonic, productive art. In L. F. Bitzer and E. Black, eds., *The prospect of rhetoric*. Englewood Cliffs, N.J.: Prentice-Hall.

Mader, T. F., Rosenfield, L. W., and Mader, D. C. 1985. The rise and fall of departments. In T. Benson, ed., *Speech communication in the twentieth century*. Carbondale: Southern Illinois University Press.

Malinowski, B. 1922. *Argonauts of the western Pacific*. New York: Dutton.

————. 1935. *Coral gardens and their magic.* 2 vols. New York: American Books.

Mangham, I. L., and Overington, M. A. 1987. *Organizations as theatre: A social psychology of dramatic appearances.* New York: John Wiley.

Marcel, G. 1949a. *Philosophy of existence.* Trans. Manya Harari. New York: Philosophical Library.

————. 1949b. *Being and having.* London: Dacre Press.

————. 1950. *Mystery of being.* 2 vols. Trans. René Hague. London: Harvill Press.

————. 1987. *The participant perspective: A reader.* Ed. T. W. Busch. Lanham, Md.: University Press of America.

Marcus, G. 1986. Critical response. *Studies in Mass Communication* 3:77–81.

————. 1989. *Lipstick traces: A secret history of the twentieth century.* Cambridge: Harvard University Press.

Marcus, G. E., and Fischer, M. M. J. 1986. *Anthropology as cultural critique: An experimental moment in the human sciences.* Chicago: University of Chicago Press.

Mead, G. H. 1934. *Mind, self, and society.* Chicago: University of Chicago Press.

Mead, M. [1928] 1949. *Coming of age in Samoa.* New York: Mentor Books.

Miles, E. M., and Leathers, D. G. 1984. The impact of aesthetic and professionally-related objects on credibility in the office setting. *The Southern Speech Communication Journal* 49:361–79.

Milford, N. 1970. *Zelda.* New York: Avon.

Miller, G. R. 1966. On defining communication—another stab. *Journal of Communication* 16:88–98.

Mishler, E. 1979. Meaning in context: Is there any other kind? *Harvard Educational Review* 49:1–19.

Morgan, G. 1986. *Images of organization.* Beverly Hills, Calif.: Sage.

Mumby, D. K. 1987. The political function of narrative in organizations. *Communication Monographs* 54:113–27.

Neumann, M. 1988a. Consuming "otherness": The politics of photographic documentary art. *Journal of Communication Inquiry* 12:45–64.

————. 1988b. Wandering through the museum: Experience and identity in a spectator culture. *Border/Lines,* summer, 19–27.

————. 1989. The "problems" of evidence in cultural studies. Paper presented at the International Communication Association convention, San Francisco.

————. 1990. Making common sense: The construction of knowledge and experience at Grand Canyon National Park. Ph.D. diss., University of Utah.

Neumann, M., and Eason, D. 1988. Casino world: Bringing it all home. Paper presented at the International Communication Association convention, New Orleans.

Newman, C. 1984. *The postmodern aura.* Evansville, Ill.: Northwestern University Press.

Norton, C. S. 1989. *Life metaphors.* Carbondale: Southern Illinois University Press.

Olney, J. 1972. *Metaphors of self: The meaning of autobiography.* Princeton, N.J.: Princeton University Press.

————. 1980. *Autobiography: Essays theoretical and critical.* Princeton, N.J.: Princeton University Press.

————. 1988. *Studies in autobiography.* New York: Oxford University Press.

Pacanowsky, M. E. 1988. Slouching towards Chicago. *The Quarterly Journal of Speech* 74:453–67.

Pacanowsky, M. E., and O'Donnell-Trujillo, N. 1983. Organizational communication as cultural performance. *Communication Monographs* 50:126–47.

Paul, R. 1988. The living dead and the puffer fish. *New York Times Book Review,* 21 August, 14.

Payne, D. 1989. *Coping with failure*. Columbia: University of South Carolina Press.

Percy, W. 1989. The divided creature. *Wilson Quarterly*, summer, 77–87.

Philipsen, G. 1975. Speaking "like a man" in Teamsterville: Cultural patterns of role enactment in an urban neighborhood. *The Quarterly Journal of Speech* 61:13–22.

——. 1977. Linearity of research design in ethnographic studies of speaking. *Communication Quarterly* 25:42–50.

Phillips, G. M., and Wood, J. T. 1983. *Communication and human relationships*. New York: Macmillian.

Pilling, J. 1981. *Autobiography and imagination: Studies in self-scrutiny*. London: Routledge & Kegan Paul.

Railsback, C. C. 1983. Beyond rhetorical relativism: A structural-material model of truth and objective reality. *The Quarterly Journal of Speech* 69:351–63.

Rawlins, W. K. 1985. Stalking interpersonal communication effectiveness: Social, individual, or situational integration? In T. W. Benson, ed., *Speech communication in the twentieth century*. Carbondale: Southern Illinois University Press.

Renza, L. A. 1980. The veto of the imagination: A theory of autobiography. In J. Olney, ed., *Autobiography: Essays theoretical and critical*. Princeton, N.J.: Princeton University Press.

Ritti, R. R., and Funkhauser, G. R. 1977. *The ropes to skip and the ropes to know: Studies in organizational behavior*. Columbus, Ohio: Grid.

Robbins, T. 1980. *Still life with woodpecker*. New York: Bantam.

Rosaldo, R. 1989. *Culture and truth: The remaking of social analysis*. Boston: Beacon Press.

Rose, D. 1987. *Black American street life 1969–71*. Philadelphia: University of Pennsylvania Press.

——. 1989. *Patterns of American culture: Ethnography and estrangement*. Philadelphia: University of Pennsylvania Press.

Roth, L. 1981. Folk song lyrics as communication in John Ford's films. *The Southern Speech Communication Journal* 46:390–96.

Sackmann, S. 1987. Beyond cultural artifacts. Paper presented to the ICA/SCA Conference on Interpretive Approaches to the Study of Organizations, Alta, Utah.

Sahlins, M. D. 1976. *Culture and practical reason*. Chicago: University of Chicago Press.

Said, E. 1978. *Orientalism*. New York: Random House.

Schutz, A. 1967. *The phenomenology of the social world*. Trans. George Walsh and Frederick Lehnert. Evanston, Ill.: Northwestern University Press.

Sennett, R. 1977. *The fall of public man*. New York: Vintage.

Shapiro, S. A. 1968. The dark continent of literature: Autobiography. *Comparative Literature Studies* 5:421–54.

Shawn, W. 1981. *My dinner with André*. New York: Grove Press.

Shotter, J., and Gergen, K. J., eds., 1989. *Texts of identity*. Newbury Park, Calif.: Sage.

Siebenschuh, W. R. 1983. *Fictional techniques and factual works*. Athens: University of Georgia Press.

Smircich, L. 1983. Concepts of culture and organizational analysis. *Administrative Science Quarterly* 28:339–58.

Smircich, L., and Stubbart, C. I. 1985. Strategic management in an enacted world. *Academy of Management Review* 10:724–36.

Spence, G. 1989. *With justice toward none: Destroying an American Myth*. New York: Times Books.

Steiner, G. 1973. *After Babel*. London: Oxford University Press.

Stoller, P. 1989. *The taste of ethnographic things: The senses in anthropology*. Philadelphia: University of Pennsylvania Press.

Stoller, P., and Olkes, C. 1987. *In sorcery's shadow: A memoir of apprenticeship among the Songhay of Niger*. Chicago: University of Chicago Press.

Strine, M. S., and Pacanowsky, M. E. 1985. How to read interpretive accounts of organizational life: Narrative bases of textual authority. *The Southern Speech Communication Journal* 50:283–97.

Sukenick, R. 1987. *Down and in: Life in the underground*. New York: Macmillan, Collier.

Taylor, B. 1988. Reminiscences of Los Alamos. Paper presented at the Speech Communication Association convention, New Orleans.

———. 1989. At work in the fields of the bomb: Critical recovery of the nuclear weapons organization. Paper presented at the Summer Conference on Interpretive Approaches to Organizational Study, Alta, Utah.

Taylor, G. O. 1983. *Chapters of experience: Studies in modern American autobiography*. New York: St. Martin's.

Toulmin, S. 1958. *The uses of argument*. Cambridge: Cambridge University Press.

Toulmin, S., Rieke, R., and Janik, A. 1979. *An introduction to reasoning*. New York: Macmillan.

Trujillo, N., and Dionisopoulos, G. 1987. Cop talk, police stories, and the social construction of organizational drama. *Central States Speech Journal* 38:196–209.

Turner, V. W. 1986a. *The anthropology of performance*. New York: PAJ Publications.

———. 1986b. Dewey, Dilthey, and drama: An essay in the anthropology of experience. In V. W. Turner and E. M. Bruner, eds., *The anthropology of experience*. Urbana: University of Illinois Press.

Tyler, S. 1988. *The unspeakable: Discourse, dialogue, and rhetoric in the postmodern world*. Madison: University of Wisconsin Press.

Van Maanen, J. 1981. The informant game. *Urban Life* 9:469–94.

———. 1988. *Tales of the field: On writing ethnography*. Chicago: University of Chicago Press.

Van Peursen, C. A. 1972. *Phenomenology and reality*. Pittsburgh: Duquesne University Press.

Ward, E., Stokes, G., and Tucker, K. 1986. *Rock of ages: The Rolling Stone history of rock and roll*. Englewood Cliffs, N.J.: Prentice-Hall, The Rolling Stone Press.

Weick, K. 1979. *The social psychology of organizing*. 2d ed. Reading, Mass.: Addison-Wesley.

Weisman, E. 1985. The good man singing well. *Critical Studies in Mass Communication* 2:135–51.

Wenzel, J. W. 1979. Perspectives on argument. In J. Rhodes and S. Newell, eds., *Proceedings of the summer conference on argumentation*. Annandale, Va: SCA.

Wood, J. T. 1984. Research and the social world: Honoring the connections. *Communication Quarterly* 32:3–8.

Wyatt, N. J., and Phillips, G. M. 1988. *Studying organizations: A case history of the Farmer's Home Administration*. Norwood, N.J.: Ablex.

About the Author

Birth: King's Daughters Hospital, Martinsburg, West Virginia, September 8, 1952. Parents both Republicans. Father: former jazz trumpeter, amateur dramatist, and bombardier on B–17s in European theater; current occupation (classified). Mother: former swing dancer and lifeguard, survivor of fire and men, now a nurse. *Youth:* In service as child to the United States Department of State. Travel and residence in Europe, early education in Rome and London. Private tutoring in field research methods, surveillance, interviewing. Avid reader, theatergoer, and soccer player. *Adolescence:* Travel and residence in the United States, continued education in Cheyenne, Philadelphia, and Hagerstown. Rhythm ace in variety of garage rock n roll bands. Active in sports, gender studies, and politics. Acquired street living and survival skills. *Career:* Properly credentialed academic currently serving in the Department of Communication, University of Utah. Author of *Casing a Promised Land,* among nine other books. Continuing education as private investigator, rock musician, and archaeologist. *Personal:* Married to the writer Sandra Goodall; avid reader, moviegoer, traveler, cultural participant. Known to be alive and well and living somewhere in the majestic surround of the American Rockies.